THE FRANCHISE

PHILADELPHIA EAGLES

A Curated History of the Birds

ZACH BERMAN

First Triumph Books paperback edition 2024

The Library of Congress has catalogued the previous edition as follows:

Names: Berman, Zach (Sports reporter), author.
Title: The franchise Philadelphia Eagles : a curated history of the Birds / Zach Berman.
Other titles: Philadelphia Eagles
Description: Chicago : Triumph Books, 2024. | Includes bibliographical references
Identifiers: LCCN 2024022973 | ISBN 9781637276259 (hardback) | ISBN 9781637276273 (epub)
Subjects: LCSH: Philadelphia Eagles (Football team)—History. | BISAC: SPORTS & RECREATION / Football | TRAVEL / United States / Northeast / Middle Atlantic (NJ, NY, PA)
Classification: LCC GV956.P44 B46 2024 | DDC 796.332/640974811—dc23/eng/20240604
LC record available at https://lccn.loc.gov/2024022973

This book is available in quantity at special discounts for your group or organization. For further information, contact:

Triumph Books LLC
814 North Franklin Street
Chicago, Illinois 60610
(312) 337-0747
www.triumphbooks.com

Printed in U.S.A.
ISBN: 978-1-63727-851-2
Design by Preston Pisellini
Page production by Nord Compo

To my grandfather,
who taught me about the joy of fall Sundays—
and so much more

CONTENTS

Part 4 The Icons

Part 5 The Standouts

Part 6 The Super Bowl Season

Part 7 The Moments

Foreword

When I first signed with the Philadelphia Eagles, I knew I was stepping into a world that was as much about the fans as it was about the players on the field. I remember vividly the day I flew into town to sign my contract. The infamous Dom, Eagles head of security, picked me up from the airport. As we drove toward the NovaCare Complex, the heart of the Eagles' operations, my excitement grew. As our Suburban climbed to the crescendo of the Girard Point Bridge, I caught my first glimpse of Lincoln Financial Field. My mind lit up with the possibilities, imagining the memories that would be made in that iconic building. The 67,000 fans roaring on a cool sunny Sunday. Just as I was lost in my daydream, a car swerved in front of us, forcing Dom to jam his brakes hard. After a quick exchange of honks and middle fingers, my welcome to Philly was over, and we were back on track. I couldn't help but smile and think, *Home, sweet home.*

Growing up in New Jersey, I've always felt a connection to the blue-collar, underdog persona that defines Philadelphia. The tough, demanding sports fans here are no different from my family. They expect excellence, they demand effort, and they cherish those who give their all. This city, this team, and these fans have a unique way of weaving together the experiences of everyone involved, creating a beautiful web of circumstance that connects us all.

This book is a tribute to that connection. It's a journey through the moments that have defined the Philadelphia Eagles over the past 25 years, told through the voices of those who lived them. From the highs of the Super Bowl victory to the challenges and breakups along the way, this curated history brings to life the characters and events that have shaped the franchise. It's about connecting the moments that made us cheer, the ones that made us cry, and everything in between.

For me, the memories of playing for the Eagles are deeply intertwined with the people of Philadelphia. The city's spirit, its resilience, and its unwavering support are what make playing here so unique. As you read these stories, I hope you feel that same connection and pride. This book is for the die-hard fans who bleed green, for the community that rallies behind its team, and for anyone who has ever screamed "Go Birds!"

Here's to the moments we've shared and the ones still to come. Fly, Eagles, Fly.

—Malcolm Jenkins

Introduction

Here's a slight confession, which seems reasonable to make before taking you through 25 years of the Philadelphia Eagles' history. This book *almost* chronicled the franchise's second Lombardi Trophy. When I spoke to representatives from Triumph Books early in 2023, the discussions were about a Super Bowl book. The Eagles were set to play the Kansas City Chiefs, and I was ready to tell the story of the team that captured the fan base's hearts in a different way than five years earlier, when I wrote my first book about the Eagles' first Super Bowl.

Then Patrick Mahomes happened, or a suspect penalty flag happened, or a slippery field happened—you pick the culprit—and that idea joined a stack of could-have-been articles and columns from my 12 years covering the franchise.

The next day, Triumph Books sent a note about touching base with other ideas.

When they raised the idea of a curated history of the franchise's last 25 years—the Andy Reid–Donovan McNabb era to present day—my first thought was about the week I had just spent in Phoenix. One of the dominant storylines that week was the meeting of these two eras. Eagles owner Jeffrey

Lurie hired both coaches in the game. Both general managers in the game started their careers with the Eagles. Both team presidents rose through the ranks with the franchise. Throughout that week, this 25-year period kept repeating itself in my reporting. I spent time in Phoenix on the phone with Joe Banner, the former Eagles team president who helped hire Reid (and the aforementioned general managers and presidents who came through the city). The game was played where Donovan McNabb now lives and where he used to host teammates when he was the franchise quarterback for the Eagles.

Even walking through the stadium in Glendale, Arizona, before the Super Bowl brought back different memories in Eagles history. I was there in September 2012 for an Eagles–Cardinals game when Michael Vick played against Kevin Kolb in the first matchup of the two quarterbacks who replaced McNabb. (Kolb was drafted to become McNabb's replacement, and Vick eventually earned the job. You'll read about that in a bit.) The next time I went to that stadium came four months later, for the Fiesta Bowl between Oregon and Kansas State, which would typically seem to be an odd game for an Eagles reporter to cover until you realize that Chip Kelly coached the Ducks and he was the Eagles' top candidate to replace Reid. (Kelly had fun with this, too, asking me if those eating cheesesteaks at Pat's and Geno's were interested in the Fiesta Bowl. In 2013, they were.) I saw Nick Foles win a big game at that stadium. I saw Jalen Hurts win a big game there, too. (Carson Wentz never won a game there for the Eagles, and he had been benched when the Eagles visited in 2020.)

All of this remained fresh in my mind when the idea was proposed to me about a curated recent history of the franchise, and it made sense. The Eagles have been around for nine decades, and they won championships in the 1940s and 1960s, but their success in the 32-team NFL during this period has elevated their prestige in the league. They have the sixth most wins in the NFL since 1999—and the second most playoff wins. They appeared in seven NFC Championship Games and three Super Bowls. The blemish is they only have one Lombardi Trophy, although that is one more than they ever had before this period.

For the past 12 years, I have been on the ground floor. I became an Eagles beat writer in 2012 for *The Philadelphia Inquirer*, where I spent seven seasons. In 2019, I joined The Athletic. In 2023, I moved to PHLY. I have attended every game during this period, home and away, with the exception of the road games in 2020 while under COVID-19 restrictions. I've traveled with the team to every NFL city—and even to London. I've been in the homes of some of the iconic Eagles, from Nick Sirianni to Fletcher Cox to Malcolm Jenkins. This has offered a unique perspective about the stories and the moments that have made these 25 years special. (I even attended the first game of this era as a 13-year-old with my grandfather, giving me a different perspective about those early years than the one I developed in the press box.)

This book is meant be a curated history—not a comprehensive encyclopedia. The focus is on the iconic characters, the unforgettable moments, and the most memorable seasons. So you'll find more on the Super Bowl season in 2017 than the 8–8 season in 2007. There is more weight paid to the past decade in particular, although appropriate attention is given to those early years when the foundation was set. The book combines new interviews, reporting from the past 12 years, and transcripts, interviews, and published reports from the preceding 13 years. The time period of a quote is identified when relevant or when it appears within proximity of interviews from a different period. If the quote was said to a different source, that source is identified accordingly.

There also is little on the pre-1999 Eagles in this book. Much can be written about those decades in Eagles history, and there are outstanding books that chronicle them. The last 25 years is the scope for this book, and as I quickly realized, that time period offered more than enough. In fact, there was no challenge in determining what to include—only what I was willing to leave out. Another anthology could go deeper on more players, moments, and teams.

The book is organized into sections on the executives, coaches, great players, great teams, and great moments. Although attention was paid to how it was organized, these are meant to be individual essays that can be consumed independently of one another. So feel free to jump from Jeffrey Lurie to Jalen Hurts to the 2017 Eagles, back to Howie Roseman, with Brian Westbrook mixed in between.

The other challenge with writing the bulk of this book during the summer of 2023 was that the story of the franchise is still developing. Soon after I agreed to embark on this journey, Hurts signed the biggest contract in franchise history and Sirianni celebrated his 42nd birthday. I'm hardened enough to know that when Doug Pederson said at a Super Bowl parade that this is their "new normal," times change quickly, but I don't have the cynicism to fight evidence suggesting the Eagles will find a way to stay relevant into late January—and perhaps even February—on a consistent basis. All that means is this will be a fun sequel to write in 2049.

PART 1

THE EXECUTIVES

1

Jeffrey Lurie

Jeffrey Lurie walked into the Eagles' locker room in the bowels of Lincoln Financial Field on January 29, 2023, after playing in the NFC Championship Game for the seventh time and clinching a spot in the Super Bowl for the third time in Lurie's ownership. He was as buoyant as an owner would be after a momentous win, although he also kept his attention on what was occurring at that moment nearly 1,200 miles away, where the Kansas City Chiefs were hosting the AFC Championship Game.

The coach for the Chiefs, of course, was Andy Reid—the winningest coach to ever work for the Eagles, whose history with the franchise was both lauded and complicated.

The cigar smoke around Lurie from the players' celebration could not obscure how clear it was to see this moment as a melding of Lurie's football life.

That stadium was only a dream 25 years earlier, when the Eagles still called the lovable (albeit rat-infested) Veterans Stadium their home. They upgraded in 2003 during Reid's run of championship game appearances, signaling a new period in the franchise's history and one of Lurie's crowning achievements in his three-decade period in the owner's box. Among the others? Hiring Reid. Celebrating around Lurie was general manager Howie Roseman, the executive Lurie believed in so much that he reinstalled him after briefly stripping him of football decision-making duties (we'll get to that later) and then watched Roseman assemble a Super Bowl roster—twice! A few steps away was Nick Sirianni, the coach Lurie hired when nobody else interviewed him and who brought the Eagles to the Super Bowl in his second season. At a corner locker, Lurie would see Jalen Hurts, a player Lurie was so resolute about drafting based on confidence in Hurts and a painful lesson from nearly a decade earlier. And if Lurie took a few strides outside to the field, where green confetti still lay, he could have looked up and seen the Super Bowl banner from the 2017 season. He could have seen the No. 5 banner honoring Donovan McNabb. If he kept walking, exiting to the stadium's front gates, he could have viewed a statue of Doug Pederson and Nick Foles calling the "Philly Special," the most famous moment from the most famous game in Eagles history. And if he had looked down Pattison Avenue and across Broad Street, past the privacy trees, he would see the top of the team's practice facility, which also did not exist 25 years earlier.

There was history of this quarter century all around Lurie, whose obsession with his franchise is the part of his ownership that he felt it was important to convey. There have been unforgettable moments and iconic characters throughout these

25 years, but Lurie is the one who has been with the franchise the entire period.

"What nobody would ever really kind of know except those really close to me is it's on my mind 20 hours a day, and I love every moment," Lurie said in a June 2023 conversation for this book. "I love waking up at three in the morning thinking, 'What if this could happen?'.... It's like loving it so much—like a child, almost—that you want to constantly massage it. Somebody once told me, 'With your passion for the team, you'll never be a really good golfer. Because you'll never devote the time to really getting better at golf.' And they're right.... A wonderful part of life, for me, is owning the team, and I just want what's best for the team and the community. I think they don't realize necessarily that it's a constant. It's not like you just turn it off."

In the conversation, Lurie brought up a statistic he found staggering and which he hoped would illustrate the nature of the franchise. Since 2001, the Eagles have been in almost a third of the NFC Championship Games (seven of 22, from 2001 to 2023). If there is anything he can strut about during his tenure, it would be that statistic, considering the Eagles had been to only one conference championship from 1970 to 2000. Lurie drew scrutiny in 2003 for suggesting that other owners and general managers in the NFL viewed the Eagles as "kind of the gold standard." A gold standard often requires finishing with the proverbial gold medal, but NFL franchises chase consistent, sustained success. Lurie noted in a 2014 interview at the 20-year mark of his ownership that he "anticipated it being difficult, but I thought if you can get to four, five, six championship games, or get to the playoffs the majority of the years, as we have, then you'd have the luck that would transcend whatever strengths or weaknesses you have." He reasoned that if the franchise maintained the proper values and passion for success, then the law of averages would play into their favor and that would "right itself over time."

That sentiment proved true when the Eagles won the franchise's first Super Bowl in February 2018. They were close again in February 2023. And the same logic seems to apply—remain a contending team capable of going deep into the postseason. Since the Eagles made the playoffs in 2000, they have only once had back-to-back losing seasons. Lurie noted that the dips are inevitable with sports franchises, but the Eagles have avoided the prolonged dips that create apathy in other markets and that once hurt the franchise with six consecutive losing seasons in the 1980s and only one winning season in the entire 1970s.

"You may have injuries or disappointments in player performance or in a poor draft choice by us or things like that, but if you stick to the culture you want, we talked about the facilities, but also the aggressiveness and the ability to analyze what makes a good roster and what kind of leaders you want on the team," Lurie said in 2023. "Stick to that and you're not going to have a long dip. You could, but you shouldn't. You should be able to find the next coach, find the next quarterback, find the next leaders on defense. You ought to be able to make up for mistakes in the draft with better drafting and smart free agency and...do not make any move because it's short-term really popular. That's a mistake waiting to happen."

Lurie had said in previous interviews that he keeps a handwritten checklist on the right side of the drawer next to where he sleeps outlining the tenets he believes are required for sustained success. "If you open the drawer, it's the first thing you see," he said in 2018. "I can't open that drawer looking for something else without it staring me in the face. And it's on purpose." The list previously featured five items and later swelled to six. (He said in 2018 he memorized the list, but he reads it for monthly reminders.) It included:

- A first-class practice facility
- A football-only stadium
- A dynamic head coach with a "great staff"
- A strong football executive and personnel staff
- A franchise quarterback
- Collaboration and chemistry in the organization and locker room

Consider that moment after the NFC Championship Game. It combined all of those elements from Lurie's checklist.

Start with the facilities, because when Lurie identified the seminal moments from the past 25 years, he first referenced the construction of Lincoln Financial Field and the NovaCare Complex. When Lurie purchased the Eagles, they played in "the Vet"—a multiuse, concrete bowl with artificial turf. It was famed for the rowdy fans of the 700 level in the upper decks, the courtroom that was opened in the stadium for said fans, and the decrepit condition relative to stadiums built elsewhere in the NFL. And that was just speaking about the 10 home games (more, if lucky) each season. For the players, coaches, and staff, a practice facility is perhaps more important, because that's the daily office. The franchise's offices were at Veterans Stadium, and they had an indoor practice "bubble" in the parking lot. In 2000, the Eagles broke ground on a new 108,000-square foot facility on the site of the old Philadelphia Naval Hospital. The complex opened one year later. It was state of the art at the time and remains a suitable workplace, even if the facility arms race accelerated to a higher gear with openings in the past decade. But everything from the locker room to the training room to the auditorium, not to mention offices for employees in both the football and business sides of the building, allowed for the Eagles to adapt to an evolving NFL landscape.

The stadium opened two years later as part of a partnership with the city and state. The open-air facility with a natural grass surface allowed for the team to generate more revenue from suites and public seat licenses while also providing a better live-viewing experience for fans in attendance.

"The moment we were able to make sure those [projects] were going to happen was a real shift," Lurie said. "Because I always talk of wanting to create a state-of-the-art franchise that had great facilities for its players and everybody, and yet it was all words at that point, because [we] obviously inherited a difficult situation with Veterans Stadium. So the moment we were able to finalize our arrangements with the state, the city, to be able to get them to start constructing NovaCare Complex and Lincoln Financial Field, fulfilled what I wanted to have for our personnel.... Until that moment it was effort and thoughts and words, but that brought it to fruition. When they opened it was a whole new frontier, a whole new beginning of the Eagles having great facilities."

This also mattered in procuring talent. Some of it might be organizational talking points, considering the impetus for signing is often the most lucrative offer or most desirable football situation—or sometimes, it's even based on geography. But Lurie purchased the team early in unrestricted free agency, and where a player worked could be a factor in a decision—even if not a top one. If nothing else, it matters for player satisfaction. Even in 2022, the NFL Players Association conducted a player survey, and facilities proved to be a major item.

"Players were going to have the option to play for whomever they wanted to play for," Lurie said of his early ownership days. "And when you have the worst facilities, you can have great coaching, you can get a quarterback that you're really excited about, but how do you explain to the rest of the world of players and agents and executives that you're going to be really competitive and aggressive when it comes to player acquisition? It was, I think, the pivot point of being a franchise, that when you [looked] inward, we had great ideas and great plans and great intentions, but until they came to fruition with facilities, you just couldn't attract the best of the best. And so that's why it was important. It's been really a harbinger of lots of great things that have happened since."

Along with the facility, Lurie identified hiring Reid as another critical moment in jump-starting the franchise in 1999. At the time, Reid was a quarterbacks coach in Green Bay and was not on other teams' head coach lists. In fact, the Packers had a vacancy that offseason and hired the coach the Eagles fired—Ray Rhodes—even though Reid was in the building. The decision to hire Reid was part of an extensive research process, but Reid won more games than any coach in Eagles history and was one of the faces of the franchise. Lurie has said Reid will one day join the franchise's Hall of Fame. Success was not promised in 1999, but Lurie's plan cemented an organizational philosophy that remains in place two decades later.

"I've been able to really find the person that I felt had great potential to be as good as any coach in football and to have the philosophy that I both learned from and also felt simpatico with from the very beginning," Lurie said. "He was the professional that brought in many other people that we were able to achieve from the coaching perspective, sort of the real upside for the Eagles."

The latter point is important, because Reid's staff was also a critical factor in the early success. Remember how Lurie's checklist included the coaching staff along with the head coach? Reid's initial staff featured eight assistants who became head coaches: John Harbaugh, Brad Childress, Sean McDermott, Ron Rivera, Steve Spagnuolo, Leslie Frazier, Pat Shurmur, and David Culley. Defensive coordinator Jim Johnson, who did not become a head coach, is one of the most influential assistant coaches in franchise history and a major part of the Eagles' success during the 2000s.

Reid's run lasted 14 years. He was eventually fired in 2012 after the Eagles bottomed out with a 4–12 record and recorded back-to-back seasons without making the playoffs—the first time that had happened under Reid. It was also a year of personal tragedy; Reid's oldest son died of a drug overdose at the Eagles' training camp.

Reflecting on any regrets he may still have from this 25-year period during the summer of 2023, Lurie mentioned that he wished he could have found a way to make it work with Reid before noting that Reid's family situation required a move away from Philadelphia and a fresh start elsewhere.

"It was very hard to replace Andy Reid. He was strong, a pillar," Lurie said. "And his situation was very, very complicated. In a normal situation, for Andy, I don't think I would have ever made a change. It was not popular to keep him year after year. I understand that. But I was very convinced that he was a Hall of Fame coach, and at that point, we'd won a lot but we hadn't won the Super Bowl. His family situation, I wish in a way that I could have found a way to help them in some way so that it didn't feel like the best outcome was for him to have a whole new move to another part of the country.... I look back and wish I were maybe more successful at trying to make that happen in a better way."

Lurie's search for Reid's replacement focused on Chip Kelly. An established college coach, Kelly came with a profile—and a self-assurance—to ease the transition from a coach who had served a 14-year tenure. Kelly also brought a different approach from Reid's, from his up-tempo style of play to an unconventional practice schedule to significant focus on sports science. He was Lurie's only hire who had head coaching experience in college or the NFL, and unlike the other three coaches during this 25-year period, he was the only one who was sought after elsewhere.

The Kelly years have become a footnote. He lasted three years in Philadelphia, and for a year and a half, he could have been elected mayor. His teams made the postseason and had two double-digit winning seasons. For a moment, it appeared as if Kelly was revolutionizing the NFL. Lurie pushed his chips in on Kelly when the coach's relationship with Roseman deteriorated. Lurie gave Kelly full personnel control and Roseman was removed from football decision-making duties (although Lurie hedged his bet by making sure he kept Roseman in the building). The Eagles faltered in 2015, and Lurie fired Kelly before the season finale when interpersonal dynamics became problematic.

"I think choosing Chip Kelly was an upside choice," Lurie said. "It was a little different than every other pick. However, the first two years were obviously very successful, with double-digit wins. But I was not pleased with his collaborative ability in the building. And I wasn't confident in his relationships with some of the players and executives, obviously, and Howie and all that kind of stuff. I wish I might have foreseen that before hiring him.... To Chip's credit, he had a hard job to replace Andy and he did an outstanding job the first two years, but I could see the flaws and I would have liked to have...maybe seen some of those before and ward those off."

The next two hires—Pederson in 2016 and Sirianni in 2021—took on similar themes. Neither coach interviewed elsewhere, yet both were offensive coordinators under head coaches with whom the Eagles had strong relationships. (Pederson worked for Reid in Kansas City; Sirianni worked for former Eagles offensive coordinator Frank Reich in Indianapolis.) The public approval rating was not especially high for either one—ESPN.com ranked Pederson the worst of the 2016 hires and gave Sirianni the lowest grades of the 2021 hires. Yet both reached the Super Bowl within two seasons, giving Lurie enough of a track record to suggest that he's adept at identifying coaches. Even dating back to Ray Rhodes in 1995, all five of the coaches Lurie hired reached double-digit wins and the postseason within two seasons. Considering the volume of coaches fired each season who fail to bring their teams to the playoffs, that statistic has become one of the hallmarks of Lurie's tenure as an owner.

"I don't know that there's a guy who in the last 20 years that has done a better job...at identifying coaches," Roseman said in February 2023.

Lurie is especially guarded about his success hiring coaches, speaking only generally and not specifically. He called it a "private thought process" and does not want to give away the "secret sauce," but he called it "very consistent in what I believe in terms of leadership and what it takes to maximize a sports franchise and a team." It is not based on scheme or even a team's offensive or defensive success in the previous season. Lurie claimed those factors are too often correlated to the talent on a given roster. In other words, Tom Brady or Peyton Manning can elevate the candidacy of the coach more than the coach might elevate the standing of the player. Lurie also insisted he is unmoved by the "hot candidate" list that comes before each hiring cycle. That might seem obvious, but you would be surprised how much public sentiment can factor into a search. Neither Pederson nor Sirianni received high marks when they were hired and both made the Super Bowl within two seasons.

"I don't care that the person hasn't been interviewed by another franchise. I don't care if they're not the hot candidate," Lurie said. "It goes back to that notion of sticking to what you think has the better chance of creating success. When Bill Walsh was picked by the 49ers, it was an unpopular choice. He was too old. He was too academic or intellectual.... And there's aspects that I really, really do believe in. And I want to be sure I don't go outside those, because you could have a tendency to say, 'Oh, that guy, his offense was unstoppable. I'm going to make him the top candidate' or something like that. Try to avoid that. If they're really able to check all the other boxes I have, then great.... There's aspects that we just feel are undervalued, really undervalued—leadership abilities to [how they] relate to those they're working with and players, resiliency.... There's a lot of clichéd ways of looking at it. But in the end, you're kind of looking at the whole person and can they be what you're hoping they can be?"

Lurie has also been critical of scrutiny about a prolonged search, given that the expected time frame to hire the equivalent of a chief executive in professional football would prompt laughter in a different industry. There is so much that must be ascertained, and the notion that a single interview—even a lengthy one, like those the Eagles are known to hold—is sufficient would be ambitious at best and potentially reckless. "What CEO search takes place in one to three weeks? It's ridiculous," Lurie asked in February 2023. Team president Don Smolenski, who was involved in the team's last three coaching searches, said much of it is relying upon research, background, and conversations that are made simply to reach the starting point. So what the Eagles learned about Sirianni *before* interviewing him is critically important.

"I think the secret sauce is involved in that evaluation of when your team is at a certain place, what can you bring in terms of coaching leadership that will vault you to have a chance to play for another Super Bowl soon?" Lurie said in January 2023. "And that's something I don't want to talk about, but there's probably multiple variables. And Nick, Doug at the time, all fulfilled those variables. I know, it's sort of not the conformist thing to do. As I said, nobody wanted Andy, nobody wanted Doug. Nobody knew about Nick, I guess, I don't know, [it] didn't make sense to me.... Just have confidence in what you think is the right way and what gives you the best chance of high success, peak success."

The success multiple coaches have enjoyed with the franchise presents a worthwhile question: Do the Eagles succeed because of the coaches they hire, or do the coaches succeed because of the infrastructure put in place by Lurie? There are some coaches who breed winning wherever they go—Reid is an example—and there are other coaches who can be a product of their environment. It's why they move on and why they cannot recreate the success from a previous place. A fascinating sliding-doors scenario would be how these 25 years would have looked had the Eagles hired their alternative candidates for each of these four vacancies. Those were believed to be Jim Haslett in 1999, Gus Bradley in 2013, Ben McAdoo in 2016, and Josh McDaniels in 2021. Each of those candidates have been head coaches elsewhere. Not a single one has brought his team to the Super Bowl. Joe Banner once compared the success of coaches to the success of quarterbacks, wherein the elite would be successful wherever they go and others would need the right circumstances to succeed.

"Whenever you win like this, or have sustained success for a period of time, it takes a lot of people, a lot of departments and sectors doing their job, improving and getting better," longtime Eagles center Jason Kelce said before the Super Bowl in 2023. "You really have to have that type of culture and type of environment. That's probably why Jeffrey has had a lot of success [with his hires]. I think it's a really well-run organization. It's not just about the coaches, who've been great. It's really from the top down. It's a well-run machine at this point."

Before the Super Bowl, the question about the Eagles' track record was posed to then Eagles defensive coordinator Jonathan Gannon, who was later hired as the Arizona Cardinals' head coach.

"Yeah, I'll tell you exactly [why]," Gannon said. "There's 32 owners, right? And I've worked for six. This isn't a slight to anybody else I've worked for, but it's really a testament to Mr. Lurie. He is committed, and all that he can do for the entire building and the structure to help the players, he's willing to do. And when you have that type of support—and not just financial support, but other things as well—typically you can put a good product in place if you have the right people."

As much as Lurie suggests he has a criterion for what he is seeking in a coaching candidate, the dynamic of the roster and the franchise at a given time also dictates the hires. After 14 years of Reid, a strong presence and track record like Kelly's, who had a radically different approach, made sense. Lurie wanted someone with "emotional intelligence" who could connect with the locker room (and collaborate with the front office) when he hired Pederson in 2016. In 2021, the Eagles were looking for an up-and-coming coach given the late start on the search, and there was a particular emphasis on teaching and player development

"They each, at the time of wanting them, fulfilled something that I thought was incredibly important for our culture or organization at that moment," Lurie said in February 2023. "And there are similarities in different ways and differences. But you got to do what's right and not do what makes sense to the noise out there or the public perceptions."

Along with the facilities and hiring Reid, the other decision that Lurie said set the foundation for this period was drafting McNabb in 1999. Lurie called the decision a "no-brainer," which might seem easy to frame in hindsight given that McNabb became the best quarterback in franchise history. But the polarizing decision, which prompted fans to boo the pick at the Theatre at MSG, came with utter conviction from Andy Reid. The coach was so convinced by McNabb that Lurie was unmoved by a personal phone call from Saints owner Tom Benson on the day of the draft to try to convince the Eagles to accept a bounty of picks so the Saints could select Ricky Williams.

All those fans clamoring for Williams in green (including Mayor Ed Rendell at the time) were never going to be satisfied, because Williams was not even the No. 1 running back on the Eagles' board. The Eagles were hellbent on drafting a quarterback, and Reid had determined McNabb was the quarterback he wanted. But Lurie said the phone call from Benson compelled him to at least bring the offer to Reid. The Saints traded the No. 12 overall pick along with third-, fourth-, fifth-, sixth-, and seventh-round picks in 1999 and first- and third-round picks in 2000 to move up to No. 5 overall that year. (The 2000 first-rounder turned into the No. 2 overall pick.) That shows the type of deal the Eagles could have commanded, and Lurie remembered the offer including a "crazy number of No. 1 picks" from the Saints, who wanted the reigning Heisman Trophy winner.

"It was like what you'd always hoped would happen," Lurie said. "But at the same time we had already discussed with Andy that this was the franchise quarterback he wanted. He was a new coach, but the reason we chose Andy was partly his offensive philosophy and his ability to develop quarterbacks, and so we literally had to decide, 'We're gonna have almost an unlimited offer from New Orleans and drop down to [No. 12] or get our quarterback that Andy really wanted.' So I said, 'Andy, this is an opportunity to have all these multiple number ones.' And he said, 'Yep, it absolutely is. Any other year. But this year, this guy has a chance to be a great quarterback for us.' And that was the end of that discussion. And it turned out to be the right move. They're not always as clear-cut, where you absolutely have one player and you know you have to have a franchise quarterback."

Lurie also noted the significance of McNabb becoming the highest-drafted Black quarterback in NFL history at the time. He said that was not a reason why the Eagles took him, but it did signal what they wanted the franchise to represent.

McNabb spent a decade as the Eagles' franchise quarterback, a run that included five trips to the NFC Championship Game. When the Eagles eventually replaced him, they initially turned to Kevin Kolb before Michael Vick became the starter. The decision to sign Vick in 2009 was one of the most polarizing during this 25-year period. Vick was a *bona fide* superstar before he was imprisoned for dogfighting charges, and the Eagles brought him back to the NFL after he was released from prison. The Eagles were set atop the depth chart with McNabb and had already drafted Kolb in the second round, so Vick was initially signed as a depth quarterback. The signing was met with resistance by fans locally and nationally. Lurie said the key for the Eagles was that Vick expressed remorse. It became national news. Lurie identified it as an important "milestone" for the franchise.

"It wasn't so much a player evaluation decision as it was giving someone a second chance that we felt really, from all indications, would be great for Michael and also excellent for the Eagles," Lurie said. "If there was a case for a player that deserved the second chance, as I said at the time, and I've said since, African Americans do not get many second chances. And why shouldn't we be proactive and lead the way? I thought that was a good identity to have because it was genuine. It wasn't like we were trying to prove something.... And so he was a wonderful locker room presence. Wonderful in the community. A pleasure to all of us to interact with. Kind of an iconic figure for young players coming to the franchise. And I think it signaled to the rest of the NFL players that the Eagles were not only a player-friendly culture that was extremely aggressive competitively but...[we were] open to things."

The Eagles eventually paid Vick to be their franchise quarterback, too, although they were clearly in the market for a potential replacement in the 2012 draft. The quarterback they ended up drafting was Foles, who remains the only one to bring a Lombardi Trophy to Philadelphia. (It came after he left and returned.) Foles is held in high esteem by Lurie and the organization—"As high-character [a] person as one can come across in any business anywhere in the world.... Nick epitomized everything you'd want," Lurie said—but the truth was that the Eagles did not set out to draft Foles that year. The quarterback they wanted and who they envisioned becoming a potential franchise quarterback was Russell Wilson. They thought Wilson would fall to their pick in the third round, but the Seattle Seahawks drafted him 13 picks before that. More than a decade later, this still sticks with Lurie. He viewed missing Wilson as one of his regrets from this era, and it later influenced the Eagles' decision to draft Jalen Hurts.

In between was the Carson Wentz era. Like Kelly, history will not look as favorably on Wentz's five years with the team because they were plagued by injury along with the inconsistency and unrest that prompted an eventual trade. But it would be revisionist history to suggest Lurie and the Eagles did not view Wentz as a franchise quarterback. In fact, in 2019, when the Eagles made Wentz the highest-paid player in franchise history, Lurie went as far as to say Wentz embodied exactly what the Eagles would want in a player commanding such a distinction. They traded significant assets to land him, and they treated him like the franchise's centerpiece—especially when Wentz was a *bona fide* MVP candidate in 2017.

Wentz's presence did not stop the Eagles from taking Hurts in the second round of the 2020 draft. An argument could be made that the pick led to Wentz's downfall. But Lurie said the Eagles were influenced by missing on Wilson in 2012, and there was top-of-the-organization conviction to make sure they do not bypass that type of quarterback if they believed they could draft him again. When Hurts emerged as the Eagles' next franchise player—fitting the profile Lurie imagined when he made that list years earlier—Lurie identified that draft pick as a defining decision for the organization.

"Because that's a franchise-changing outcome," Lurie said. "And it's very consistent with our philosophy.... If you can find a young quarterback that can exhibit what you're hoping to achieve and just needs development, it doesn't matter the situation. You should acquire that player. And this is where it really helps to not try to make popular decisions. I mean, we knew that it was not going to register on the popularity scale. But it was a no-brainer for those of us that wanted to continue to be very, very disciplined in what we believe in. I think you're the product of your own history. And we went away from it, not pulling the trigger on Russell Wilson in that draft when we were unanimously ready to take him and we were all just ready to put the word in and let's go, and we overestimated, or underestimated, one franchise that got the benefit of it. We weren't going to let that happen."

That leads to the executive part of Lurie's checklist. The role has evolved during the 25 years and, at times, what exactly it encompasses has been nebulous. Reid had final say on football decisions for much of his tenure, so he was effectively the chief personnel decision-maker even when the Eagles had a general manager during his tenure (Tom Heckert at one point, then Howie Roseman). But the two executives who are most prominent during this era for the Eagles are Banner and Roseman.

Banner helped implement some of the organizational and team-building philosophies that remain in place to this day, and Roseman has emerged as one of the most powerful and influential executives in football. The main difference is Banner's purview included the business and the football side while he was team president, whereas the Eagles split those responsibilities after Banner's 2012 exit. Roseman and Smolenski have led the football and business sides, respectively, ever since. (The outlier for Roseman was the 2015 season when Kelly was in charge.) Lurie went out of his way to emphasize the importance of the front office in organizational success.

"It's really underrated because...it's not the forward-facing part that the fan recognizes, but I do," Lurie said. "If I didn't have good presidents and general managers, it would not take hold the way it has. The success would not have been the same. And it's unheralded."

Lurie praised Banner, a childhood friend, for bringing an outside-the-industry perspective that helped with renovating the organization, navigating the construction of the stadium and practice facility, and bringing an innovative approach to salary cap management and roster construction.

Lurie said the "next wave" was the Roseman-Smolenski arrangement. Roseman started in salary cap management under Banner before learning scouting during his ascent in the front office. Lurie has credited Roseman with embodying what's required in a modern football executive. His point is that the role has grown so large that it is no longer simply about sitting in an office watching film—even if that's part of the job. It's managing an entire football operations department. That stretches from salary cap allocation to the use of data and analytics to strategic roster-building to parts of the operation that fans might not consider, such as the performance staff, medical staff, or equipment staff. And that is in addition to the traditional roles of a general manager.

"You can have real advantages in emphasizing it, and so the general manager in our case really is head of football operations," Lurie said. "There are multiple departments and at the same time, they've got to be on top of player acquisition and salary cap and all that. It's a multivariable job, but if it was just football scouting, it wouldn't be what we need."

Roseman has survived multiple regime changes, which has made him a polarizing figure. He has continued to earn Lurie's loyalty, leading to suggestions that he's bulletproof. There have also been whispers of Lurie's involvement in personnel decisions, considering he is not an absentee owner. There have been other owners who are the butt of jokes about coming in off a yacht and telling the front office who to pick; Lurie is the opposite. He is not a Jerry Jones figure making all the roster decisions, but he is in draft meetings and in the draft room and is aware of what's happening with the roster. Even if Lurie would dispute characterizations of how or whether he tipped the scale on decisions, it is blatantly clear that this is not a hobby for him. As he said, it's an obsession.

Lurie is a strong advocate for the use of analytics, and the Eagles have been viewed as one of the league's leaders in incorporating data into decision-making. When Lurie was pressed in the spring of 2022 about decisions in which he was involved, he cherry-picked a few that would make his hit rate seem so strong that he should make every decision. When viewing a collection of his remarks on this topic, it is clear Lurie likes to tout the importance of collaboration in decision-making—one of the items on his checklist. It is an idea that is sensible in theory but can be ambiguous in practice. Someone's finger is always on the button. Since 2016, that finger has clearly been Roseman's, and Roseman is responsible for the good and bad—whether it is drafting Hurts in the second round in 2020 or Jalen Reagor 32 picks earlier.

"It's a misnomer to think one person is actually making the pick," Lurie said in 2022. "It's an organization. And if we miss, the organization misses. Maybe we collaborated, and there was a reason that it wasn't seen as a good scheme fit. Or maybe there was a medical reason...that didn't end up happening. Or maybe it was a misevaluation in some way. Today's NFL, I can't think of any team—I'm sure there's exceptions—with one person doing that."

Lurie added that there is "always a sort of controversy over hitting and missing on a draft pick," but he focuses more on the process when considering the fallout. How were the players evaluated? How was information gathered and sorted? How did the departments collaborate? To those points, Lurie suggested Roseman "deserves a lot of credit."

The reality of collaboration is that when teams win, collaboration is often touted, and when teams lose, it is often said that more collaboration is needed. As the saying goes, victory has a thousand fathers, and losing is an orphan. But it is accurate to suggest that the Eagles tend to be less influenced by public perception than they could be, a characteristic in which Lurie takes pride. It would be easy to make consensus-based decisions and, if they were to fail, point to the fact that there were few detractors at the time. Sometimes, the best decisions are the obvious ones. Good luck finding an objection to the Eagles drafting DeVonta Smith in 2021, for example. But Lurie made the point that his ownership coincided with the proliferation of sports talk radio as a populist approach to watching sports. It would have been easy to allow the loudest voices on the airwaves to influence decision-making, and team officials would be lying if they suggested they are unaware of what the populist opinion might be on a big topic. Yet some of the big decisions and great players (and coaches) spotlighted in this book were not winning fan polls when they first joined the organization.

"Be proactive and don't just do what's popular, but sometimes do what you think is right," Lurie said. "And I think that's been the guiding principle really ever since I bought the team.... Stick to your principles, stick to what correlates with winning, and don't worry that you're at times making short-term unpopular choices. That should be the last thing you ever think about."

For a cross-sports reference, he pointed to the Boston Celtics' decision to draft Larry Bird in 1978, even though they needed to wait a year for Bird to leave Indiana State. The Eagles have long been on the cutting edge of valuing the team's future draft picks more than a standard draft chart might suggest, and they do it with this concept in mind: do not make short-term popular decisions.

Spend enough time listening to Lurie, and you will hear how other franchises exert more influence than a popular opinion. He likes to cite Bill Walsh and Red Auerbach as examples of coaches and executives he admires, and he referenced the Golden State Warriors and Miami Heat as organizations whose cultures are worth emulation.

It was not lost on Lurie that other franchises might view the Eagles—or at least parts of their operations during the past 25 years—that way. By the time Lurie left the stadium he helped build on that night of the 2023 NFC Championship Game, the Chiefs had clinched a spot in the Super Bowl. The game featured two coaches who were first hired by Lurie, two general managers who broke into the NFL in Philadelphia, and even two team presidents who rose through the ranks in the Eagles' front office. And Lurie pointed to a tree with branches of former Eagles coaches and executives spreading around the NFL. The gold standard franchise seems to be whichever one is hoisting a silver Lombardi Trophy at the end of each year, but the franchise Lurie owns is different now than it was 25 years ago.

2

Joe Banner

To understand Joe Banner's time as Eagles president, consider the story about the 1998 trade for Hugh Douglas. During the negotiation, Banner dealt with then Jets coach Bill Parcells, a towering figure in the NFL with several Super Bowl rings and an authoritative presence. Banner was still a relative unknown in the NFL without a traditional football background. Parcells took an aggressive approach in the initial trade talks with Banner—"Kind of a bully about the whole thing," Banner remembered—and pushed hard for a first-round pick. Banner was adamant that the Eagles would not trade a first-rounder. The two sides agreed to a second- and fifth-round pick as compensation while the Eagles negotiated a contract extension with Douglas. Banner played hard to get while trying to iron out the contract. Parcells wanted to close the deal and grew impatient.

"I'm going to dinner at 8:00 tonight," Parcells told Banner, although Banner remembers some choice words mixed in (at a loud volume, at that). "So at 7:59, I'm just telling you right now, I'm turning off my phone. And if you haven't called me by 7:59, there's nothing in the world you could do that would end up with Hugh Douglas being a Philadelphia Eagle. So you decide, but I'm not sitting around here on hold, waiting for you to make up your mind. You got until 7:59."

At 7:58 PM, Banner called Parcells and told him they had an agreement. The two teams could document the trade and make it official. Banner had known well before 7:58 that they had a deal in place, but he waited until the last minute on principle.

"I wanted to show him that he couldn't kind of push me around or intimidate me," Banner said. "Me personally and then us collectively, we didn't want anybody else to get a sense that we were pushovers or we weren't tough. Probably part of the reason that we, I, got perceived as being so tough."

The end result was the Eagles acquiring one of the top players in franchise history for a reasonable price, as Banner was wont to do. It was an example of the Eagles exploring the trade market and finding an underappreciated asset, which became a marked characteristic for the Eagles during the Banner era (and subsequently under Howie Roseman). It shows how Banner needed to overcome a perception that he came from a nontraditional background, which followed him throughout his time in Philadelphia. The tough negotiation and impulse to make sure he could not be pushed around were also characteristic of Banner's time with the Eagles.

Remember the elements that Lurie identified as critical to the Eagles establishing their foundation 25 years ago? Banner was directly involved in each of them. He was the frontman in the stadium deal and practice facility construction. He oversaw the study that helped the Eagles identify and hire Andy Reid. He was part of the decision to draft McNabb. And Banner instituted strategies and philosophies that helped the Eagles construct the rosters in those early years—which Howie Roseman has carried on two decades later.

"The league was just dealing with a new hard salary cap, so to be at the forefront of being able to figure out how best to manage that, I think, gave us a big advantage that we've continued to have," Lurie said. "Anything you can think of, business or football, needs a whole different approach. And it had to fit the vision I hoped for with the franchise. Joe was really instrumental in executing and managing a lot of it. I don't think he gets enough credit for that and being supportive of Andy."

Before the Eagles hired Reid in 1999, Banner organized a study that would try to make the coaching search more scientific. It was based upon the idea that the league was not particularly good at hiring coaches, considering the six to eight openings per year and how many jobs turned over because of inadequate hiring. They studied every head coach who had won two or more Super Bowls and learned that there was "nothing in common" regarding their approaches to playing the game, ages, or even styles of play.

What they found were similar characteristics that went beyond football, from leadership to an obsessive preoccupation with every detail to the ability to evaluate other coaches and effectively manage them. There was a strong conviction about how they played the game—it wasn't one way, but it was an irrefutable, unmovable belief in a given philosophy that they used and taught.

"That study obviously led directly to hiring Andy Reid," Banner said during a January 2023 interview. "We started with believing the process was broken."

Banner's approach to the salary cap gave the Eagles an advantage during the early 2000s, when they were consistently signing ascending players to early contracts that would lock the player into the franchise—often at a salary rate that would have been less than the player could have commanded on the open market. The *New York Times* called Banner the "Joe Montana of the salary cap."

"The idea was to neutralize the leverage in the negotiations," Banner said during an interview in the summer of 2023. "The risk is you shift the injury risk. You're making a projection on the player's development when you go early. So we started signing players two years early, which at that point was legal. The second part of the strategy was we were very open: 'We will sign you early. We will therefore take the risk of injury. We will take the risk of your development and in return for that we want a discount on the average of the deal.' And this was not a secret. It was not sprung on anybody. We spoke openly about it. And frankly we had some people [who] said no, and we didn't do those deals early. Some of those players we lost and some of those players we just signed later. But most people at that point, there's financial security and the guaranteed money motivates them to find that concept pretty appealing."

The thought was if a player would command $11 million on the open market and the Eagles signed him for $9 million by executing the deal earlier, then after five deals they would have $10 million in savings that could be allocated elsewhere.

"You're not being unfair, you're not fooling anybody; you're actually providing earlier financial security for the player in return for maybe a little bit smaller gross earnings," Banner said. "But you start doing that year after year, by the time you've done it for two, three, four years, you now have $10, $12, $15 million more in cap room than you should have based on the accumulation of these discounts you're getting in return for doing the deals early."

There were other roster-building strategies that came from Banner. He was a strong proponent of trading—and Howie Roseman has followed in his footsteps by earning the distinction as one of the most aggressive general managers in the league. The Eagles acquired players such as Douglas, tackle Jason Peters, linebacker Takeo Spikes, and wide receiver Donte Stallworth during his tenure. (Terrell Owens was also technically acquired in a trade after a clerical issue with his free agency.) They also were quick to trade aging veterans to generate some type of return (even if it was modest) rather than cutting them. The Eagles made 25 trades involving players from 1999 to 2010.

In the draft, Banner was often a proponent of trading back. He said he was dogmatic about this approach and would move up under the right circumstances, but Banner believed in drafting with volume. He liked targeting players with injuries in the middle to late rounds, believing they were undervalued for that reason. Trent Cole was an example of a player who the Eagles landed in the fifth round because of what Banner deemed this market inefficiency. They liked players from small schools, believing that was also an inefficiency. Todd Herremans was drafted this way from Saginaw Valley State. A number of times, both strategies failed, but the Eagles viewed these methods as a way of finding starting-caliber players at backup prices.

Banner also believed in trading for future picks, which were often discounted. In 2008, the Eagles dealt their first-round pick to Carolina in exchange for a second-round pick, fourth-round pick, and first-round pick the following season. That gave them the flexibility to acquire Peters. When they traded A.J. Feeley and James Thrash before the 2004 draft, they did not acquire picks that spring. They landed a second-round pick and fifth-round pick in 2005, which seemingly went at a discounted rate. In 2001, they turned a third-round pick and a sixth-round pick into a second rounder the following year. That was how they landed Sheldon Brown. Banner laughed at the notion that a future pick was worth one round less. A dollar today might be worth more than a dollar tomorrow, but there is no pick inflation in the NFL. There's only job preservation.

"The league is devaluing these future picks too much," Banner said. "We were always looking for the opportunities in those things."

The Eagles made their share of mistakes in roster management during the Banner years. There were picks that missed, trades that backfired, and ill-fated signings. The same is true for every team. But Banner wanted it to be an organizational emphasis not to let a failed decision affect the aggressiveness of the next decision. He said one of the tenets was the willingness to accept a mistake and move on, rather than compound a problem by prolonging it. He came into the league without a background in football and he tried to turn this perspective into an asset. Whereas the differences might have drawn ridicule from those who had only ever worked in football, the different background allowed him to think and act differently.

"Jeff and I have watched games for years as fans and we had an aggressive mindset," Banner said. "We didn't understand why football was so different about the inclination to make trades or get creative, get aggressive. There were things that just weren't happening to football then even to this day, they don't happen as often as they should. One of the pieces separating the Eagles is just fearlessness about doing it."

The willingness to challenge conventional wisdom is one way Banner would like his Eagles tenure to be remembered. It extends from hiring a head coach who has never been a coordinator or head coach to the application of analytics in decision-making to the way the stadium deal was structured to the selling of naming rights to the practice facility to simply how he believed winning football should be played. The reason those fans wanted the Eagles to draft Ricky Williams over Donovan McNabb was because of the way the running game was viewed in 1999. But Banner looked at the numbers and openly wondered why coaches and analysts called to run the ball so much if a good running team averaged 4.5 yards per carry and a good passing team averaged 7.5 yards per play.

"It didn't seem like anyone was asking such a simplistic question," Banner said.

Or maybe they didn't like who was doing the asking.

"Because Jeff and I didn't have a background in football, I think it contributed to a lot of the questions that we got," Banner said. "'They're coming in here telling us that you should pass the ball more. Who the hell do they think they are?'"

Banner heard commentators discuss how teams must establish the run and wanted to pull his hair out. If a disproportionate amount of games are won by the team leading at halftime, wouldn't it behoove a team to be aggressive *early* rather than try to play catch-up? So pass to build a lead, and then run when the lead is established. And build a defense that is built to play with a lead.

"I think people forget how many things were kind of just considered truths way back then that we ignored and turned out to contribute in a big way to our success," Banner said.

As Lurie explained, the early years of this period came during the proliferation of sports-talk radio. Banner was often a lightning rod for fans. Reid and Banner established a good guy–bad guy routine that allowed for Reid to maintain the good will he needed in the locker room. Even though Reid had final say on personnel, contract disputes were often put on Banner's shoulders. His public demeanor did not help—Banner liked to win an argument and would not be described as warm and fuzzy—and he became the face of bottom-line decisions. When a popular player departs, it's hard for management to win the popularity contest. Nobody cheers in the stands for salary cap prudence or winning a negotiation. Banner's view was that winning or losing would determine public perception. If the Eagles won, fans would be thrilled. If the Eagles lost, they would not.

"The irony is we ended up winning and getting criticized anyway," Banner said. "We hadn't really contemplated that was one of the options that we would win and get criticized anyway."

This does not necessarily leave Banner free from decisions he regrets. He wishes there was more patience with Sean McDermott, who was fired as defensive coordinator after two seasons following the enormous shadow left by Jim Johnson. McDermott went to Carolina and eventually became a successful head coach. Banner personally regrets the way Brian Dawkins' time in Philadelphia ended—he said it's "not fair" for the decision to be pegged on him, as it had been publicly—but it was hard for Banner to see the way it materialized.

And then there were the what-could-have-been decisions that every executive has with player personnel. One that has never been reported was that the Eagles "briefly" talked about signing Drew Brees as a free agent in 2006. It did not make much sense because McNabb was entrenched as the franchise quarterback and Brees was signing somewhere to be the starter, but Banner said they identified the rare opportunity to acquire a transcendent player in free agency. As it does Lurie, the decision to wait on drafting Russell Wilson in 2012 still rankles Banner.

As team president, Banner considered identifying talent to hire as the most important part of his job. The Reid decision was the big one, but Banner also brought in Roseman when Roseman had just graduated law school. He hired Smolenski from minor league hockey. And there were a number of other hires in different departments who later became team presidents, football executives, and head coaches. Banner viewed this as his most important contribution to this period of Eagles football. In fact, part of his eventual departure in 2012 was the desire to promote Roseman and Smolenski and split Banner's role into two jobs—one on the football side, one on the business side.

"I think the reason it worked was overwhelmingly because of my success in being able to hire other people who were really good," Banner said. "Just looking at my own time at this, I think that is the most important, valuable thing I did."

With time, those evaluations have aged well. Reid is one of the best coaches in NFL history. Roseman helped deliver the Eagles their first Super Bowl and is regarded as one of the league's best general managers. Several players acquired during Banner's tenure as top executive are among Eagles greats (and are featured in this book), and similar books on other franchises would include coaches and executives who started their careers in Philadelphia during Banner's reign.

Like agreeing to the Douglas trade, sometimes the gratification is delayed until the last minute.

3

Howie Roseman

Howie Roseman strolled the field in the Houston Texans' stadium before an Eagles game in November 2022. At that moment in the season, one might have suggested Roseman actually had water and not turf under his feet. The Eagles were undefeated, the last team without a loss in the NFL. Roseman's offseason transactions produced sterling results and helped eventually earn him the NFL's Executive of the Year award for the second time in his career. A group of Philadelphia fans cheered toward Roseman and drew attention to a sign that suggested Roseman was forgiven.

"I'm f—ing forgiven for your first f—ing Super Bowl?" he asked.

The retort was met with cheers from the group. It also revealed Roseman's complicated history as Eagles general manager. Roseman's résumé was atypical for a top football executive. He has twice assembled Super Bowl rosters in the years he was honored, yet he also effectively lost his job for a year when he was stripped of football decision-making responsibilities. He has survived the dismissals of three head coaches—a rarity among executives—yet he also played a major role in the hiring of the coaches who led the Eagles to the Super Bowls. He's been loved and ridiculed, and he now has an indelible place in franchise history and is one of the most notable sports figures in Philadelphia.

"I think experience is a great tool. I really do. And I think adversity is a great tool," Roseman said on the day before he departed for the Super Bowl in Arizona in February 2023. "I can say that now—not necessarily when you're in that moment. But I think if you can find a way to use those moments productively, you can continue to get better. And I feel like I can continue to get better personally. I don't feel like I've hit a level where I'm not learning new things or open to new ideas. I'm not saying that to pat myself on the back. It's just the reality of it."

Roseman's biography is one that is far more relatable than it is replicable. As a kid in Marlboro, New Jersey, Roseman dreamed of becoming a general manager. His persistence as a child has become legendary; he sent letters to every NFL franchise while in high school, and if he received a rejection letter, he sent a thank you for the rejection. He famously wowed Jack Elway, a college football coach and the father of Hall of Famer John Elway, on an airplane with his football knowledge. He made it his life's work to become an NFL general manager, even when it seemed he possessed little conceivable reason to believe he would become one. He did not play football other than throwing with friends. He did not grow up in a football family. He did not have a connection with an NFL franchise. What he offered was a mix of intelligence, creativity, and persistence, and as Jason Kelce will tell you, nothing gets in the way of persistence.

"Ever since I was little I had this direction, and I don't know why," Roseman said. "I didn't really have anyone around me and obviously I've been knocked down a bunch of times.... You had to be passionate and determined to get here. Sometimes I wish I was able to take my foot off the gas a little bit. But as my wife reminds me, 'I am who I am,' and I kind of dove into it at this point in my life."

He attended the University of Florida because it was, at the time, the top football program. Roseman treated the NFL Draft like it was a final exam well before you could find endless draft information by scrolling through your phone. He wrote notes, compiled rankings, and broke down positional needs for every team in the NFL. He was not shy about disagreeing with picks, including when he threw his notes when his (then) beloved New York Jets selected Kyle Brady No. 9 overall in 1995. He scouted in unorthodox ways, too. There was a fourth-floor parking garage where he could watch Gators practice from a distance. He turned to his roommate during one of their viewing sessions and said, "There's a running back wearing No. 21 who will one day become better than Herschel Walker." That player was Fred Taylor, who became a top-10 pick and rushed for more than 10,000 yards in the NFL. He sat in his living room with the same roommate when a report surfaced about an NFL player who would be released. The club received no compensation—they just let him go for free—and Roseman wished the league was more imaginative.

"There's not enough trades in the NFL," Roseman told his roommate. "They don't know how to value people and picks, and once I get there, I'm going to make more trades than you've ever seen."

His other roommate was similarly like-minded. Jedd Fisch, another football-obsessed New Jersey native who did not play at the college level, also attended Florida because that was where Steve Spurrier coached. Fisch and Roseman bonded over their shared ambition—and the seemingly impenetrable barrier to entry. While Roseman rose through NFL scouting, Fisch developed as a coach. He was an NFL coordinator and is currently head coach at the University of Washington.

"The thing that both of us had was a relentless attitude, and we wouldn't take no for an answer," Fisch said in a 2014 interview. "You have to have the personality that you accept 75 rejection letters as long as the 76th letter says, 'We'll bring you in for an interview.'"

Roseman and Fisch studied football while others played, giving Roseman an analogy he liked to use: "Do you want the heart surgeon who had bypass surgery, or do you want the one who has studied it the longest?"

What Roseman needed was someone who would put him at the operating table. That proved to be Joe Banner—after Jets general manager Mike Tannenbaum gave him an interview. Banner and Tannenbaum actually had a running joke about Roseman's doggedness, remarking that when they meet with Roseman, it should probably be in a public space. When Roseman met with the Jets, he encountered Bill Parcells, who told him that the only Howie he had ever met was Howie Long. The Hall of Fame defensive lineman was listed at 6'5" and 268 pounds. Roseman wrestled at 119 pounds in high school. He was ready to add a new "Howie" to Parcells' list.

Banner could only offer an internship working with the salary cap for Roseman, who had graduated from law school at Fordham University and took the bar exam as a backup plan. That gave Roseman a foot in the door in the Eagles' offices (then Veterans Stadium, later the NovaCare Complex). His title changed throughout the years, and he graduated from a small space on the desk of an administrative assistant to one of the most expansive offices on site. But he proved he just needed to get in, considering he lacked any NFL connections. He would take it from there.

Roseman progressed from salary cap staff counsel (2000 to 2002) to director of football administration (2003–'05) to vice president of football administration (2006–'07). Even though his entry was in cap management, he itched to build a team. He learned scouting during this period and was a sponge for the roster management ideas and strategies of Andy Reid and Banner. By 2008, Roseman was vice president of player personnel—a role that required him to manage the college scouting staff and run draft meetings. The term "football guy" can be nebulous, but this was decidedly a job with football responsibilities. When Tom Heckert, who had been the general manager from 2006 to 2009, left for Cleveland in 2010, Roseman was promoted to general manager. Even though Reid maintained final say on personnel and Banner remained influential in football decisions, Roseman, at age 34, was the youngest general manager in the NFL.

"I love Howie's energy and his eagerness to grow in the profession," Reid said when Roseman was introduced in 2010. "You've seen how we've done it on the coaching side; you've seen how we've done it on the player personnel side of it. His eagerness to learn and then his ability to evaluate are second to none. Then you can add in that Howie mentioned here about being a cap expert and all of those things. That's just icing on the cake from that side of it. His effort and energy, I think you will find out over time here that it is second to none."

The team regressed in Roseman's first three seasons from 10–6 and in the postseason in 2010 to the ill-fated "Dream Team" in 2011 when the Eagles loaded up the roster during the lockout and finished 8–8 to cratering at 4–12 in 2012. That's when Reid was fired. But instead of a clean sweep of the front office, Lurie kept Roseman, and they spearheaded the coaching search together. Lurie also endorsed Roseman's player evaluation and essentially absolved him of blame from decisions that included 2011 draft picks that did not last beyond two seasons and lucrative signings that went awry, such as Nnamdi Asomugha. Lurie also credited Roseman with the 2012 draft that provided a critical foundation for the Eagles—bringing Fletcher Cox, Mychal Kendricks, Vinny Curry, and Nick Foles. It's impossible to separate the general manager from those decisions, but what mattered was that he remained a central figure in the organization—and a critical one for Lurie, considering longtime decision-makers Reid and Banner were gone. Roseman was even further emboldened with more personnel power.

"What I had to do was really look at the 2010, 2011, 2012 drafts, offseasons; I really wanted to evaluate everything," Lurie said at the time. "I keep voluminous notes on talent evaluation on not just who we draft, but who is valued in each draft by each person in the organization that's working here. I came to the conclusion that the person that was providing by far the best talent evaluation in the building was Howie Roseman. I decided to streamline the whole decision-making process for the 2012 draft and offseason, and that's the first draft and offseason I hold Howie completely accountable for. The mistakes that were made in the 2011 draft have little or nothing to do with Howie's evaluations, and I think it was important for me to own up to the mistakes that were made and understand where they were coming from and it was awfully clear."

It would not be the last time Lurie defended Roseman in a similar way.

The Eagles hired Chip Kelly in 2013. The new coach had control of the 53-man roster, but Roseman was in charge of the 90-man roster—so roster decisions other than who made the team were technically his call. The Eagles had 10 wins in 2013 and 2014, and those years included shrewd draft picks (Lane Johnson, Zach Ertz), signings (Connor Barwin, Malcolm Jenkins), and trades (Darren Sproles). But the relationship between Roseman and Kelly deteriorated and reached critical mass after the 2014 campaign. Lurie decided to embolden Kelly, giving him full roster control and taking Roseman out of football decision-making duties. But Lurie did not outright dismiss Roseman. He insisted that he saw Roseman's talent and wanted Roseman in the building, even offering him a raise and a new title. It was not as if Roseman was scheduled to return to power. In fact, the organizational hope at the time was to succeed with Kelly. If that occurred, Roseman would likely have been elsewhere. Roseman's office was literally moved to a different part of the NovaCare Complex, a point that Jason Kelce reminded fans about years later when defending Roseman in a Super Bowl parade speech.

Lurie's rationale was that to properly evaluate Kelly, the coach needed to have a hand-picked personnel executive with whom he'd be working every day. For his part, Roseman told former NFL general manager Thomas Dimitroff in a 2022 podcast interview that his lesson from the experience was the importance of spending time to build trust with a new coach and ensuring the communication was "person-to-person" instead of delegating in between. Roseman had been a shooting star in the industry, with a new title seemingly every two years and outpacing more experienced executives to a coveted job. This was a public setback, and it included criticism and reevaluation.

"When you get an opportunity at a really young age and the arrow's pointing up and you don't really get a chance to step back, and [then] something like this happens, there's humility in it," Roseman said in 2018.

That 2015 season turned into the football equivalent of a gap year for Roseman. He traveled around the world meeting with executives from different sports, from San Antonio Spurs general manager R.C. Buford to Chelsea FC director Mike Forde. He reassessed his priorities and how he would do the job. There were organizational lessons and football lessons. But there was also an understanding of how big the job had become, which Lurie had emphasized. A general manager—or executive vice president of football operations, however you want to frame it—has so many decisions to make and so many people to manage that there can be a misconception suggesting he is simply sitting in front of a screen watching film of a left guard from Middle Tennessee State all day. The scope of the job in the present day includes player evaluation, yes, but it also includes salary cap management, implementing data and science into decision-making and overseeing the medical staff and training staff and equipment staff, while also being a public face of the organization.

"I think during that year, when you have the opportunity to talk to people in Major League Baseball, in the NBA, in the NHL, in the EPL, and even working outside sports, you see that it's hard to have one person who just makes every single decision and runs every single department," Roseman said. "Sometimes we forget...it's big business. We're managing payroll, we have a bunch of resources, and we're trying to hire a lot of good people. Really, I think maybe we're the last sport that doesn't [split up the jobs] as much."

When the Eagles collapsed under Kelly in 2015 and Lurie elected to fire the coach, Roseman was moved back to the football side of the building and entrusted to help find a coach (Doug Pederson) and re-assemble a roster. The priority was to find a franchise quarterback, which led to a series of moves to acquire Carson Wentz. He also stripped the roster of Kelly's high-profile decisions from 2015 and rewarded core Eagles such as Johnson, Ertz, Curry, and Jenkins with contract extensions.

Roseman has been praised—perhaps sometimes in a backhanded way—for his survival instincts, although he reflected in 2023 about a boldness that came from the 2015 experience because he had lost his job. He came out the other side with an understanding that it could be taken from him, so he should at least commit to doing it his way.

"I think sometimes when you get these jobs, you do worry a little bit about job security—and not because of my relationship with Jeffrey at all—but I think when you go back to '15 and basically you're kicked in the dirt and you already see, this is what it feels like, and you feel that way and have regret over some of the things you didn't do," Roseman said in 2023. "So from my perspective, because I've felt that feeling, which is a terrible feeling...the worst part of that is having regret about not doing stuff. And so if we do stuff and it's aggressive and it doesn't work out, I can live with that. If we don't do stuff because we're worried about the repercussions of it, that'll be hard."

Roseman's second act as general manager included some of these bold moves. He remained aggressive with trades and the organization took a salary cap approach of restructuring deals by turning base-year salaries into bonuses that could be spread over the life of the contract. The thought process was akin to getting a mortgage versus paying in cash—they were not paying the player less, but they would extend those payments over a few years and thus have more cap space to spend on contracts. They also added voidable years to deals to prolong such bonus payments.

It started when Roseman shipped out many of Kelly's 2015 additions, including DeMarco Murray, Byron Maxwell, Kiko Alonso, Sam Bradford, and Eric Rowe. The Eagles targeted ascending players in the 2016 free-agent market who were not the top available players at their positions but proved to be core players for the team's growth, such as Brandon Brooks and Rodney McLeod. A series of trades (with those Kelly cast-offs as bait) helped Roseman move higher in the draft so he could take Wentz. With a skeleton scouting crew, the Eagles added two more eventual Super Bowl starters in the draft—Jalen Mills and Halapoulivaati Vaitai—along with contributors Isaac Seumalo and Wendell Smallwood. The Bradford trade helped the Eagles land a first-round pick in the deal for Wentz. The Eagles went 7–9 in Pederson's first season, but they cleaned their salary cap and had a chance to add legitimate talent around Wentz. Roseman could not help but lament the players who had been let go, including DeSean Jackson, LeSean McCoy and Jeremy Maclin. "I don't have a DeLorean time machine to go back in time and get some of those guys back," Roseman said then.

There are times he might have wished he could have a DeLorean to go back to 2017, because it seemed every move by Roseman that offseason turned to gold. He rebuilt the wide receivers with Alshon Jeffery and Torrey Smith at the start of free agency. He lured Foles to be the backup quarterback—and as Lurie would note, the Eagles were willing to eat the cap hit on Chase Daniel's contract to ensure the upgrade at backup quarterback—and watched Foles eventually win Super Bowl MVP. He signed defensive end Chris Long and cornerback Patrick Robinson on the same day at the league meetings, and the two veteran lottery-ticket signings proved to be key contributors for the Eagles. In fact, Long forced an interception and Robinson recorded a pick-six in the NFC Championship Game victory over Minnesota to help turn the momentum toward the Eagles. Roseman traded for Timmy Jernigan before the draft to help build the defensive line. Even post-draft additions such as running back LeGarrette Blount proved valuable, and the acquisition calendar continued during training camp when Roseman traded for cornerback Ronald Darby, early in the season when kicker Jake Elliott was signed off Cincinnati's practice squad, and at the trade deadline when he acquired Jay Ajayi. Those moves also helped the Eagles hoist the Lombardi Trophy. Combined, Roseman has cited this offseason with teaching him and the front office a valuable lesson about roster building: talent acquisition is not confined to obvious pressure points like the first week of free agency and draft weekend. It's anytime until the trade deadline—a principle Roseman is not shy to remind those who are critical when the Eagles' roster is incomplete in March or May.

"Sometimes it just doesn't roll where it's the first day of the league year and all of a sudden you're addressing everything and you feel really good," Roseman said. "I think for us that's the one thing about '17. That was a great lesson for us as a staff: if you can't do it right in the moment, you're going to have opportunities throughout."

Roseman did not have the same luck with veteran acquisitions in 2018, which could serve as evidence that those lottery ticket signings do not always cash in. But the 2018 draft, with the benefit of time and maturity, might be his best draft as general manager. The Lombardi Trophy rested on the draft table for everyone to see as a guide, and their hope was that the draft would produce core players for their next Super Bowl. The irony was the Eagles did not have a second-round pick going into the year because of the Wentz trade, they traded out of the first round to secure future draft inventory (a move of which Banner would certainly approve), and they were drafting at the bottom of each round because they won the Super Bowl. The odds were stacked against them landing four core players—especially with only five overall players selected—yet that's exactly what happened. Second-round selection Dallas Goedert, fourth-round selection Avonte Maddox, fourth-round selection Josh Sweat, and seventh-round selection Jordan Mailata all signed contract extensions with the franchise. Even the other pick the Eagles made, Matt Pryor, contributed and was traded for a future draft pick. Within the NovaCare Complex offices, the lessons from that draft were about prioritizing value over need (Goedert was selected as the top pick even though Ertz was entrenched on the roster) and recognizing the importance of development (Mailata offered tantalizing tools as a 6'8", 364-pound rugby player but had never played organized football when the Eagles drafted him).

During the 2019 offseason, Roseman committed to Wentz as the Eagles' franchise quarterback with a $128 million contract extension and allowed Foles to leave in free agency. He then made a number of moves trying to extend the Eagles' Super Bowl window. Lucrative contracts to aging high-profile veterans DeSean Jackson and Malik Jackson did not materialize as expected, and contract extensions to Super Bowl contributors such as Alshon Jeffery backfired. The Eagles were a nine-win playoff team that needed an infusion of young talent. It seemed 2020 offered an opportunity for that to happen. The COVID-19 pandemic altered the Eagles' strategy in free agency, with Roseman sensing an opportunity to take a win-now approach. (The big moves the team made, which included acquiring Darius Slay and Javon Hargrave, eventually paid off in a significant way.)

And then came the 2020 draft, which was one of the most polarizing weekends in Eagles history and included perhaps the best and worst of the Roseman era. In the first round, the Eagles clearly needed a wide receiver in a loaded draft at the position and selected Jalen Reagor over Justin Jefferson. The public consensus at the time was to take Jefferson, who had been a star on the national champion LSU Tigers. The Eagles wanted Reagor thinking he was a better deep threat as an outside receiver, purportedly because of how the coaching staff thought he would fit in the offense. Roseman had final say and picked Reagor, who was traded after two seasons while Jefferson became a superstar.

In the second round, the Eagles shocked fans and analysts alike when they took Jalen Hurts while Wentz was entrenched as the starting quarterback. With the memory of waiting too long to draft Russell Wilson in 2012 and seeing Foles win the Super Bowl as the backup quarterback, Roseman selected Hurts even though the public reaction was critical and it created a potential firestorm within his own quarterback room. Roseman had notified Wentz earlier in the day that they were interested in potentially drafting a quarterback and offered considerable public support for Wentz. The suggestion was that the Eagles showed their support for Wentz with the contract they paid him. But any doubts about Wentz were exacerbated when he bottomed out in 2020 and was benched before the season ended.

Wentz demanded a trade after the season. The Eagles became Hurts' team and a difference in vision between Pederson and the front office led to the Super Bowl–winning coach's ouster. So the coach was gone, and the quarterback was soon to be elsewhere, yet Lurie remained committed to Roseman as general manager. After a four-win season and going onto Roseman's fourth coach, this brought further scrutiny upon Roseman and the roster he built.

"I think you've really got to look at the big picture of have you analyzed every single draft pick and street free agent and everybody?" Lurie said that winter. "Have you compared it to other teams? Have you compared it to other successful teams, and do they have two-, three-year drop-offs with less volume? Are the picks that you're talking about seen in the long run or just in a one-year period?...You take whichever organization you want and look at it over a multi-year period, you're going to see highs and lows of drafting, you're going to see highs and lows of free-agent acquisition, and you're going to have to make your own determination of do they have the right people in the building? Is that two years of not having good first-round picks related to people in the building or is that because the two players that they actually were going to draft got taken just before and they are All-Pro players in the league? I have to be much more in-depth and complex about the analysis. Luckily for me, I sit there and I get to see exactly what took place and takes place."

The reality of the Eagles bottoming out at 4–11–1 was it set up Roseman for a stage of roster building where he flourished. Roseman's shortcomings in the maintenance stage can occur when he's too attached or when he's not necessarily taking the longest view in the room. When he's building, he operates with a detachment and creativity that can help separate him from his peers. Perhaps part of those so-called survivor instincts is knowing how to climb out of a mess.

"Coming out of '17, we win a championship and it's like, 'Let's run it back. Let's give these guys a chance to go back-to-back,'" Roseman said. "And you know at some point you're gonna have to pay the price. It's just the reality of it.... And so I think it's different where you are. We learned a lot of lessons about that moment.... You think about the things that we could have done better and I could have done better personally."

Roseman's 2021 and 2022 offseasons propelled the Eagles back to Super Bowl contention. Even though the Wentz trade was not viewed as an organizational achievement at the time—the Eagles were forced to trade a player they identified and paid as their franchise quarterback—Roseman landed a third-round pick and a first-round pick and eventual cap relief for a declining asset. He made a series of trades with the Eagles' top draft pick to move back in the first round and add a future first-round pick, and he was still able to land DeVonta Smith. In 2022, he used their newfound cap space to sign Haason Reddick; he again maneuvered in the draft by trading picks to land A.J. Brown, Jordan Davis, and a future first-round pick and future second-round pick; and then he was opportunistic after the draft when he signed James Bradberry and on cut-down day when he traded for C.J. Gardner-Johnson.

Nothing mattered more than developing Hurts into a signal-caller, especially with lingering gossip that the Eagles were trying to acquire Russell Wilson or even Deshaun Watson via trade before the 2022 campaign. Short of landing an established quarterback, Roseman's commitment to surround Hurts with *bona fide* talent meant the Eagles had perhaps the NFL's finest roster when Hurts became the quarterback they hoped.

"To turn it over the way he has…is a real tribute to him," Reid said. "I don't think he gets enough credit for what he does. Howie's done a great job in a tough place. My hat goes off to him."

Roseman had long outpaced the preconception that came from his nontraditional background. He had become recognized as one of the sport's top executives.

But a common refrain is that he benefits from the support of Lurie, emboldening the general manager to take risks that another general manager with less job security or organizational support cannot take. Roseman insists he's "not on scholarship," but that argument also misses a critical understanding of Lurie's expectation in his football executive. Lurie's belief in Roseman does not allow the general manager to be more aggressive as much as Roseman's aggressiveness fosters Lurie's belief in him. It's the cause—not the effect.

"If he were any less bold, he wouldn't be my general manager," Lurie said. "I believe you really need to identify what can make you really successful and go for it. And then if it's not, if it's a missed call, a player that gets injured, a misevaluation, you then get back together and figure out how you can make up for that in a big way.… I mean, there's 32 teams. You don't want to be 8–8."

This is a sentiment Roseman has shared throughout the years, when he has compared the NFL to a bell-shaped curve. The league is designed for teams to become mediocre. Roseman fears mediocrity. The winning occurs on the right side of the curve. And the teams that finish on the left side of that curve, as disheartening as it may be, are rewarded with assets to build quickly. Look at the Eagles' two drafts after they finished with four wins, when they landed Lane Johnson and Zach Ertz in 2013 and DeVonta Smith and Landon Dickerson in 2021. It helps considerably to have a boss who is willing to stick with him despite those bad teams, which is a luxury other general managers might lack. And that is where Lurie will discuss focusing on the process that has helped the team avoid prolonged dips.

"We're very fortunate here to work for someone in Jeffrey who believes in us and doesn't ebb and flow when we have terrible years," Roseman said. "When I think back, sometimes those terrible years do lead you to opportunities that we have now. I definitely don't want to go through them again. But I think that you've got to reflect in those moments and make sure that you get back to doing the things that are really right."

After the Eagles won Super Bowl LII, Roseman walked through the locker room with the potent intoxication of victory and vindication. His shirt was untucked out of his suit. A Super Bowl Champs cap was on his head. There was a sense of satisfaction that could probably only be understood by someone who took his particular journey. He had the last laugh on anyone who had laughed at his expense.

"Nobody can ever say we're not world champions. Ever!" Roseman said.

And he was right. He always kept that in his pocket in case anyone needed a reminder.

PART 2

THE COACHES

4

Andy Reid

On Andy Reid's first night as head coach of the Philadelphia Eagles in January 1999, he dined at Frederick's, an Italian restaurant in South Philadelphia. A priest sat a few tables away and came to say hello to the man in charge of Philadelphia's largest Sunday gathering.

"Hey, Coach.... Boo!" the priest said, before smiling and giving another offering.

"Just wanted to make you feel at home," he said.

Reid recounted this story in the foreword of the book *A Sunday Pilgrimage*, and similar anecdotes have been told over the years. Like a story Reid shared with *The Philadelphia Inquirer* in 2007 about his first season in 1999—a 5–11 campaign that built the foundation for the next 13 years. Reid is well known for his exhaustive hours. He left Veterans Stadium late one night and was stuck in traffic due to a Philadelphia Flyers game being played next door. Reid was on the phone with Marty Mornhinweg, who was then the San Francisco 49ers offensive coordinator and later served the same position for Reid in Philadelphia.

"I said, 'Marty, these people, they want to kill me. I mean they really want to kill me. It's crazy,'" Reid recalled in the *Inquirer* story. "He goes, 'Ah, it can't be that bad.' I said, 'No, it's a wild, wild deal.' I'm pulling out of the parking lot and one of the hockey games is getting over, and I'm right there at the gate at the Vet ready to make a right turn to get on [Interstate] 76, and it's backed up traffic. All of a sudden, these two cars of guys are hanging out the window going, 'You fat son of a gun. Go back to Green Bay.' They're just going crazy.

"I said, 'Marty, can you hear that?' He goes, 'What?' I said, 'Here, listen,' and I held the phone outside the car window. And then they really put on a good show. I brought the phone back in and I said, 'Marty, did you hear that? Marty? Marty, are you there?' He goes, 'That was the most unbelievable thing I've ever...heard in my life.'"

So it says something about Reid as a coach—and about his temperament—that he lasted 14 years in Philadelphia. He won more games than any coach in franchise history. By the admission of owner Jeffrey Lurie and then team president Joe Banner, the pair who hired Reid, his presence helped incite the organizational success the team would enjoy over the next decade. Reid will go into the Eagles Hall of Fame one day. He'll probably have a spot in the Pro Football Hall of Fame. And though his career might be remembered for what happened *after* he left Philadelphia and took over the Kansas City Chiefs, where he's won three Super Bowls and built a dynastic run, his mark in Philadelphia cannot be forgotten. It was where he established himself as a head coach and instituted a culture and a philosophy that still permeates within the NovaCare Complex.

In fact, when the Eagles moved on from Reid after 14 years, Lurie brought Reid to the cafeteria to meet with employees. Reid had been the only coach to occupy the team practice facility at that point and there was a generation of emerging Eagles fans who associated the coach affectionately known as "Big Red" as a face of the franchise. (I was 12 when Reid was hired, and I covered his final season in Philadelphia.)

"You have no idea because he many times didn't want to share himself with the press or in a way in which he had to protect his own players [and] protect the way he was as a coach," Lurie said when Reid was fired. "Having worked side by side with him for 14 years, this is a gem of a person and incredibly dedicated to making the Eagles the franchise we have been. It was no easy task, he left no stone unturned, and his dedication was incredible. His work ethic was incredible and his ability to work with others was incredible. He had the love and respect of every individual in this organization. And I don't say that lightly, because I think if you were to interview owners and other franchise operations around the league, not everybody could say that. This man is amazing to work with, smart and dedicated himself, and the record will speak for itself. History will focus on exactly what he's been able to accomplish and what the team has been able to accomplish. I look forward to the day we all welcome him back and introduce him as a member of the Eagles Hall of Fame, because that's inevitable."

Reid was not a popular hire in 1999. In fact, Green Bay had an opening and did not even interview Reid, who had been the Packers' quarterbacks coach. They hired Ray Rhodes, who was dismissed in Philadelphia. Eagles president Joe Banner organized a study to make the coaching search scientific and found traits that led the Eagles to hire Reid. Reid famously brought a binder with pages accumulated throughout his coaching career while preparing for the opportunity. It included a ranking of potential coaches for every role on his staff. He kept notes for speeches on specific moments of the season. Lurie and Banner saw a leader and someone with the temperament for the role. (It was believed that top football executive Tom Modrak favored Pittsburgh Steelers defensive coordinator Jim Haslett.)

"It was surprising to me that other teams weren't super interested in him because we tried to hire Andy as our offensive coordinator and [the Packers] wouldn't allow him to come," Lurie said in January 2023. "So we knew he was [the Packers'] most treasured asset at the time. And then he was our first choice to be head coach, and nobody else was interviewing him. So it was kind of like, 'Hmm. Why is that?' I was a young owner. So you don't always know why others have priorities in different directions."

Reid did not reveal to the public what was in that binder. For someone who once penned a newspaper column and had admired famed *Los Angeles Times* columnist Jim Murray, Reid was a master at controlling his message through the media and remaining unmoved by public pressure. At his opening news conference, he said, "You have to trust me," about his plan. And the 40-year-old coach stuck to his convictions. He assembled one of the best coaching staffs in the NFL, including eight future head coaches. His most important assistant did not become a head coach: Jim Johnson, his defensive coordinator who was critical to the success during the first decade of Reid's tenure.

When there was public pressure to take Heisman Trophy–winning running back Ricky Williams—and even the potential to stockpile draft picks in a trade with New Orleans so the Saints could acquire Williams—Reid was steadfast in selecting Donovan McNabb as his franchise quarterback with the No. 2 selection. Reid and McNabb were linked. It was part of the way Reid viewed team building, adhering to a philosophy that remained through his 14 years in Philadelphia and has continued in the decade since.

"I want two offensive tackles, a quarterback, two pass rushers, two corners, and I'll figure the rest out," Reid would say in job interviews, according to a *Sports Illustrated* article in 2016. His roster moves mostly backed this philosophy.

Reid made sure to put his imprint on the team from the start. He oversaw an intense training camp at Lehigh University. After veteran George Hegamin was demoted from a starting spot on the offensive line and bolted from the team, Reid made Hegamin push a blocking slide upon his return. It was an example of who was in charge. Reid put his stamp on the team.

Reid lost his first four games in 1999, and he was 2–7 before he finally inserted McNabb into the lineup. McNabb finished 3–4 as starter, including two wins to close the season. Those victories helped carry momentum into the 2000 campaign.

"The thing I was probably the proudest of was those last couple games that first year," Reid said in a 2007 *Philadelphia Inquirer* article. "It could have very easily gone the other way if the veteran players like Troy Vincent, Bobby Taylor, and Duce Staley jumped ship. Troy, he knew. He had seen the good, the bad, the whole deal, but he hung right in there. All those older guys, they hung right in there and said, 'We're going to keep trusting him even though he's working our tail off and he's relentlessly preaching to us about this and that. We're still going to trust him.' Those last two games, I went, 'Wow, we can do this thing now.'"

Year 2 was an example. The Eagles made a splash in free agency when they signed Jon Runyan to a six-year, $30-million contract that made him the highest-paid offensive tackle in NFL history at the time. It also signaled the Reid-emphasized organizational philosophy of building the team along the lines of scrimmage and showed that the franchise could compete for top free agents. With McNabb entering his first full season as the starter, a strong offensive line in front of him, and a standout defense under Johnson, the Eagles finished the season 11–5 and made the NFC divisional round. They appeared to be an up-and-coming club—and a well-hydrated one, at that—when the campaign started with an onside kick against Dallas in the "Pickle Juice" game. The 109-degree temperature was even more scorching on the old Texas Stadium's turf, so the Eagles consumed pickle juice to combat the heat. The 41–14 shellacking of the rival Cowboys foretold a promising season under Reid.

By Year 3, the Eagles were one of the NFL's best teams and Lurie saw enough to give Reid control of personnel. He was one of the most powerful coaches in the NFL, and his imprint on the organization was undeniable. The Eagles again reached 11 wins with the help of a defense that finished No. 2 in the NFL in points allowed. They even won the NFC East for the first time since 1988—beginning a run of four consecutive division crowns. The success continued in the postseason with a victory over Tampa Bay in their opening-round postseason before they upset Chicago in McNabb's return to his hometown. That set up a date with the St. Louis Rams, the best team in the NFL. The Eagles came within a touchdown, but McNabb was left watching the confetti fall on the opponent. But the franchise's promise was apparent in the NFL, with a third-year coach and quarterback on the brink of the sport's biggest game.

That set up the 2002 Eagles, a team that seemed destined for the Super Bowl. It was the final season in Veterans Stadium, and the farewell included one of the best teams to ever play in the lovable concrete bowl. The Eagles set a franchise record for points while winning 12 games. Ten players were voted into the Pro Bowl. And their defense might have been even better, limiting opponents to the second-fewest points in the NFL. They quieted the Rams, the team that beat them in the championship game one year earlier, by limiting Kurt Warner and Co. to only a field goal in a December victory. And they did it while starting third-string quarterback A.J. Feeley after McNabb and Koy Detmer suffered injuries in the previous two games—both wins, of course. In the divisional round of the playoffs, they held NFL sensation Michael Vick out of the end zone in a convincing win over the Falcons. That set up the final game at the Vet—the NFC Championship Game against the Tampa Bay Buccaneers. The script couldn't have been written any better. And when the Eagles scored on the second play of the game, it seemed as if they were destined for a victory. The game turned on a Joe Jurevicius 71-yard reception on a third down late in the first quarter to put Tampa Bay in position to take a lead, and the Eagles never recovered. When Ronde Barber returned an interception for a touchdown late in the fourth quarter to seal the Bucs' upset, the Eagles were no longer the ascending franchise on the doorstep. They were Sisyphus with the boulder rolling down the hill.

"It felt like we let the city down," linebacker Ike Reese told *The Philadelphia Inquirer* upon reflection in 2019. "The people that filled the stadium were what gave it the mystique, and we wanted to win a Super Bowl for them that last year. That hurt for a lot of us. I know I had tears leaving that stadium. History wasn't going to be written the way it should have been written."

The Eagles did not look like the same heavyweights in 2003, starting 0–2 and needing a miraculous Brian Westbrook 84-yard punt return in Week 7 to keep the team at .500. That return sparkplugged the team to a nine-game winning streak that helped the Eagles finish with a 12–4 record and again earn the top seed. The improbable victories continued in the postseason when, facing elimination, the Eagles converted a fourth-and-26 to keep their hopes alive against the Green Bay Packers. Go around Philadelphia decades later and bring up "fourth-and-26," and any self-respecting Eagles fan would know exactly what you mean. It's one of those ubiquitous phrases in an Eagles fan's lexicon. Brian Dawkins intercepted Brett Favre in overtime to help the Eagles preserve the victory. All they needed to do to reach the Super Bowl was beat the Carolina Panthers. But the boulder rolled back down the hill. The Eagles could not even score a touchdown in the championship game. The 14–3 loss was the third consecutive defeat one game shy of the Super Bowl. The fan base had become fatigued by promising autumns preceding disappointing Januarys.

Going into the 2004 season, the Eagles operated like a franchise determined to depart from the doorstep. They acquired Terrell Owens to give McNabb the best wide receiver of his career. They signed Jevon Kearse to offer Johnson one of the NFL's most athletic pass-rushers. (Banner viewed the Kearse signing as perhaps the most significant given the position.) Jeremiah Trotter returned to Philadelphia after a two-year absence. The Eagles were loaded—and they played like it. They won their first seven games of the season, with Owens topping 100 yards in five of them. He was the dynamic playmaker that brought McNabb to a different level. The McNabb-Owens combination was unlike anything else during the Reid era. McNabb had the best season of his career, throwing for 31 touchdowns and finishing with a career-high 104.7 passer rating. Owens suffered a bad leg injury in Week 15, at which point he was tied for the NFL's lead with 14 touchdowns. The injury would typically end a season. Owens pleaded for the Eagles to make the Super Bowl and he would return. They finished 13–3, and Reid passed Greasy Neale for most wins in franchise history.

Owens' absence did not stop McNabb and the Eagles from cruising through the NFC playoffs, defeating Minnesota by 13 points in the divisional round and then limiting Vick and the Falcons in the NFC Championship Game. The convincing all-around performances allowed for a moment to exhale for the core players who had fallen short during the previous three seasons. Hoisting the NFC trophy on their home field gave them an indescribable satisfaction—Reid included.

"I think it even makes it more worthwhile that we had to do it four times to get over the hump," Reid said after the victory.

But there was still one more game. Owens, true to his promise, returned for the Super Bowl. He said he was 81 percent. (He wore No. 81.) The Eagles were nonetheless heavy underdogs against the New England Patriots, Lurie's childhood team (and a franchise he once tried to purchase) and the defending Super Bowl champions. The game was tied 7–7 at halftime, with both teams scoring a touchdown in the second quarter. (Tight end L.J. Smith caught the score.) It remained tied at 14 at the end of the third quarter, although the Patriots started to move the ball more effectively by throwing quick passes to eventual Super Bowl MVP Deion Branch. The problem for the Eagles offense was turnovers. An interception and a fumble stymied drives in the first half, with the interception coming in the red zone. Another interception in Patriots territory in the fourth quarter when the Eagles trailed by 10 points made the team's chances look bleak. Jim Johnson's defense forced a three-and-out with less than six minutes to go, getting the ball back to McNabb. But he needed to move quickly. Instead, the Eagles moved methodically. They huddled and seemingly took their time on a 13-play drive. Patriots coach Bill Belichick famously wondered if the scoreboard was correct. By the time the Eagles scored a touchdown to cut the deficit to three points, the clock had already dipped below the two-minute warning. The defense forced a three-and-out while the Eagles exhausted their timeouts, giving McNabb and the offense one last gasp with 46 seconds remaining in the game. It was too little, too late. McNabb threw an interception on the third play, and Reid's only appearance in the Super Bowl in Philadelphia ended one win short.

Reid hit a relative lull after the Super Bowl. The 2005 season cratered with Owens' disenchantment—he was unhappy with his contract, was sent home from training camp, bristled during the season, and was dismissed from the team during the season. Adding to the Super Bowl hangover was an injury to McNabb that halted his season. The Eagles' 6–10 mark proved to be their worst during the 2000s.

Reid's teams seldom stayed down. He flipped that record in 2006 and made the postseason and reached the divisional round, although another McNabb injury meant the team needed Jeff Garcia to get there. McNabb's injuries continued into 2007, when an 8–8 finish led to two of three years without a winning record.

There was also turbulence in Reid's family life. Two of his sons were in legal trouble from separate incidents that occurred on the same day in January 2007. Reid took a five-month leave of absence. At the sentencing, a Montgomery County judge called the Reids a "family in crisis."

"In a game, once the whistle blows and you're playing the game, now the human element is there, and it's how you've trained them," Reid told *Philadelphia Magazine* in December 2007 when asked about how a coach obsessed with details manages when he has no control over addiction. "Some days they are going to throw an interception or miss a tackle.

You didn't train them that way. But you live with it, and you keep on teaching them. That's why we're here, we're here to be teachers. And so you do the same thing at home, you teach them and then let them go. You blow the whistle and let them play. Sometimes it works out, and sometimes it doesn't."

Entering his 10th season with the Eagles, in 2008 Reid was already the winningest coach in franchise history and had matched the mark for longest tenured. And even if there might have been fatigue from the fan base about Reid clearing his throat, reciting injuries, and saying "time's yours" in his news conferences—and perhaps those fans grew a distaste for his game management, too—there remained strong ownership support.

"When you first start off, you're just trying to make it to the next year. 'How will I make it to three years in this league?'—the average of a head coach. You're planning for the future," Reid told the *Philadelphia Daily News* before the 2008 season. "Then you hit this point—I don't know if it's Year 7, wherever it is—where you're going, 'Man, I love every minute of this.' You're not even thinking about when you're going to end. At least, that's not where I'm at; at my age and years here, you appreciate every day even more now than you did back then. You're still working hard. That part hasn't changed. The work level hasn't changed."

Reid made a bold move in November 2008 when he benched McNabb during a loss to the Baltimore Ravens that dropped the Eagles to 5–5–1. But Reid stuck with his franchise quarterback, who led the team to a Thanksgiving rout and won four of five games entering the postseason. Requiring help on the final day of the season, the Eagles responded to a series of beneficial outcomes with a 44–6 trouncing of the rival Cowboys to clinch the playoff spot. Reid then continued his postseason proficiency by leading the franchise to consecutive road victories in the playoffs to reach the NFC Championship for the fifth time in the Reid-McNabb partnership. The Eagles had a one-point lead late in the fourth quarter before the Cardinals scored a go-ahead touchdown with just under three minutes remaining in the game. They couldn't have known it at the time, but the franchise would never come that close to the Super Bowl again under Reid.

A significant change occurred during the 2009 offseason when Jim Johnson took a leave of absence due to a cancerous tumor on his spine. Sean McDermott replaced Johnson first on an interim basis, and then eventually as the permanent coordinator before the season. Johnson passed away in August 2018.

Also in the summer of 2009, the Eagles made the polarizing decision to sign Michael Vick after Vick served 21 months in prison. He was initially the third quarterback behind McNabb and Kevin Kolb.

The Eagles went 11–5 that season, although they lost their season finale to Dallas and then fell to their rival again one week later in the opening round of the playoffs. A quarterback decision was coming, and that loss proved to be the end of an era. Reid and McNabb had been linked throughout the coach's career, but he traded McNabb to Washington on Easter night. It was Kolb's turn to become quarterback.

That offseason also saw Lurie, Banner, and Reid agree to promote Howie Roseman to general manager. Reid maintained personnel control, but Roseman's rise in the organization brought him to its most powerful front office position.

Kolb's tenure as the top quarterback lasted one game. When he suffered a concussion in the season opener, Vick looked like he came out of a time machine—and was refined in Reid's system—and emerged as the Eagles' answer at quarterback.

Vick was one of the best players in the NFL that season and authored some of the most memorable moments of the era, including a sterling performance on *Monday Night Football* against McNabb and Washington and the "Miracle at the New Meadowlands." The Eagles even won the NFC East. The dream season fizzled after Christmas. A game postponed to a Tuesday because of a snowstorm brought the Eagles a startling upset to Minnesota and a little-known reserve quarterback, and they lost their season finale. Then came an opening-round playoff loss to Green Bay at home, ending what once appeared like a dream season with a thud. (Or, to be literal, an interception.)

It was the final postseason game of Reid's tenure.

Following the loss to Green Bay, Reid shook up his coaching staff. McDermott was dismissed, with Jim Johnson's shadow considered a challenging complication for a successor. But instead of hiring an established defensive coordinator, Reid made a bold move. Reid hired defensive line coach Jim Washburn even before the coordinator was hired, boxing the Eagles into a particular scheme. And then Reid made the bolder decision to move offensive line coach Juan Castillo to defensive coordinator, an unorthodox hire that caught everyone—including the players—by surprise.

"The offensive line coach?" cornerback Asante Samuel asked *Philadelphia Inquirer* reporter Jeff McLane in February 2011.

And that was not even the biggest story of the franchise's offseason! After the NFL lockout, the Eagles embarked on a string of high-profile acquisitions that captured the league's attention. They traded Kolb to Arizona in a deal that included Pro Bowl cornerback Dominique Rodgers-Cromartie—and he was not even the top cornerback acquired. The Eagles made the headlining signing when they lured top free agent Nnamdi Asomugha to Philadelphia with a $60 million contract.

Combined with other big-name signings all done in a flurry, backup quarterback Vince Young dubbed the new-look Eagles the "Dream Team." The label was innocent, but it was never forgotten—especially when the season proved to be a nightmare.

The Eagles were 4–8 in December. They won the last four games of the season, although Lurie thought clinging to that late surge as the reason for optimism would be "fool's gold." He called the 8–8 finish "unacceptable," but he elected to keep Reid because of the coach's track record in Philadelphia.

It didn't get better. The 2012 season was a disaster.

It started with tragedy when Reid's son, Garrett, died of a drug overdose in training camp. Reid returned to work after the funeral. "I'm a football coach, that's what I do, and I know my son wouldn't want it any other way," Reid said that summer.

The Eagles started 3–1, but they lost 11 of their next 12 games. Reid fired Castillo midseason. He dismissed Washburn, too. The worst season of Reid's coaching career was his last. He was dismissed after the season finale.

Years later, Lurie wished Reid could have continued as a coach. But the owner noted that given Reid's family situation, a change made the most sense. It reinvigorated Reid. Although some close to him thought he could benefit from time off, Reid was unemployed for less than a week. The Kansas City Chiefs hired him. He was in the playoffs in his first year. He never had a losing record with the Chiefs. He won his first Super Bowl after the 2019 season.

Reid returned to Philadelphia during the 2014 offseason to speak at a coaching symposium at the University of Pennsylvania. He was honest when asked about identifying shortcomings at the end of his Eagles tenure.

"About a year ago, I found out what I wasn't good at because [I was] out the door," said Reid, now the Kansas City Chiefs coach. "I went back, and I looked at it, and…I drifted away from the thing I love doing most, and that was coaching."

Reid identified the focus on personnel and surrendering play-calling responsibilities to Mornhinweg as getting away from what he does best. When he was hired by Kansas City, he called plays and ceded personnel control.

"I'm not saying [it was] the wrong way to go; we had a lot of success in Philadelphia," Reid said. "But where I was in my career, this is what I want to do. And it worked out where I could actually do that."

As successful as he was in Philadelphia, Reid reached a different level when he left. He was quickly hired by Kansas City and thrice won the Super Bowl—including beating the Eagles in February 2023. By that point, Lurie had already hoisted the Lombardi Trophy. Both the owner and the coach separately achieved the success they could not reach together.

"Jeffrey gave me every opportunity to be successful," Reid said at the Super Bowl. "And that's all you can ask for. Everything doesn't last forever. So we all had our time there. And Jeffrey was very honest with us. I think we saw what Jeffrey saw. And sometimes change can be good. And it can be good for both the team and the coach."

5

Chip Kelly

On Thanksgiving Day 2013, Chip Kelly was asked a rather innocuous football question about whether it's inaccurate for one to think a quarterback is more susceptible to injury on a read option than standing in the pocket. Kelly rerouted the question with a life philosophy—a "Chip-ism," if you will—one that seemed to explain much about his tenure and how it might be remembered.

"I don't care what other people think," he countered. "It doesn't bother me. I mean, to spend time for me to think about what someone else thinks is counter to anything I've ever believed in my life. If I believe what other people think, then that means I value their opinion more than I value my own."

In Kelly's three years as the franchise's head coach, he offered a version of this answer multiple times. And he seemed to adhere to it—for better and for worse.

Attention is a reality of coaching in the NFL. There is less interest in the head coach at Manchester (New Hampshire)

Central High School than there is in the Philadelphia Eagles—although having spent a day once with Bob Leonard, Kelly's coach at Manchester Central, I can attest it's also nice to learn about the coach at Manchester Central—yet Kelly liked to treat any question that veered toward the personal nature with defiance. He explained that he viewed it from the perspective of the Navy SEALS: "I do not advertise the nature of my work, nor do I seek recognition for my actions.'" But there could often be a public message to convey as a head coach, like a politician crafting his approval rating.

"If you're thinking about crafting," he said, "you're not spending enough time on your job."

"He doesn't worry about other people," Hall of Fame coach Tony Dungy once said. "To me, that's what makes him unique."

It works when you win...but not when you lose.

Ask an Eagles fan now about the Chip Kelly era and prepare for the bitterness. In the scope of 25 years, it was a fleeting period. It arrived with a bang and ended with a thud, and in between there were peaks that made you think the revolution was being televised. At the nadir, there wasn't just frustration with the football team—there was a distaste, which is even worse.

After the Eagles fired Andy Reid following 14 years, they commenced a search that saw Chip Kelly emerge as the clear No. 1 target. In fact, Eagles beat reporters (including the one writing this book) quickly booked flights to Phoenix to cover the Fiesta Bowl, where Kelly's Oregon Ducks topped Kansas State. After the game, Kelly joked about the interest in the Fiesta Bowl at Pat's and Geno's—two popular cheesesteak spots in South Philadelphia. It was a good line, as Kelly was wont to offer, but he knew full well why the reporters were there. Because the next day, Kelly met with the Eagles. Other teams were interested, including the Cleveland Browns. Kelly decided to stay at

Oregon. The Eagles moved on and were close to hiring Seattle Seahawks defensive coordinator Gus Bradley. But Kelly had a change of heart one week later, and the Eagles landed their top candidate—and the hottest name on the coaching market.

"I'm all in," Kelly said at his opening news conference. "I think it was [Hernán Cortés] who burned the boats. I've burned the boats so I'm not going back. I'm in. I'm an NFL coach and this is where I want to be."

When asked specifically about personnel control and who has final say—Kelly or Howie Roseman—Kelly explained that his role would be "clearly defining what we want." He had specific parameters for positions. But he insisted that he's a "football coach"—"not a general manager" and "not a salary cap guy." Those were Roseman's duties, and the two would need to work together.

Kelly once remarked that he "was probably a pain in the ass as a little kid" because he "questioned everything," and that was how the Eagles seemed to operate at the beginning of Kelly's tenure. It was refreshing for some, intimidating for others. But it was always interesting. Kelly referred to a Latin term *mutatis mutandis*—it translates to "things having been changed that have to be changed"—almost as an operating principle when he first became a head coach. He wanted to know how everything worked and why. Sometimes it made sense. Sometimes it required change.

When Kelly arrived, what seemed remarkable was how *different* it all was. Kelly downplayed any allusion to revolution. And it's inevitable that when there is one way of operating for 14 years, there will be change. But Kelly brought a brand of football that represented an adjustment in the NFL. It could be heard at practice, with music in the background offering a daily concert to the South Philadelphia natives surrounding the

NovaCare Complex. It could be seen on the schedule, with practices on Tuesday—typically an NFL day off—and Saturdays—typically a day for walkthroughs. It could be seen by the level of insight into players' bodies, ranging from hydration tests to sleep monitoring. And of course, it was evident with an offense that did not huddle—those were, as Kelly deemed, committee meetings—and played at a pace that made the NFC East seem like the Pac-10.

"If the answer is, 'That's how we've always done it,' I just want to know the 'why.'" Kelly said during his first year. "Just explain why you're doing it. A lot of times...people... can't explain why they're doing it in a certain manner. If they don't understand how to do it in a certain manner, then they don't know how to fix it when it breaks. I think you've got to have an understanding of what it is."

So much of coaching is about navigating the unexpected. Kelly was tested in his first summer with the team when wide receiver Riley Cooper was videotaped shouting a racial slur at a concert. The front office left the discipline up to Kelly, who briefly sent Cooper home but kept him on the team. That was a polarizing decision—Cary Williams engaged in a scuffle with Cooper in an early season practice and made clear in no uncertain terms that the incident was not exactly forgotten—and it was a curious way for Kelly to use early career equity.

But winning tends to help shape a narrative, and that was what Kelly did in his first season with the Eagles. The season opened on *Monday Night Football* in front of a national audience when the offense ran 54 plays in the first half and the Eagles scored 26 points with a brand of football that had seemed foreign to the NFL. Kelly said they don't count plays—only points. But the rest of the NFL did. "I don't think it can get too much faster than that," quarterback Michael Vick said after the game. And when Vick was asked if the NFL had witnessed the start of a revolution, he answered, "Maybe so." At the end of the first quarter, Vick thought it was halftime.

The notion that Kelly needed a running quarterback was tested that season when the Eagles turned to Nick Foles after Vick's injuries, although Foles was a revelation in the system. He threw 27 touchdowns and two interceptions, including a seven-touchdown performance on the way to the Pro Bowl and the NFC East crown. LeSean McCoy led the NFL in rushing and set the franchise's single season rushing record. DeSean Jackson had the best season of his career. The offense benefited from all five starting offensive linemen starting every game, which the team viewed as a credit to Kelly's emphasis on sports science. The Eagles finished 10–6 and lost to the New Orleans Saints in the playoffs, but Kelly's approval rating was soaring.

As is often the case in NFL organizations, there was more to the story behind the scenes. The Kelly-Roseman relationship was deteriorating, and Kelly's influence swelled. He had decided he wanted to part ways with DeSean Jackson, who was one of the team's most dynamic players. Whispers of a potential trade or release of Jackson grew louder during the 2014 offseason, which was an otherwise strong free agency period for the Eagles with the signing of Malcolm Jenkins and acquisition of Darren Sproles. The Eagles released Jackson, getting no compensation for an in-his-prime player coming off the best season of his career. Kelly called it "purely a football decision" and said the timing had nothing to do with an NJ.com report linking Jackson to gangs, which was published an hour before the Eagles cut Jackson. Lurie put the decision in Kelly's hands.

"Chip and his people were incredibly clear that for us to get better we need to take a step back and reconfigure the wide receiver position," Lurie said in 2014. "And for Chip on offense, it just wasn't a good fit with what he asks wide receivers to do."

This would not be the last time Kelly unceremoniously parted with a high-profile player.

On the field, Kelly picked up where he left off in 2014. The Eagles won five of their first six games. During the sixth game, a shutout of the rival New York Giants, NFL Films caught Kelly telling a down-the-roster safety, "Culture will beat scheme every day." That became a rallying cry for the way Kelly's Eagles were viewed at that time. Jackson was gone, and Jeremy Maclin stepped into the top receiver spot and had the best season of his career. Even when Foles was injured, the offense continued to flourish when Mark Sanchez moved into the starting job. The Eagles' special teams excelled with offseason upgrades. More than anything, it appeared Kelly—and his system—was the star.

The high-water mark might have come on Thanksgiving 2014. The Eagles and Cowboys both entered the game 8–3. The Eagles dominated their rivals on national television with Sanchez starting at quarterback in an all-around performance that included 464 yards of total offense while forcing three takeaways and registering four sacks. Philadelphia was the first team in the NFC to reach nine wins.

The Kelly era went downhill after that day.

The Eagles lost their next three games, first when the Seattle Seahawks appeared to be the more physical, tougher team in front of a Philadelphia crowd, and then the following week when the Cowboys avenged the Thanksgiving loss and took control of the NFC East. To add disgrace to the decline, the Eagles' playoff hopes were lost in Week 16 against Washington when they could not stop Jackson during a 126-yard performance. The Eagles won a meaningless Week 17 game to finish with double-digit victories, but there was no way to spin the final month of the season.

"Ten and six, not going to the playoffs, is just like being 4–12," Kelly said.

Changes were coming. Nobody knew how drastic they would be.

The front-office discord that had been brewing behind the scenes reached its crescendo in the days after the season. In his end-of-season press conference, Kelly only noted Roseman's salary cap acumen when discussing his job and called Tom Gamble, Kelly's right-hand man in the front office, "an outstanding football man." Gamble was then fired, creating more front-office drama. Finally, Kelly was given full control over the Eagles' roster and Roseman was removed from football decisions.

"We had to over two years understand where we're at: Where are we going to maximize Chip Kelly's vision and system—or were we going to counteract it?" Lurie explained that offseason. "It's a gamble to go from good to great because you can go from good to mediocre with changes. But I decided that it was important enough to adopt the vision and philosophy of integrating the scouting with the coaching on a daily basis."

The offseason was one of the most chaotic in recent Eagles history. First was trading McCoy, who was in the prime of his career and had broken the franchise's all-time rushing record. The player the Eagles acquired? Kiko Alonso, a linebacker who once played for Oregon. It was the second consecutive offseason that Kelly jettisoned an iconic Eagle (with a big personality) who predated him. (When Kelly was asked later that offseason about the type of player he desires, he answered, "We want a bunch of guys that love playing football, not what football gets them.")

Then Kelly traded Foles for oft-injured St. Louis Rams quarterback Sam Bradford—and he threw a 2016 second-round pick into the deal as a sweetener! The price the Eagles paid demonstrated their inexperience in the front office. The Eagles viewed it as a worthwhile risk considering Bradford had been the No. 1 pick in 2010. Kelly thought it was akin to the New Orleans Saints signing Drew Brees after injury. (And there was speculation that Bradford was added as a chip to try to acquire Kelly's ideal quarterback: Oregon's Marcus Mariota, who was available in the draft that year and was expected to be a top-two pick.) The Eagles lost Maclin in free agency, leaving them bare at wide receiver. And with extra money to spend, they signed Cowboys star DeMarco Murray to replace McCoy in a move that was polarizing among Eagles fans with a distaste for Dallas. They also splurged on cornerback Byron Maxwell, and the free-agency spending created a new identity for the Eagles.

Come draft weekend, the Eagles could not land Mariota—"It was like driving into a nice neighborhood and looking at a house, and they tell you the price and you walk away," Kelly said—and they built around Bradford in 2014.

What's most remembered from the preseason was Bradford's perfect opening drive in the third preseason game, but what was perhaps more important was a hit in the preseason opener. Baltimore pass rusher Terrell Suggs crashed into Bradford's surgically repaired knees after the quarterback handed the ball off on a read-option, a staple in the Eagles' system. The Eagles moved away from that concept thereafter, and it affected their offense. Murray was more used to running with the quarterback under center than in shotgun, leaving a disconnect with the franchise's prized free-agent signing, who seemed to be an awkward fit in Philadelphia. (When Murray sat out of practice one day, Jenkins brought him a chair in a not-so-subtle message.) Maxwell struggled in coverage in the season opener, which did not help build any confidence about a revamped defense. The

Eagles lost three of their first four games. A three-game losing streak in November dropped the Eagles to 4–7, including an embarrassing 45–14 loss to the Detroit Lions on Thanksgiving Day. It was startling to see how far the Eagles had fallen from one Thanksgiving to another. When Kelly defended the players' effort, a reporter asked Kelly if the problem was the head coach. "I don't know," Kelly said. "I don't have that answer." It seemed that Kelly might not make it to Year 4, or at least that his seat was scorching. Behind the scenes, the confidence in Kelly was eroding.

The building was not a harmonious place. Lurie's annual holiday party was moved to accommodate the coaches. Lurie had T-shirts printed before a game against New England that read 53 ANGRY MEN. The Eagles were eliminated from postseason contention with a loss to Washington in Week 16. The next day, Kelly was asked about his dual role with personnel control and being head coach. "I'm not the general manager," he said, and he argued semantics insisting he also had control of the 53-man roster before the change with Roseman and the only difference was that he added control of the 90-man roster. Kelly is not interested in perception, but the moves that led to the downfall were clearly at Kelly's urging. In some ways, Kelly the personnel chief sunk Kelly the coach. In that same news conference, Kelly was asked if he would cede control of the 90-man roster.

"The owner decides whatever he wants," Kelly said. "It's his team; he can do whatever he wants."

One day later, Lurie decided what he wanted. He fired Kelly—and he made clear who was responsible for the decisions and the results.

"I wanted to make Chip accountable for everything he wanted to have happen," Lurie said during a news conference after the change. "And one of the ways to make him accountable was to have him make those decisions, because that is what he insisted on decisively doing. So if you want to make those decisions, be accountable for them, and that's the direction it took. There was a risk involved in allowing Chip to have that kind of say over player transactions. However, risk-reward. Sometimes the risks don't work, and in this case it didn't work."

Lurie cited disappointment in the trajectory of the franchise. He wanted a coach to "open your heart to players" and value "emotional intelligence." But Lurie said he did not regret pushing the chips in on Kelly. (Years later, Lurie said in an interview for this book that his regret was not recognizing the lack of collaboration within the building sooner.)

"I think it was the necessary way to go to find out if Chip was the right guy," Lurie said in the spring of 2016. "No question I have that it was the right way to dissect whether Chip was going to be the right guy going forward or not. We dissected it and decided with some of the great things he brought, he wasn't the right person going forward."

But Kelly's time in Philadelphia was not for naught. The Eagles' emphasis on sports science started with Kelly's implication and understanding of data. His coaching staff included the addition of offensive line coach Jeff Stoutland, who became one of the great assistant coaches in franchise history. And there were two years of memorable football, with big victories and an entertaining brand of offense that made the Eagles a must-see attraction. It ended with a crash and some of the collateral damage hurt the franchise, but that should not entirely obscure all that occurred during those three years. It's not a stretch to suggest that the Eagles would not have won the Super Bowl two years later without some of the decisions and changes that Kelly made.

Kelly spent one year in San Francisco and eventually became head coach at UCLA. His offense continued to evolve, and he's spoken highly of Lurie and the organization since his exit. He is no longer beloved by Eagles fans. But Kelly always understood that they love you when you win and they don't when you lose. He never seemed overwhelmed by perception. The opinion he valued most was his own.

6

Doug Pederson

To recognize Doug Pederson's role in Eagles history, all you need to do is walk inside Lincoln Financial Field's front gates and look for the nine-foot statue of a coach wearing a visor and headset with a thick, overflowing mane. He has a play sheet in hand, and he's discussing a critical fourth-down play with his quarterback.

Pederson is literally immortalized in Philadelphia with a bronze statue. (It was gifted by Bud Light, for the record, as opposed to commissioned by the Eagles.) Calling a trick play—"the Philly Special"—on fourth down at the goal line in the Super Bowl is a revealing characterization of a coach whose autobiography is titled *Fearless*.

Pederson is the first—and only—coach to win a Super Bowl in franchise history. That alone makes him iconic. But his relationship with the franchise stretches beyond that magical 2017 season. He was the first starting quarterback for the era of

Eagles football covered in this book, from 1999 to present day. That was the first time in his career he was viewed as more than a backup. He started as an NFL coach in Philadelphia, transitioning from the high school ranks. He was first hired as an NFL head coach by the franchise. And he made the postseason in three of five seasons as head coach. Only Andy Reid, Dick Vermeil, and Greasy Neale coached more games on an Eagles sideline. He played in the NFL before he came to Philadelphia and he's coaching in the NFL beyond Philadelphia, but Pederson will forever be linked with this franchise.

"Obviously [I] have a lot of fond memories there," Pederson said in 2022. "And what we did in 2017 is something we'll always remember."

Pederson first entered the Philadelphia lexicon when Reid signed him as the veteran placeholder at quarterback. He kept the seat warm for Donovan McNabb while giving Reid someone familiar in the locker room. Pederson only spent one year with the team, offering exposure to the market and the organization when it was setting the foundation that would remain in place two decades later. It was Pederson's first chance to be an opening-day starting quarterback, although his identity as a player was as a backup quarterback—and as a future coach. Reid identified him as someone who could go into coaching, but he did not go from an NFL locker room to an NFL coaching staff.

Pederson's first foray into coaching was actually with a high school team in 2006. After he retired from his 14 seasons in the NFL, Pederson returned to his offseason home of Shreveport, Louisiana, and became the head coach at Calvary Baptist Academy. The NFL had eyes on him—the San Francisco 49ers offered Pederson a job during his first year at Calvary—but the school's athletic director had hired Pederson with the expectation that he wouldn't pack his bags for the NFL in a week or a month or a year. Pederson obliged, under one condition: "I'm only going to take one job if I get an offer. If Andy Reid calls me, I'm gone."

The small high school in the northwest corner of the state became a breeding ground for Pederson's coaching ideas. He found ways to apply NFL concepts in an digestible manner for teenagers. He could take risks with unique formations, writing in his book, *Fearless,* about one play with 10 players on the line of scrimmage stretched sideline to sideline, and when the quarterback yelled "shift," a few players would step off the line of scrimmage so they were legal. Defenses would be flummoxed. He attempted fake field goals and trick plays. He learned not to overthink—if a curl flat works on consecutive downs, why not keep running it?—and he recognized the importance of connecting with varied constituencies. There were the players and parents, teachers and administrators, and Pederson needed to be more than someone drawing plays on a whiteboard. He required emotional intelligence. Pederson went 40–11 in four seasons with two appearances in the state semifinals. He walked into the athletic director's office in 2009 with the one job he couldn't refuse.

"I got the call," he said.

Reid wanted him in Philadelphia.

Pederson spent two years as the Eagles' quality control coach, which is the lowest rung on the NFL's coaching ladder. He spent two years as the quarterbacks coach, working closely with Michael Vick and playing a role in the decision to draft Nick Foles. When Reid was fired in 2012 and hired in Kansas City, he brought Pederson as offensive coordinator. Even though Pederson was not the primary play-caller, this was the natural ascension in the coaching ladder and put him on the doorstep of becoming an NFL head coach.

Look back at the hot coaching candidate lists after the Eagles dismissed Chip Kelly in December 2015, and Pederson was not atop them. No other team requested to interview him. (That would not be the last time the Eagles hired a coach who was not desired elsewhere.) After their experience with Chip Kelly, the Eagles valued familiarity and a strong recommendation from Reid was helpful.

The Eagles interviewed Adam Gase, who was hired in Miami. They were believed to have heavy interest in Ben McAdoo, who was promoted by the rival New York Giants. Super Bowl–winning coach Tom Coughlin was also a candidate. Pederson was still coaching in the playoffs when the request came in from the Eagles, and he admitted he had not prepared to be interviewed by a team at that point. His agent helped him assemble a binder with information and he considered his coaching philosophy, but part of Pederson's charm is his amiable demeanor. He met with Eagles officials the morning after the Chiefs beat the Houston Texans in the opening round of the postseason, and he knew most of the faces in the room from his time working in the Eagles' building. (This extended to Jeffrey Lurie's son, Julian, who Pederson trained as a high schooler.) The familiarity helped the interview—and Pederson was able to laugh at himself. At one point, as he explained in his book, he expressed how he was looking forward to returning to training camp at Lehigh University. They informed him that camp had since been moved to the team's practice facility. "I got it," Pederson responded, sharing that he was all in for a summer at the NovaCare Complex. He had to present his first speech to the team. Among the notes he shared were four concepts: create energy every day; eliminate distractions; attack everything, from practice to sleeping to eating to preparing; and fear nothing. One week later, word started to spread that

Pederson would be the next coach. After Kansas City lost to the New England Patriots in the divisional round, Pederson declined comment to reporters (including this one) waiting to speak with him in the Gillette Stadium visitor's locker room. When he boarded the bus, Lurie called and officially offered him the job. Two days later, he signed with the Eagles on his 24th wedding anniversary.

"[Doug] checked the box on everything we looked at from football intelligence, overall intelligence, strategic thinking, communication skills, collaboration skills, genuineness, comfortable in your own skin...leadership abilities," Lurie said. "Those were the obvious ones. It was pretty easy."

The question of personnel control was raised, which was noteworthy not only because of the way the Kelly era ended (and Roseman's reintroduction into power) but also because all three coaches Lurie hired were eventually handed final say on personnel. Lurie emphasized the "collaboration," and when asked who would break the tie, Lurie raised his hand.

Pederson's first press conference included a notable guest. Standing on the side, watching the questions fired at the first-time head coach, was former Detroit Lions head coach Jim Schwartz. Pederson had tabbed Schwartz as his defensive coordinator in what amounted to an arranged marriage. They did not have a relationship prior to that point, but Schwartz was Pederson's most important hire—the defensive coordinator for an offensive-minded coach often is. Pederson called Schwartz "the head coach on defense" and envisioned a partnership like the one Reid shared with Jim Johnson. He built a quarterback incubator on the offensive staff, with Frank Reich as offensive coordinator and John DeFilippo as quarterbacks coach. Between Pederson, Reich, and DeFilippo, the Eagles had three coaches who had been offensive coordinators and quarterbacks coaches in the NFL and two who had been longtime NFL quarterbacks. For a team with designs on acquiring a young quarterback, this was the type of infrastructure it felt was necessary for development. Pederson was willing to keep certain Kelly assistants who were well regarded by the organization, including offensive line coach Jeff Stoutland. There was also an emphasis on including former players on the staff—eight overall, including Pederson.

"They understand the dynamic...of the locker room," Pederson said during his first year with the team. "They understand what it means to be a teammate, a leader on the football team."

The Eagles re-signed incumbent starting quarterback Sam Bradford in March 2016 and signed Chase Daniel, who had been the backup in Kansas City when Pederson was offensive assistant, similar to how Reid once acquired Pederson. Daniel knew the offense and could help the adjustment. The blockbuster trade for Carson Wentz crowded the room and made clear the direction the franchise would ultimately steer. Pederson initially indicated that Wentz would be on a Donovan McNabb–like timeline and wait and develop. When Wentz impressed the Eagles that offseason and the Vikings offered a first-round pick for Bradford before the season, Wentz ascended to the top of the depth chart. The Pederson-Wentz era would commence from day one.

Although the season began with promise when the Eagles won their first three games, they lost seven of nine from Weeks 5 to 15 to clinch a losing campaign. But there were two losses during that stretch that resonated beyond 2016. After a lopsided 32–14 blowout by the Cincinnati Bengals in Week 13, Pederson questioned his team's effort. He did not mention players by name, but he sent a hard, public message to his group. Two weeks later against the Baltimore Ravens, the Eagles were down by seven points when Wentz dove past the goal line for a touchdown with four seconds remaining. Instead of sending his kicking unit onto the field to tie the game, Pederson instructed the Eagles to attempt a two-conversion and try to win in regulation. The conversion failed, but the aggressiveness—and the willingness to be bold with a data-driven decision—foretold what would come the next season. So did the last two games of the year, which the Eagles won back-to-back to finish 7–9 and at least carry goodwill into the offseason.

That first season also tested Pederson in ways that a coach can only experience when he is on the job. There were high-profile player arrests. One of his top free agents, Brandon Brooks, missed time because of an anxiety condition. Nelson Agholor, a second-year player who had been a first-round pick, experienced a crisis of confidence that compelled Pederson to bench him for a week. There is much a head coach can prepare for, reflected in those binders brought to interviews, but the measure of a coach is often how he responds to the unknown and unplanned.

Pederson kept most of his coaching staff together after the 2016 campaign. The focus was on building talent around Wentz, and Roseman fulfilled his end of the bargain with a strong offseason that gave the Eagles—and Pederson—a promising roster. Implicit in those changes was a need for improvement. Reid arrived with a five-year plan. Pederson conceded he would not be granted that type of window.

"Sometimes when you're building a [Super Bowl] roster…it takes three years, four years, five years in, and if you constantly change, I don't see how you can get there," Pederson said during the summer of 2017. "With that being said, there has to be consistency and there has to be improvement this year. I get that. I'm not naïve to that or anything."

Pederson remarked in that same interview that the 2017 Eagles had more talent than his Super Bowl teams with the Packers. He contextualized the statement by explaining that so much needs to go right to win besides talent—injuries, chemistry, roster development, good coaching—but that the ingredients were present for the Eagles to be more than a middling team.

"If we go 8–8, is that a successful year?" Pederson said. "I don't coach to be average—I'll tell you that."

The scrutiny on Pederson reached a crescendo before the season when analyst Mike Lombardi, a former NFL executive who worked for the Eagles in 1998 before Reid came to the franchise, said Pederson "might be less qualified to coach a team than anyone I've ever seen in my 30-plus years in the NFL." In a market like Philadelphia, this became a major story. Pederson said he knew little about Lombardi's comment and Lurie held an impromptu news conference that coincided with the firestorm. He offered an endorsement of Pederson that day, dismissing Lombardi's comments as "clickbait."

"He took over a team that had some locker room issues with the previous head coach. He lost his starting quarterback [eight] days before the start of the season and was asked to use our young third-string quarterback," Lurie said. "He had to put together a coaching staff. My personal evaluation of the coaching staff that he put together, or inherited, but was open to inherit, is outstanding. I mean, really outstanding. That's a huge credit because quarterback analysis, locker room chemistry, and the ability to put together a top-notch coaching staff, those are three real key ingredients. I think he aced them all. Yes, there's going to be growing pains with any first-year head coach. We had that with Andy [Reid], we had it with Chip [Kelly], we've had it no matter who it is. I see [Doug] as someone who can keep improving. He's a listener. He's a collaborator. I think he has terrific relationships with the players. The future is in front of him, and it's there for the taking."

For what it's worth, Pederson wrote in his book that Lombardi sent him a note after the NFC Championship Game later that year. "The first rule of any informed opinion is to never begin with the end in mind. And I violated that rule. For that, I extend my sincere apology," Lombardi wrote, per Pederson.

Even if Pederson needed to convince the public, he did not need to convince the locker room. The players were in Pederson's corner, even showering him with Gatorade following a Week 1 victory in 2017.

"That's Philly. Second-year head coach—pressure's on him, pressure's on us," left tackle Jason Peters told *The Philadelphia Inquirer* after the game. "Doug is kind of like an Andy Reid guy. He mentored under Andy Reid, and he's more of a players' coach, and when you have a players' coach, you tend to play harder for that guy. He knows how it feels to get tired, so he'll take something off a little bit. You tend to lay it all on the line for a players' coach like that."

There were more moments that could have been reserved for Gatorade showers in 2017 when the Eagles went 13–3 and won the Super Bowl. It was that type of season for the Eagles and for Pederson. His emotional intelligence had been a key factor when Lurie hired him and was present throughout the season, especially with the way he managed the locker room. But Pederson's game-day coaching was also a major value add. Pederson had been the play-caller since day one even though he was never a primary play-caller in the NFL, and he suggested calling plays was the best part of his job. He would meet with Reich for 90 minutes the night before games to discuss the call sheet, and he focused on remaining aggressive. That could come in an unconventional way, such as the same call on back-to-back plays—remember his lessons from Calvary Baptist Academy—or with the way they dressed up different play designs.

"I think you either have it or you don't," Pederson said. "If you just look at what I've done in two years, you'd probably call me unorthodox with some of the decisions I've made on fourth downs and going for it, two-point conversions, things like that.... Sometimes you just don't do the norm, just don't do what everybody expects you to do and sometimes that can help you."

The in-game aggressiveness was also an advantage. The Eagles were No. 2 in the NFL in 2017 with 26 fourth-down attempts, although fourth-down calls are often dependent on the situation. They were No. 1 in fourth-down aggression when the win probability is between 20 and 100 percent outside of the final minute of each half, as calculated by data analyst Ben Baldwin, and the Eagles' aggressiveness set a trend. Part of this was an organizational emphasis to utilize data in decision-making that went to the top with Lurie, but Pederson was receptive. It earned Pederson a clever moniker for his gutsiness, and it was exemplified in the Super Bowl with the Philly Special that combined so much that went well for Pederson that year: the aggressive decision (a fourth down on the goal line in the Super Bowl!) and creative play design (a pass to the quarterback!).

"You saw a driven Doug Pederson, a man who went for it on fourth down...in the Super Bowl...with a trick play!" Jason Kelce screamed in his Super Bowl speech. "He wasn't just playing just to go mediocre. He's playing for a Super Bowl."

Pederson heard from other coaches after the Super Bowl who applauded an approach that most of them had defied. It's easier to play it safe, to take a field goal, than it is to walk the tightrope of aggressiveness.

"Those were some ballsy calls in the Super Bowl, man, on the biggest stage," Jon Gruden told him, according to Pederson's book. "There's not many people that make those calls, if any."

But there was also the way he navigated challenging situations, such as Carson Wentz's season-ending injury. He knew when eyes were on him and how his attitude could be reflected in the locker room. He did not publicly express concern—only confidence for Foles and sympathy for Wentz.

"I'm going to lead this football team," Pederson said shortly after Wentz's injury. "It falls more on my shoulders than it does these players. That's why they need to stay encouraged. That's why they need to stay excited about this opportunity we have in front of us."

He tried to keep the team loose—in the ways only he could. Sometimes, that was kicking a trash can in jest to lighten the mood one day after Kelce did the same in practice. He would call on certain players to speak in team meetings. He would take input from his leadership council. He adjusted the team's weekly schedule and offseason approach from Year 1 to Year 2. He ended every meeting with ice cream for the team—and made sure to include Häagen-Dazs vanilla, which is his favorite flavor.

"Doug Pederson is just himself," Lurie said then. "And at times, that's very humble, and at times, it's just very real. At times, that's very bright. At times, it's tough. But he does it in a true, genuine way and I think players really respond to that in today's world."

In some ways, Pederson's life turned into what happened before the Super Bowl and what happened after the Super Bowl. A Lombardi Trophy can do that to a coach, like a singer who has a hit or an actor with a blockbuster. What comes next? The book, the speaking engagement, the fame, the adoration—it did not seem part of the script 24 months earlier.

"You kind of sit back, my wife and I might have a conversation like, 'Man, this is kind of cool,'" Pederson said in June 2018. "It is cool to be mentioned that way. For a guy who didn't have probably a lot of support coming into this job initially, to be on the other end of that spectrum is cool. But I know what it took for me to get here. And I have to continue that for myself."

Pederson did not want the Super Bowl to define him. He also knew staying at the top can be as challenging as getting to the top. And the conditions that were in place in 2017 changed in 2018. He lost key members of his coaching staff, including Reich and DeFilippo. Wentz was recovering from a torn ACL and there was Foles' looming shadow, as the Super Bowl MVP experienced a summer of fame. The roster changed. Pederson told the team during the Super Bowl that an "individual can make a difference, but a team makes a miracle." A similar sentiment was set to be a guiding principle in 2018. He asked the players if they were *a* reason the Eagles won or *the* reason the Eagles won.

Pederson had shirts made that read EMBRACE THE TARGET. But few know the right buttons to press after reaching the mountaintop. The references to the Super Bowl were unavoidable. They were also cumbersome. Externally, the celebration never seemed to end. The Super Bowl banner was unveiled in Week 1 of the 2018 season—against the Falcons, who the Eagles beat in the playoffs in January of that year to propel the magical run. That was for the fans. The veterans on the team asked Pederson for the Super Bowl signs to come down in the locker room. They did not need to see the reminder in the back of the room every day.

"The decision [was] just to move on, move past, move to 2018," Pederson said.

The Eagles were a middling team for much of the 2018 season. They lost games they seemingly would have won a year earlier. They did not have the same luck overcoming injuries in 2018. The veterans they signed in free agency akin to lottery tickets did not cash in the way Chris Long and Patrick Robinson did. The coaching staff took time to adjust. Stuck at 6–7 in December, the Eagles decided to sit Wentz, who had a back injury that became progressively worse. It seemed as if their season was finished—until Foles rescued them, leading the Eagles on a four-game winning streak (with the help of a strong defense) to earn a wild-card bid in the final week of the season. The late-season march to the postseason included a wild-card win in Chicago and a narrow loss to New Orleans in the divisional round, and it was generally viewed as a superb coaching job by Pederson.

Entering the 2019 season, Pederson seemed to be in a good groove as head coach. As much as he wanted 2017 to be the new normal, there's little normalcy during a year when a team is the defending champion. The 2019 offseason seemed to take on a more normal pace, and Pederson did not need to replace his coaching staff nor navigate a tricky quarterback situation. (Foles had moved on, and Wentz was finally healthy.)

Pederson outlasted all of the seven coaches who were hired in 2016, giving him the last laugh after he had been named the worst hire from that cycle. He was a low-maintenance coach in a league where head coaches often took on outsized roles with more success. His assistant coaches appreciated that he did not micromanage, and his players valued the way he listened to them when making decisions.

"I think a lot of times, people's egos get in the way, and they feel like they've got to have their hand in everything," linebackers coach Ken Flajole, who was a defensive quality control coach in Green Bay in 1998 when Pederson was a backup quarterback, said of Pederson during the 2019 offseason. "That's not Doug. Doug expects you to do your work, and do it right, but he's very good that way.... I would say this: his ability to put his ego in his back pocket and put the team ahead of power struggles, or however you want to say it, is probably a pretty good reason why he's been successful."

Pederson's relationship with Wentz was most critical. Wentz endured a turbulent 18 months with two season-ending injuries and the way Foles rallied the team both years. Even with a nine-digit contract and strong organizational commitment, Wentz had fence-mending to do in the locker room after reports of a high-maintenance personality. Pederson had long said that he and Wentz were "married," and he envisioned a partnership like the one between Brady and Belichick in New England. That required development—as a quarterback and a leader—from Wentz, and Pederson needed to maintain the trust and confidence.

"You've seen the great ones [head coaches and quarterbacks] in the NFL that have been together for a long time," Pederson said. "It's not always easy. There's going to be heated discussions, but you know what? It's like anything. Any family structure. You're going to have an argument but you're going to walk out and you're going to be united when you go out on the football field. That's the thing. Just being able to have those conversations, and just continue to cultivate that just goes a long way with the head coach–quarterback combination, and again, the ones that have been successful have done that, have built that lifelong relationship that we have begun here."

The 2019 season took on a similar pattern to 2018. The Eagles could not separate in the standings for much of the year and they did not have the same resilience from injuries as they did in 2017. But the Eagles again used a late-season push to make the playoffs. This time, Wentz led them—with a group of no-name receivers that seemed to validate the franchise's confidence in the quarterback. Wentz was set to start in the postseason for the first time. He lasted one quarter before a concussion forced him out of the game, and the Eagles' anemic offense could not prolong the season. They scored nine points in the loss, leaving a bitter last taste about an offense that had been mediocre throughout much of the season.

In the days after the postseason loss, Pederson said offensive coordinator Mike Groh and wide receivers coach Carson Walch would return for a third season in their roles. He backtracked but didn't retract...until 24 hours later, when Pederson dismissed both coaches—with whispers that he was implored to make changes. Pederson did not hire a formal offensive coordinator, instead creating a reworked offensive staff that was supposed to meld together different ideas for 2020. Shortly after the staff was assembled, the COVID-19 pandemic forced the staff to be sequestered in their homes. The offseason program was virtual. So was the creation of this new offense.

During the draft, the Eagles tried to solve their hole at wide receiver by drafting Jalen Reagor (notably over Justin Jefferson, who the coaching staff purportedly thought was more of a slot receiver). In the second round, they shocked football fans by taking Jalen Hurts—a bold pick that later paid dividends, although its unintended consequences for Wentz helped contribute to the franchise quarterback's downfall. Training camp was delayed because of the pandemic, and when the team finally took the field, Pederson was quarantined at home because he contracted COVID-19.

It did not take long for the season to go awry. The Eagles surrendered a 17–0 first-half lead in their season opener to lose 27–17 to Washington on an afternoon when Wentz turned the ball over three times. After losing Week 2, the Eagles tied their third game of the season—a result notable because Pederson elected to punt the ball in the opponent's territory in the final minute of overtime. The coach who wrote *Fearless* played for a tie. The Eagles were 3–7–1 and spiraling in the second half against Green Bay in Week 13 when Pederson made the decision to bench Wentz. By that point in the season, there were reports that the coach and quarterback were butting heads. He made the decision to stay with Hurts, who showed promise in the final few games of the season. In the season finale, with the Eagles playing on national television and out of playoff contention, Pederson made the decision to bench key players and relieve Hurts at halftime. There were health-related reasons behind some of the benchings, and Pederson said he wanted to give loyal reserve Nate Sudfeld a chance to play, but it appeared to the football world—and even to players on the sideline—that the Eagles were tanking for draft position.

On the day after the season, Pederson conducted exit meetings as usual. He held his season-ending news conference with Roseman as usual. He was expected to return for 2021, with a meeting scheduled with Lurie as the last item on his schedule. Schwartz stepped down as defensive coordinator, giving Pederson a major hole to fill on the coaching staff. And clearly after an offensive performance that ranked 28 out of 32 teams in DVOA (defense-adjusted value over average) and 26th in scoring, offensive changes would be required, too. But the meeting was not a formality. More time with the owner revealed what Lurie termed a "difference in vision." One week after the typical "Black Monday" firings in the NFL, the Eagles dismissed the only coach who had led them to the Super Bowl. The marriage had run its course—seemingly for both sides.

Lurie was candid and reasoned, relying more on logic than the concept of fairness. In fact, Lurie said the decision was not based on whether Pederson deserved to get fired. "He did not deserve to be let go," Lurie admitted. But the owner viewed the franchise with a broader lens than a head coach entering Year 6 would.

Pederson, coming off a four-win season and needing new assistant coaches, was not necessarily looking for a rebuild. He valued familiarity and promoting from within. He needed a strong year in 2021 because two seasons with a losing record often puts a coach on the hot seat. Lurie wanted to reset, focusing less on maximizing the 2021 season and more on sustaining success. That required procuring draft picks and cleaning up the team's cap situation.

"I would say the difference in vision is much more about where we're at as a franchise," Lurie said about firing Pederson. "It's a transition point, and we've got to get younger, and we have to have a lot more volume of draft picks, and we have to accumulate as much talent as we possibly can that is going to work in the long run with a focus on the midterm and the long term and not on how to maximize 2021. And it's almost not fair to Doug because his vision has to be: What can I do to fix this right away, and what coaches can help me get to a smoother 2021. My vision is much more: How can we get back to the success we've had and what we're used to in the next two, three, four, five years? It's not a difference of opinion. It's a difference of where we're both at, and I really feel it was in both of our interests to proceed on our own paths that way."

Pederson spent the 2021 season out of coaching. He lived in Florida and experienced civilian life for a change. It was an important year for him to have personal time. He became a grandfather and watched his son get married. He lost his brother. He was back on the interview circuit in 2022. This time, he had a Super Bowl and strong résumé to point to in interviews, giving him some clout. The Jacksonville Jaguars hired Pederson, and he brought the team to the postseason in his first year.

"It just was a really good time for me to step away, refocus and regroup myself," Pederson said, "and come back with a lot of energy and passion, and pour everything I learned in five years into this job, and make it the best I can be.... Have a little more fun with what we do, and don't be so stressed out all the time."

When he was asked at the 2022 scouting combine what he would like to do differently the second time around, Pederson flexed in a way that a Super Bowl–winner might be permitted to.

"Besides win another championship?" Pederson shot back.

Pederson and the Jaguars played the Eagles in 2022. Hanging above Pederson on the visitor's sideline was a banner commemorating the Super Bowl he brought to Philadelphia. The franchise showed Pederson on the screens at Lincoln Financial Field, and he received a hearty ovation—even in an opponent's garb. He gave his jacket to Jason Kelce after the game. Former players embraced him. A few trick first downs away stood a statue depicting him making one of the gutsiest calls in franchise history. Pederson still has not seen the statue in person. He's waiting until retirement, when he'll assuredly be welcomed back in Philadelphia. Because Pederson is immortalized in bronze, ever a franchise icon.

7

Nick Sirianni

In the second quarter of Nick Sirianni's first postseason win in January 2023, he raced near the goal line while the Eagles attempted a two-point conversion after securing a four-touchdown lead. When an official told Sirianni where he was allowed to stand, the then-second-year coach's response instantly became a meme.

"I know what the f— I'm doing!" he said.

Yes, he does. But that was not the way Sirianni had always been viewed.

Two years earlier, the Eagles had made Sirianni a surprise hire to replace Doug Pederson. Sirianni was not atop the pundits' expected coaching list. He had not been a primary offensive play-caller and only spent two seasons as an offensive coordinator with the Indianapolis Colts. He did not interview for any other head-coaching jobs. In fact, after the Colts lost in the postseason and the coaches had some time off during the coach-hiring cycle, Sirianni took a family vacation to Fort Lauderdale, Florida, and did not pack a suit. When the Eagles called to arrange an interview, they allowed him to dress casually. The interview went eight hours. They asked him back the next day. At the start of the week, most Eagles fans could not have picked Sirianni out of a lineup. By the end of the week, he was set to become the head coach for the city's most popular franchise.

"We are so incredibly excited for the coach you are," Lurie told him on the phone call when he offered him the job, "and the coach you can become."

Sirianni still needed to offer the Eagles fanbase who knew little about him similar confidence. It did not go well.

Introductory press conferences are not a reliable indicator of coaching success, so enlarging their importance would be impractical. But they are nonetheless a first impression—especially when the coach is not yet a household name. Sirianni's press conference was atypical for a few reasons. COVID-19 protocols were in place, so the gathering was virtual. This took away some of the performative elements of the ordeal. There's an energy that can come from standing in front of a crowd and reading a room, and part of Sirianni's charm is his ability to connect with those around him. Instead, Sirianni was in an empty auditorium watching a screen. Also, the biggest topic at the time was the uncertain status of franchise quarterback Carson Wentz. This would not necessarily be Sirianni's decision to make, yet it was a question that demanded answers. Plus, there are natural nerves that come in this setting. A first-time head coach in a demanding media market can become a combustible combination.

Sirianni stumbled through the session, offering a long-winded opening statement before rambling answers to questions.

The press conference became an immediate punchline. Lost in the laugh track was legitimate substance that proved clairvoyant two years later, when the core principles he first introduced—connect, compete, accountability, football intelligence, and fundamentals—helped shape a Super Bowl–caliber team.

Sirianni's core principles became a walking tagline for the coach. You cannot spend any time around the Eagles' facility with Sirianni in charge and not hear them echoed. But if you want to learn their origin, it helps to visit the western New York town of Jamestown on the tip of the state, about 75 miles south of Buffalo between Lake Erie and the Allegheny National Forest. And their roots come from the West Ellicott neighborhood where Fran and Amy Sirianni raised three future coaches.

"I can trace every core value back to the Sirianni household growing up," Sirianni once said.

Connection? How about the family's kitchen table where the track athletes Fran coached would come over on Thursday nights for spaghetti dinners?

"Nick has an ability to connect with everybody," former NFL quarterback Kellen Clemens said during a 2021 interview. "He does because he cares. And I think that's one of the biggest things that you have to be able to do at that level. You're coaching guys that are in their mid-to-late thirties and you're coaching guys that are in their early twenties. And everybody's at different times in their careers, has different experiences, different expectations, but Nick has the ability to reach everybody, to connect with everybody."

Compete? Sirianni is the youngest of three brothers and competed in every sport, whether in their front yard or on their street corner or in the schoolyard or at Lakewood Beach for summer basketball games. There's a stop sign in front of his home with which he once collided while catching passes, requiring stitches around his eye.

"He was always the little brother," Amy said. "He had to fight his way through stuff.... They didn't abuse him. But he was a pest, just like little brothers are."

Seemingly every story with his friends involves some type of competition.

"I could be coaching in this division for 30 years and play the Cowboys 60 times," Sirianni said in 2021, "and I could never catch the amount of times I've competed against [friend] Tommy Langworthy."

Fundamentals? He's a coach's son, after all—and the son of teachers. That fact is important because his parents consider teaching the family business. All three Sirianni boys—Mike, Jay, and Nick—married teachers. The parents did not find this to be a coincidence.

"Teaching is coaching; coaching is teaching," Jay said. "I think you see that when Nick [is] talking about 'fundamentals, fundamentals.' That's teaching. I think that's the teacher's background that he's gotten from a family of teachers."

While in college at Mount Union, Sirianni would spend summers on the corner of Southwestern Drive running routes on the open field and going through plyometrics learned under the tutelage of his father. He would also lift weights, and it was then, at the local YMCA, that he met NFL coach Todd Haley. Haley had a summer home at nearby Chautauqua Lake. They were introduced by the facility director, who saw the connection between a local D-III wide receiver and pro coach.

"So it all started off, well, 'How do I make myself a better football player?' That was where I first met Todd," Sirianni said. "Todd was very open to helping me out, and I really admired that he would want to help me out. I remember it started off like, 'Give me some wide receiver drills to do,' talking through some routes and stuff like that."

Haley and Sirianni stayed in touch. When Haley was hired as the Kansas City Chiefs' head coach in 2009, Sirianni was an assistant at Indiana University of Pennsylvania. He contacted Haley, who responded with an invitation to meet at the combine for an opening at quality control coach. The IUP coaches knew Sirianni would not stay and rise on the college coaching ladder. He was too impressive of an interviewee—and too promising of a coach.

"He's on his journey now," said Paul Tortorella, then IUP's defensive coordinator and now their head coach. "He's going to be going to places."

Football IQ? Sirianni did not have a pedigree. He was not a former player and did not grow up around professional football. He did not make it to the NFL based on name. It was his football acumen and his ability to teach the concepts to the players.

"Here's what stood out: I didn't have to double-teach," said Charlie Weis, who was the Chiefs' offensive coordinator with Sirianni, during a 2021 interview. "Because one of the things when you have a young guy who's doing stuff, some things you have to spend a lot of your time going back in and fix them or add on to what they said. And usually, I was allowed to just worry about adding on the X's and O's, a game plan and schematics, and the thought process. I didn't have to spend much time tweaking fundamentals and techniques because he had that pretty well covered."

Brian Daboll, another offensive coordinator in Kansas City, noticed Sirianni's "energy," "attitude," and "ability to deal with players." And that was during a 2–14 season marked by tragedy on the team, so it was not as if Sirianni rode the waves of success.

"You could tell right from the beginning...his arrow was pointing up. And fast," Daboll said.

When Andy Reid was dismissed by the Eagles in 2013 and landed in Kansas City, he brought his own staff, and Sirianni went looking for work. He landed in San Diego, a pivotal stop in his career. It connected him with Frank Reich, who was then a Chargers assistant and became a work version of a big brother for Sirianni. He worked directly with Philip Rivers, one of the NFL's top quarterbacks. He met Shane Steichen, whom he would later bring to Philadelphia.

Reich soon became the Eagles' offensive coordinator, and after the Eagles won the Super Bowl in February 2018, the Indianapolis Colts hired him as head coach. Reich knew who he wanted as his coordinator: Sirianni. That was the first time Sirianni ran an offense. He did not call plays in Indianapolis, although he helped put the system together with Reich. And when the Eagles needed a new coach in 2021, Reich's input was valuable. Sirianni received a sterling recommendation.

Sirianni brought in Steichen as offensive coordinator and Jonathan Gannon as defensive coordinators, both young up-and-coming coaches with whom he had previously worked. This was not a staff full of head-coaching or coordinator experience. It was a staff that fit Sirianni's personality. Sirianni devoted his early months focused on those core values he often recites, creating the sense of connection that might prove valuable when it would be easy to question or crack.

That came quickly. After the Eagles' impressive season-opening win over Atlanta, they lost five of six games. Hurts seemed a clumsy fit in a pass-happy offense. A conservative defense resembled a summer passing camp for opposing quarterbacks. At 2–5, Sirianni's public approval rating might have been at its nadir. Andy Reid could have empathized from his first year. When the players returned to work the following week, Sirianni had a particular message he wanted to reinforce.

"I said the results aren't there right now, but what's going on here is that there's growth under the soil. I put a picture of a flower up, and it's coming through the ground, and the roots are growing out," Sirianni explained. "The roots are continuing to grow out. Everybody wants to see results. Shoot, nobody wants to see results more than us, right? We want to see results, too. But it's really important that the foundation is being built and that the roots are growing out. And the only way the roots grow out every single day and they grow stronger and they grow better is if we all water, we all fertilize, we all do our part, each individual, each individual coach, each individual player, everybody in the building, that we do our part to water to make sure that, when it does pop out, it really pops out and it grows."

The analogy was more specific behind closed doors, but the public messaging was panned. A city with a Rocky Balboa statue doesn't necessarily use botany for motivation. But the message resonated with the team, even if they were not gardeners. They maintained belief in Sirianni. He earned their trust. Four days later, the Eagles dominated the Detroit Lions. In the postgame locker room, respected team leader Jason Kelce brought the team together: *Roots on three!*

The momentum continued with the Eagles winning seven of nine games to earn a spot in the postseason. The fertilizer, though, might have been a change in the offense. Behind the scenes, Sirianni made an unselfish decision. He ceded play-calling responsibilities to Steichen, recognizing that he had been spread thin and he preferred to allocate his attention to game management decisions and overseeing the entire team. Sirianni later emphasized that he was still responsible for the offense; to use a restaurant analogy, he set the menu and Steichen picked the dishes. Sirianni said there's nothing he enjoys more than putting a game plan together, which he still did. But he wanted to broaden his scope.

"I just didn't feel like I was doing a good enough job communicating. It wasn't any particular 'a-ha' moment or anything like that," Sirianni said in the summer of 2022. "I trusted Shane. All the work's done Monday through Saturday to get ready for it, and they knew how I wanted to run plays."

Nonetheless, other coaches might have resisted such a change because of pride or ego. Not Sirianni.

"I think that's where a lot of problems happen in the NFL is from an ego standpoint," Sirianni said. "It's what is the best thing to do. If I said I'm going to stand on a table and run these plays that we ran with Philip Rivers, because that's what we do, that's an ego thing to me."

The offense also shifted into a run-heavy attack, leaning on the strength of the roster: Hurts' legs and a top-of-the-league offensive line. The Eagles finished No. 1 in the NFL in rushing despite overleveraging on passing early in the season. This showed that Sirianni could adapt. And the turnaround validated the way the locker room viewed Sirianni.

Those changes were good enough to reach the postseason. Once there, it was clear they were a class below the NFL's elite teams. The Eagles were overmatched in a 31-15 loss during which the Buccaneers led 31-0 at the end of the third quarter. Hurts struggled against Tampa Bay, completing only 50 percent of his passes for 140 yards and two interceptions through three quarters before statistical inflation when the game was out of reach. It was clear that afternoon that the Eagles had come a long way in Sirianni's first year, but there was much to improve.

The Eagles needed an infusion of talent entering Year 2 of the Sirianni era—particularly at wide receiver and pass rusher.

Howie Roseman took care of that with high-profile acquisitions, including a blockbuster draft-day trade for star pass-catcher A.J. Brown (and a subsequent $100-million contract extension) to go along with the start-of-free-agency signing of Haason Reddick, a Camden, New Jersey, native and Temple product who had proven he could wreak havoc on the quarterback. There were other opportunistic moves, such as the signing of veteran cornerback James Bradberry and cut-down day trade for defensive back C.J. Gardner-Johnson. Combined with another year of development with the roster and continuity on the coaching staff, there was considerable optimism in Philadelphia.

Throughout the offseason, there had been speculation that the Eagles would acquire a high-profile quarterback such as Russell Wilson or Deshaun Watson. The Eagles did not land either quarterback—it seemed more because of those quarterbacks' preferred destinations than whether the Eagles were interested—and the season was billed as a chance to evaluate Hurts with a full arsenal of offensive talent. A similar logic was applied to Sirianni, and the head coach welcomed the expectations that came with the loaded roster. When he had interviewed for an assistant job at Mount Union at his alma mater years earlier, Larry Kehres—the head coach whom Sirianni idolizes—asked his former player what offense he would run. Sirianni started answering before Kehres slammed the table.

"You don't even know what type of players we have here!" Kehres told him. More than a decade later, Sirianni still recites the story with the prevailing takeaway—players matter more than plays. So he adjusted the offense to fit their personnel, especially considering Brown's prodigious talent.

Sirianni also sought to find more emotional stability in his second season and avoid the "ups and downs" that come with prosperity and despair. In professional football, you're seemingly one week—or even one play—away from either extreme. He shared an example that traces back to his discomfort from flying. His vacations as a kid were road trips, so he didn't board airplanes until college. He learned to look at the flight attendant when turbulence caused angst, figuring the flight attendant was in the air every day and would know when to panic. So when the flight attendant remained calm, Sirianni did not worry. If the flight attendant appeared distressed, Sirianni had cause for concern. He wanted to apply that approach to coaching.

"All eyes are on you. How you react after wins. How you react after losses. How you react with the team," Sirianni said during the summer of 2022. "You're setting the tone there. Your energy at all times is [reflecting on] the team. Until you're in that seat, you don't understand...everybody is looking at you at all times."

He was mindful of how he communicated and took stock of when he went too far. As a rookie head coach, Sirianni wore a BEAT DALLAS T-shirt before his first rivalry game, as if he had returned to Mount Union preparing for a game against John Carroll. Such a gimmick was unnecessary in the NFL. It enlarges one week relative to another, which Sirianni did not want. And it brought unnecessary attention. Before the first Eagles-Cowboys game in 2022, he showed the shirt to the team.

"This was stupid on my part last year!" Sirianni told his team, as recounted in a team video, and he tossed the shirt behind him.

He held himself accountable, which allowed him to hold others accountable. During the Eagles' meetings, the player at fault on a given play is identified in front of the room. If the coach is at fault, he's identified. It goes back to his time as an education major at Mount Union and trying to understand different ways people learn. It can be visual. It can be verbal.

And it can come by making them feel responsible when it's their responsibility.

"I think it's a way to get people's egos out of the way," Lane Johnson said in 2022. "It doesn't matter who the player is, just hold them accountable. I think it makes a team better in the long run, that approach."

For much of the 2022 season, Sirianni did not need to worry about how he reacted to defeat. The Eagles enjoyed a charmed start to their season. They won their first eight games—and the games were not particularly close, with six of those eight victories by more than a touchdown. To show the strength of the overall roster, they all came in different ways. The Week 1 win over the Detroit Lions required a 38-point onslaught, with Hurts passing for 243 yards and rushing for 90 yards. A.J. Brown introduced himself to Eagles fans with a 10-catch, 155-yard effort. Four nights later, the Eagles beat the Minnesota Vikings with the help of three interceptions on defense and the unit allowed only seven points.

The Week 3 visit to Washington was marked by a familiar face on the other sideline: Carson Wentz. It was the first time the Eagles faced their former franchise quarterback. Because it was a road game, Wentz did not get the Philadelphia welcome. The Eagles defense spoke for the fans. "Get after him. That was it," Reddick said of the Eagles' game plan for Wentz that day. "Hit him early and often. Try to get him flustered." That's what happened. The Eagles sacked Wentz nine times—the most he had ever been sacked in a game—and they hit him 17 times. It was a sign of how menacing the Eagles pass rush would become that season. They finished 2022 with a franchise-record 70 sacks.

The reunion tour continued in Week 4 when Pederson visited Philadelphia with the Jacksonville Jaguars. The reception for Pederson was positive from both the fans and his former players, but Sirianni outlasted his predecessor behind a rushing offense that accumulated 210 yards and four touchdowns. That was an example of how the Eagles adapted their style and personnel.

They signed a kicker off the street (Cameron Dicker), and he hit the game-winning field goal in Week 5 in Arizona. The offensive line dominated during an overpowering 13-play, 75-yard fourth-quarter drive in a Week 6 win over Dallas in which the Eagles repeatedly called the same running play. Convincing victories over Pittsburgh and Houston pushed the Eagles to 8–0, giving them the best start in franchise history.

"I've been 8–0 before and lost a national championship," Hurts said after the win in Houston, his hometown. "We haven't accomplished anything yet."

No, but they appeared to be a juggernaut. They had the best roster in the NFL. Hurts took the leap into becoming one of the best young quarterbacks in the NFL. And Sirianni became more of an asset than a punchline. The Eagles had one lone hiccup before Christmas Eve—a Week 9 loss to Washington in which the Commanders controlled the clock and the Eagles committed uncharacteristic turnovers—but they otherwise pushed to 13–1. Sirianni's sideline emotion came off as brash but also relatable to a passionate fan base. There was one game when it was especially apparent. The Indianapolis Colts fired Reich, and the Eagles played them shortly thereafter. When the Eagles snuck away with a late-game victory, Sirianni ran to the stands and hollered at the fans, "That s— was for Frank Reich!" He needed to regain his composure when he entered the locker room. "I'm emotional because I love Frank Reich," he said after the game.

No season is easy, though. And the Eagles were tested in a major way come December, when Hurts sprained his throwing shoulder in a win against Chicago. Just like 2017, they were dealing with a quarterback's injury with the postseason approaching. (This time, the injury was not a season-ender.) The Eagles lost two games with Gardner Minshew starting, including a 20–10 loss to the New Orleans Saints on New Year's Day with only 67 rushing yards. Hurts' injury affected the running game perhaps more than the passing game, and Sirianni needed his star quarterback to return to clinch a bye in the postseason. Johnson's absence because of a torn adductor was also a factor. Hurts rushed back and did just enough in the season finale to finish with an NFC-best 14–3 record, giving the Eagles a bye week to regain swagger for the playoffs.

The homefield advantage was critical. In a meeting with the coaches before the season, Lurie told his staff that their goal was to get the No. 1 seed to play at home in the postseason. Sirianni's reaction? "He didn't blink!" Lurie said.

Sirianni is maniacal about preparedness for specific situations, and he holds meetings in which he'll call on others in the room using the Socratic method to see what they would do in a given situation. The Eagles were dangerous on fourth downs with the use of the "Tush Push"—their version of a quarterback sneak in short-yardage situations in which Hurts dives behind an overpowering offensive line. He also has the help of teammates behind him pushing his back side, if needed. (Hence the moniker.)

"His atmosphere or culture that he's built within this building is a really big reason why the coaches have flourished, why the players have flourished," Kelce said in January 2023. "That's what a head coach's main goal is. Whether he's calling the plays...or managing the game, his No. 1 job is to facilitate a team, an organization that's focused on improving, that's focused on working, that comes in the building with energy, that's motivated to get better. These things far outweigh what play we call on third down, and I think Nick does a phenomenal job of that and I think he deserves all the credit in the world for that."

The home-field advantage—and the advantage of the NFL's best roster—was apparent in the playoffs. Hurts looked like a superstar. Johnson danced his way through the injury while celebrating a 38–7 rout of the New York Giants. That's when Sirianni confirmed that he did, in fact, "know what the f— I'm doing." The Eagles were back. They scored five touchdowns, rushed for 268 yards, and completed 10 of 14 third downs. "It's just that juice, man. That swag," Jordan Mailata said. "It helps when you get your star players back, for sure."

The star power continued in the NFC Championship Game. Haason Reddick, who had emerged into one of the NFL's elite pass-rushers, pummeled San Francisco 49ers quarterback Brock Purdy on the opening possession when the 49ers oddly tried to block him with a tight end. Purdy was injured on the play and left the game. Backup quarterback Josh Johnson was knocked out of the game early in the third quarter. The 49ers used running back Christian McCaffrey at quarterback, and they had no answers for the Eagles. San Francisco was limited to 164 yards and only seven points. The Eagles rushed for four touchdowns, controlling the clock. Sirianni gave the Eagles an advantage with in-game decisions. Just like five years earlier, it was a party at Lincoln Financial Field with a ticket punched to the Super Bowl. Unlike 2017, there were no dog masks in the locker room this time. They were favored all the way through. "Tale of two different teams," Johnson said. "We were underdogs in '17. This year, we have a heavily loaded roster. Expected to do good things."

"We thought we had an opportunity to be really great," Lurie said in the locker room after the game. "It was taking advantage of a perception that we had a chance to be an outstanding team and a mix of veterans in their eighth, 10th, 12th year with a lot of wonderful young players, including a quarterback who's that way. We really felt there was a great opportunity. But you got to get the right players. And we have the right players. They're outstanding."

While Lurie spoke, though, he knew what potentially awaited in the Super Bowl—Andy Reid, the winningest coach in franchise history. (He also happened to be the coach who left Sirianni unemployed upon taking over in Kansas City.)

After two weeks of hoopla and four decades of work, Sirianni's emotions reached a crescendo in the minutes before he was set to coach on the biggest stage. It might have become a meme to the general public to see tears stream down Sirianni's face while Chris Stapleton sang the national anthem, but for Sirianni, it was a moment of reflection and appreciation for where he stood—and what it took to reach that point.

"I've dreamed about this since I've been two years old," Sirianni said. "I said to our guys, 'Some of you guys have been dreaming about this since you've been two, some of you since you've been in peewee football, some of you since high school, college or even when you got to the pros. But we've all been dreaming of it.' And growing up in a family with a dad that's a football coach, older brothers that played football, this is what you dream of, being in this moment. Just emotional because there's a lot of work, not just by myself, but a lot of people. Starting with my wife and my kids, my brothers, my dad, and just so many people—coaches that I've had, teammates that I've had that helped me get to that moment."

The Eagles met the moment—at least at the start. The offense reached the end zone on three of five drives in the first half, with Hurts outdueling Patrick Mahomes (other than an inopportune fumble that was recovered and returned by Kansas City for a score) and Brown showing why he set records for the Eagles. The Chiefs offense only scored once. The Eagles entered halftime with a 24–14 advantage, and at that moment, it would have been sensible for the Philadelphia police to consider greasing the poles on Broad Street.

Inside the locker room at halftime, teammates told each other it was a 0–0 game. They offered the reminder that Mahomes was on the other side. The season had been marked by mismatches. They knew the Super Bowl wouldn't remain one. There was another complicating factor. The State Farm Stadium grass field played like a skating rink. The Eagles' franchise-record 70 sacks that season was aided, in part, by nursing leads and forcing opponents to become one-dimensional. But it was difficult for players to maintain their footing during the Super Bowl. ESPN later reported the turf had been overwatered. The conditions affected both sides, but it was a noticeable deterrent for the Eagles' pass rushers.

"I'm not going to lie; it was the worst field that I've ever played on," Reddick said after the game. "It was very disappointing; it's the NFL. You would think it would be better so we could get some better play, but it is what it is.... If you said I'd beat my man a couple of times, just try to turn the corner, I was slipping. I just couldn't turn the corner."

A 10-point lead is not safe against Mahomes and the Chiefs. It's barely a lead. And the Eagles defense was out of answers in the second half. The Chiefs scored on every possession, leaving the secondary flummoxed and the pass rush dormant. Meanwhile, Sirianni's offense ran out of consistent firepower. They settled for a field goal on their first drive after halftime. Sirianni chose to punt on a fourth-and-3 at the Eagles' 32-yard line down one point in the fourth quarter, a decision he defended but one that proved ill-fated. The Chiefs returned the punt to the 5-yard line, and the Eagles faced an eight-point deficit.

To the Eagles' credit, they tied the game. Hurts led the Eagles on an eight-play, 75-yard drive, rushing for both a touchdown and a two-point conversion to bring the score to 35–35 with just more than five minutes remaining. Sirianni's swagger was warranted.

Except in order to win, the defense would need to make a stop. Their best chance came when Kansas City was forced to a third-and-8 from the 15-yard line with 1:54 remaining in the game. Hold the Chiefs to a field goal, and the Eagles would have a chance to win the game. The defense forced an incompletion, but excitement turned to bemoaning a flag thrown on James Bradberry. Defensive holding. Fresh set of downs. It was a polarizing penalty, considering it occurred at such a big moment in the game.

"I was hoping they would let it ride," Bradberry said after the game. "But it was holding."

"That's game," Kelce muttered to himself on the sideline, as captured on an NFL Films video. "We're going to call that?"

The Chiefs drained the clock to 11 seconds and kicked a go-ahead field goal. All the Eagles had time for was a feeble Hail Mary attempt that fell short of the end zone. Reid hoisted the Lombardi Trophy against the Eagles. Sirianni was left with the same pain the opposing coach felt two decades earlier.

In the postgame locker room, Sirianni's message to his team focused on the adversity they had overcome and finding a way to "use this pain, use this failure to motivate us and make it a strength."

Sure enough, the confetti was used for that reason entering the 2023 season—literally. Sirianni showed an image of red and yellow confetti falling at the Super Bowl at the start of the offseason program, a reminder of the bitterness of being left at the altar and a north star for how far they sought to reach. The loss stung Sirianni, who would blurt an expletive in his office on the occasions he rehashed the game. It was not to create pain. It was to become calloused, to learn, to be ready for it again.

"To me, it's very healthy to do that," Sirianni said during the summer of 2023. "It's healthy to—as Frank Reich used to say to me—drag yourself through the mud.... This is the accountability piece of our program. It's healthy to drag yourself through the mud. To get real dirty, and to be like, 'Oh, I messed that up.' But then there's got to come a time where you get yourself out of the mud and you realize you're here for a reason and you're confident in your abilities and to move on. But there is a healthy portion of dragging yourself through the mud, because that's how you get better. 'What did I screw up? What are the things I didn't like about what we did?'.... So, of course, I've had those with that game. I've probably watched that game an obsessive [number] of times."

He studied other teams' seasons after losing the Super Bowl, seeking lessons. No two teams are the same from one year to the next. The Eagles experienced one of the drawbacks of success: players and coaches were in demand elsewhere. Key contributors such as Javon Hargrave, Miles Sanders, Gardner-Johnson, T.J. Edwards, Marcus Epps, Kyzir White, and Isaac Seumalo signed with other clubs. The exodus of defensive starters led to considerable turnover on the depth chart.

The changes spread to Sirianni's coaching staff, too. Steichen was hired as the Colts' head coach. Gannon landed in Arizona as head coach—a controversial exit because he spoke to the Cardinals general manager leading up to the Super Bowl without the Eagles' knowledge. Sirianni promoted quarterbacks coach Brian Johnson to offensive coordinator, keeping continuity on offense for Hurts. He made an external hire on defense, bringing in Sean Desai to oversee the unit. There were no position coaches on defense who had been a coordinator, and Sirianni tried to mitigate the lack of experience by hiring longtime NFL coach Matt Patricia as a senior defensive assistant.

For the first two months of the season, the changes did not affect the Eagles in the standings. They opened the season 5–0 and then went a league-best 10–1. And the wins came against some of the NFL's heavyweights. On the surface, the Eagles appeared to be the best team in the NFL. But they survived more than decimated opponents. Winning can be a deodorant, obscuring the odor. Perhaps Sirianni could sense something was awry.

He didn't show it. Sirianni gloated during the high-water mark—a Super Bowl rematch in Kansas City in Week 11. The Eagles outlasted the Chiefs to keep the best record in the NFL, and Sirianni hollered at the Chiefs fans on his way off the field.

That proved to be the Eagles' Super Bowl. Because two weeks later, when San Francisco visited Philadelphia for a rematch of the NFC Championship Game, it seemed like the 49ers' Super Bowl. This time, the Eagles did not knock out the 49ers' quarterback. Instead, San Francisco knocked out the Eagles. They outplayed and outcoached Sirianni's team in a 42–19 blowout, and the Eagles' season was never the same.

Two weeks later, Sirianni demoted Desai and replaced him with Patricia. Never mind that it was not Patricia's defensive scheme or the fact that the Eagles were 10–3 at the time. Sirianni thought a change in leadership was needed. The decision weighed on him, although not nearly as much as it anchored the Eagles. They were suffering a historic late-season collapse, and Sirianni had few answers. The offense lacked the firepower from the previous season. The defense could not make stops.

The Eagles lost five of six games, including Weeks 17 and 18 to teams with losing records. They lost control of the NFC East, needing to travel for the postseason.

In theory, a trip to Tampa Bay—a team the Eagles had dominated in September—offered an opportunity to reset. Instead, the Eagles discovered that the bottom was even lower than they knew. A listless 32–9 loss included no second-half points. It was a fitting conclusion to a more than monthlong meltdown. They lost six of their last seven games by an average score of 15 points. Sirianni went from coach-of-the-year lists to hot-seat lists.

"Obviously we were on a big slide," Sirianni said after the postseason loss. "Any time that's the case, I always look at myself first. And I didn't do a good enough job. Obviously, we lost five in the last six and lost today. And it was almost like you couldn't get out of the rut.... And that's all of us. We'll have to look ourselves in the mirror and accept that and find answers, find solutions. But obviously, when you start 10–1 and you get into what will happen for us and obviously that the expectations were high.... I'll look at everything."

Lurie did, too. The Eagles did not formalize Sirianni's return until nearly a week later. By that point, Sirianni dismissed both coordinators. He ceded control of the offense, which he concluded grew "stale." He hired established coordinators on both sides of the ball—and Lurie suggested the decision to do so was a major factor in keeping Sirianni for Year 4.

"Nick's conscious desire to have top-notch coordinators under him really drove a lot of the strategy and he was hellbent on making sure we had the best," Lurie said at the NFL league meetings in March 2024. "[I'm] highly encouraged by both his analysis of where we're at, no excuses, a fundamental understanding of what needs to be better than the last five or six weeks of the season, and not only a return to our championship-caliber performance and execution, but improve on that, too."

Even more, Lurie still saw the coach who impressed him in his Palm Beach home three years earlier during a decisive job interview. He saw three postseason appearances, plus a trip to the Super Bowl.

"I do know until we were hitting that streak of not playing well at the end of the year, we were 31–7 in the previous 38 regular season games," Lurie said. "To say the least, that's exceptional. And that's starting with taking a team that had a four-win season in our final year with Doug [Pederson] and taking it to a playoff team right away, and then to the Super Bowl, and then to a 10–1 beginning.

"Very disappointing ending, but I don't make light of 31–7 in the [NFL]. That's extraordinary. The ingredients I've always seen with Nick are very obvious—the ability to connect, the ability to be authentic, incredible work ethic, high football IQ. All the reasons he was hired in the first place have been almost magnified in the first three years."

Remember, Sirianni was hired not only for the coach he was, but for the coach he could become. After Year 3, there were clues—but there were still questions. He already rebounded from a dubious first impression. He colorfully suggested he knew what he was doing. In February 2024, he was ready to prove it again.

"We've won a lot of football games, but we didn't win the last month of last season, so it's a reboot and a re-prove for me and for this football team," Sirianni said.

When there's turbulence, he wants all eyes on him. And Sirianni's lasting impression resonates more than the first one.

PART 3

THE QUARTERBACKS

8

Donovan McNabb

DONOVAN MCNABB STOOD AT MIDFIELD OF A STADIUM HE'D indoctrinated as a franchise quarterback. He clinched a bid to the Super Bowl on that field. He spent most of his Eagles career on that field. And on this night in September 2013, his jersey was being retired. Andy Reid, the coach with whom he is forever linked and who believed in him enough to bypass an unprecedented offer of a bounty of draft picks (and eventually traded him a decade later), was coaching on the opposite sideline for a different team. His longtime teammates were on the field with him, including Brian Dawkins—the defensive leader often linked with McNabb during an era of unimaginable success and one painstaking void. Nobody would ever wear No. 5 again, an honor earned by the best quarterback to ever play in Philadelphia.

"No. 5 will always love you!" McNabb screamed to the crowd.

The statement prompted some punchlines, but it was noteworthy because it carried enough baggage to fill McNabb's flight back home to Arizona. A complicated relationship existed between No. 5 and those to whom the statement was directed.

"I look at the relationship just like a marriage," McNabb said when he retired. "You have some great times; you have some tough times. Hey, one thing is for sure, and I've said it before and I'll say it again, I told the fans that I would bring a championship here. My goal was to have that parade down Broad Street. Now the Phillies did it first, and I apologized to the fans because that was my goal. I felt like I let them down. The thing for me is I don't regret anything that happened throughout my career here. For the fans, they thoroughly appreciate the effort that I gave and what I gave them out on the field. It's about the product."

It is true McNabb never won a Super Bowl in Philadelphia. Neither did Dan Marino in Miami. Neither did Jim Kelly in Buffalo. But McNabb experienced a decade-long run in which he was consistently one of the best quarterbacks in the NFL, and he helped turn around the franchise. The Eagles had a revolving door at quarterback between Randall Cunningham and McNabb, a time period that included a stretch of false hope with Rodney Peete and Ty Detmer and Bobby Hoying and Koy Detmer.

"I just so happened to be a guy that was here in Philadelphia before Donovan got here," Dawkins said, "and I remember the times, I remember what those feelings felt like before [McNabb] got here."

Then Reid came in 1999, and he wanted a quarterback. The Eagles did not need to worry about quarterback for another decade. That's the type of security that NFL franchises dream about—and that's ultimately the story of McNabb's time in Philadelphia.

"Simply put, when all is said and done," Lurie said in 2013, "this man, No. 5, Donovan McNabb was a franchise-changing quarterback, and those words are not spoken very often."

McNabb's complicated relationship with Philadelphia dates back to the 1999 draft. The Eagles were determined to acquire a quarterback to build around from a draft rich in the position—the top three picks were quarterbacks—and Reid had identified McNabb as the quarterback he wanted. The Eagles liked McNabb more than Tim Couch, who went No. 1 overall, and thought McNabb's skill set and temperament would fit in Philadelphia. And they definitely liked him more than Texas running back Ricky Williams, the Heisman Trophy winner who attracted the infatuation of a vocal group of Eagles fans. That included the most popular sports radio show in Philadelphia and some of its dedicated listeners. And it included Ed Rendell, then mayor of Philadelphia, who phoned in to the show to advocate for Williams and implore fans to call the Eagles to push for them to take the running back.

Eagles fans were not alone in their interest in Williams. The New Orleans Saints offered all their draft picks to trade up to draft Williams. Lurie said in an interview for this book that late Saints owner Tom Benson even called him directly on draft day to try to persuade the Eagles to take the deal.

When NFL commissioner Paul Tagliabue announced that the Eagles had selected McNabb, a vocal collection of Eagles fans who traveled up to New York City for the draft responded with boos. The booing was in response to the Eagles' strategy more than McNabb himself—it's not as if fans were disgruntled by McNabb's Syracuse performance against Rutgers. This was a time when the notion of building around a running back was still prevalent. But the booing stung McNabb early in his marriage with Philadelphia, and it remained linked to McNabb throughout his time in Philadelphia. "Let's put the booing to rest," McNabb said years later. "That was back in '99. That was the beginning of an era, and this is the end. So I guess that made me stronger as a man."

McNabb had a chance to write his own story. He played 11 seasons in Philadelphia, 10 of which he was the opening-day starter. He set franchise records for passing yards and passing touchdowns and reached six Pro Bowls, but what was most remarkable during McNabb's decade as the starting quarterback was how much the franchise won. In those 10 years, the Eagles went to the postseason eight times, the NFC Championship Game five times, and the Super Bowl once. The Eagles won only one postseason game in the six years before McNabb arrived and did not win one in the seven years after he left, but they won nine postseason games that he started. There were qualms about the way he played—his completion percentage, in particular—and there was no Lombardi Trophy in the end. But he was 99–56–1 as a starting quarterback in Philadelphia.

"As a quarterback, you get criticized no matter what you do anyway," McNabb said when he retired. "If you win, you didn't throw enough completions. If you lose, it's your fault. That is what you take on. That is the job you take, and I loved every bit of it. It never bothered me if I got criticized. It never affected anything that I did out on the field. One thing that I tried to display to my teammates was that it didn't affect me. I was going to continue to work hard, no matter if we won or lost. So [was I] over-criticized? I don't look at it that way. Most of the people across the country do, but one thing I will say playing here in Philadelphia, as a quarterback, you get measured by your wins and losses, and we sure won a lot."

The winning started soon after McNabb became a full-time starter. The Eagles' initial plan was for McNabb to learn behind Doug Pederson, who was signed as a veteran bridge quarterback with a background in Reid's offense (and who eventually became the head coach who led the Eagles to their first Super Bowl). McNabb played sporadically through the first nine games of the season while learning Reid's offense and acclimating to the NFL. The Eagles lost seven of their first nine games and fans—even though they had booed him on draft day—were eager to see the player who was supposed to be a franchise savior.

But in the 10th game of the season, Reid inserted McNabb into the lineup. The Eagles won with McNabb, in his first start, showing the type of dual-threat ability that was rare in the NFL.

By 2000, McNabb was one of the best quarterbacks in the league. He had a career-high 629 rushing yards—at the time, the fourth most rushing yards by a quarterback since 1970. He brought the Eagles to the playoffs and finished second in MVP voting. He was in his age-24 season, and the future looked promising. McNabb had a strong offensive line with Tra Thomas and Jon Runyan as bookend tackles, and there was synergy with Reid even while the Eagles' offensive weapons were evolving.

In 2001, the Eagles repeated with an 11–5 record, and McNabb led the franchise to their first of four consecutive trips to the NFC Championship Game after upsetting the Chicago Bears in the divisional round. Playing in his hometown, McNabb passed for two touchdowns and rushed for one. "This is a feeling right now I somewhat can't explain," McNabb said after the game, according to the Associated Press. The Eagles lost in the championship game to the St. Louis Rams, who were 11-point favorites. McNabb stopped in the tunnel to the locker room and watched the confetti fall on the Rams. It was his way of inflicting pain on himself, with the plan to one day experience green confetti falling from above.

The Eagles' conviction in McNabb as their franchise quarterback was exemplified in September 2002 when they inked him to a 12-year, $115 million contract extension. Like most NFL contracts, the years and dollars were never fully realized. But the nine-figure contract was representative of a pact that remained strong until late in the decade.

Two months after he signed the new deal, with the Eagles boasting one of the best records in the NFL, McNabb broke his right ankle early in a game against the Arizona Cardinals. He refused to exit, though, throwing four touchdown passes while clearly laboring. That toughness was referenced a decade later when he retired.

The Eagles kept winning with backup quarterbacks, and McNabb returned in time for the postseason. He had a chance to feel that green confetti and avenge the prior season's defeat against the Tampa Bay Buccaneers in the final game at Veterans Stadium. The Eagles could only muster 10 points, and a late comeback attempt was stymied by a Ronde Barber interception that was returned 92 yards for a touchdown.

Once again, the Eagles were NFC bridesmaids.

It happened again in 2003. Another 12–4 season looked good, but the postseason was what mattered. When McNabb helped push the Eagles to the championship game with a miraculous fourth-and-26 conversion to Freddie Mitchell in the divisional round game, it seemed the fairy tale would come true. Alas, it was another loss. This time, the Eagles were held to three points. McNabb threw for 100 yards. It was clear going into the postseason that McNabb needed better weapons.

Two weeks later, McNabb and Terrell Owens gathered at the Pro Bowl in Hawaii and imagined a partnership. It took some machination on the Eagles' part, but it finally happened that spring. And the initial results were better than even the most optimistic fans could have expected. McNabb set career highs in passing yards, touchdowns, and completion percentage with Owens as a *bona fide* No. 1 target and the best pass catcher of the McNabb era. The Eagles were the best team in the NFL. It was the best McNabb ever looked.

There was a dose of gallows humor, then, when Owens injured his ankle and leg in Week 15 that season. The Eagles seemed to have lost the elixir that had been a force in 2004, and they were back to the underwhelming receiving corps that had been the reason to bring in Owens in the first place.

But they still had McNabb. They still had Brian Westbrook and a standout offensive line. They still had Brian Dawkins and Jeremiah Trotter and Jim Johnson's defensive line. And McNabb helped push the Eagles to the Super Bowl at last, beating the Minnesota Vikings in the divisional round and Michael Vick and the Atlanta Falcons in the NFC Championship Game. That night, January 23, 2005, with the windchill at zero, McNabb finally hoisted a trophy into the Philadelphia air. He called it his fondest memory in Philadelphia.

"That was something that we fought for a couple times," McNabb said upon retirement. "That brings back memories of the effort you put in. Guys came out to Arizona and we spent a week or two. Guys we spent time with here in Philadelphia, we went out to dinner together, invited each other over to each other's houses. It was the bond that we built from '99 on. We felt like it was a weight off of all of our shoulders to finally get it done. That right there just brought a tear to me, because I haven't watched that game nor the Super Bowl since. To see that highlight again brings back special memories."

The Super Bowl wouldn't bring back those same memories. Even though McNabb threw for 357 yards and three touchdowns with Owens back in the lineup, he also had three interceptions in the 24–21 loss to the New England Patriots. The Eagles famously went on a nearly four-minute scoring drive late in the fourth quarter, down by 10, when they weren't hurrying up and Patriots coach Bill Belichick was left wondering if the scoreboard was correct. McNabb was sacked four times in the game and hit four times. It's become an urban legend that he vomited in the huddle, which McNabb denied.

"I did not throw up in the game," McNabb said in a 2020 Bleacher Report interview. "Roll the video tape. The film don't lie. In 15 years later since the Super Bowl, no one brought the video up. Because it did not happen."

But McNabb was in the Super Bowl for the first time, and he was only 28. It could have been the start. Instead, it was never the same.

McNabb's relationship with Owens deteriorated in 2005—as did Owens' relationship with the organization—and McNabb could not recreate the magic. He also endured more injuries. The 2005 season ended with a sports hernia. He tore his anterior cruciate ligament in 2006. Between those two seasons, McNabb missed 13 games. The Eagles started to envision a succession plan.

In the second round of the 2007 draft, the Eagles drafted Kevin Kolb. It was not known when he would take over, but McNabb's career in Philadelphia appeared to be on the clock. It did not help that the Eagles again failed to make the postseason. And the McNabb era reached a critical juncture during the 2008 campaign when the quarterback was benched during a loss to Baltimore. It was temporary, and McNabb returned the following week to lead the Eagles to a Thanksgiving victory and eventually back to the NFC Championship Game. The Eagles lost to Arizona, and McNabb never won another playoff game in Philadelphia.

The 2009 campaign was McNabb's final one in Philadelphia. The Eagles signed Michael Vick during the preseason as the third quarterback, leaving them with two potential starters behind McNabb on the depth chart. After Philadelphia lost to Dallas in the opening round of the playoffs, the franchise was ready for a transition. McNabb was traded to Washington—an NFC East rival—on Easter Sunday.

McNabb returned to Lincoln Financial Field the following year and received a standing ovation. Washington upset the Eagles that day. It was the last true highlight of McNabb's career. Washington traded him to Minnesota in 2011, which was his final season in the NFL. He did not return to the NovaCare Complex until he was honored in 2013. McNabb is the best quarterback in franchise history, yet the context of that decade—both good and bad—was clear in his comments.

"The big result is obviously we didn't win," McNabb said. "But the thing that stands in my mind is you had 53 men out there putting everything on the line to fulfill a dream. When you step out on that field playing a Super Bowl, as a kid in the backyard, playing King of the Hill, playing flag football, playing tackle on the cement, and then you're throwing that last pass saying, 'This is me in the Super Bowl throwing to win the game with a touchdown or making that big hit,' whatever it may be. That was a dream that we all had, and we felt leading up to that, that was the best week of my career because it felt like everybody in that locker room could take a deep breath because we made it.

"Now, it wasn't everything. We didn't put the sugar on top or the cherry on top. We know that. But one thing is for sure, that we can say when we're all done and we look back on jerseys or pictures when we were younger and a little slimmer—because I still maintain my sexiness—but we can say we played in a Super Bowl. We've been to five NFC Championships. For us, we've been to Pro Bowls, but the thing that sticks out in my mind and probably Dawkins and everybody else, when it came to the 2000s, there were only three teams that had a high winning percentage, and we were one of them. That's one thing that nobody can ever take away."

What also cannot be taken away apparently is the love that No. 5 will always have for Eagles fans—even if it is a complicated love story.

9

Michael Vick

It is rare for a remember-where-you-were moment to occur during the preseason, but that's exactly what happened on August 13, 2009, when the Eagles signed Michael Vick after the star quarterback had served 23 months in federal prison and had been suspended indefinitely by the NFL for running a dogfighting operation.

The news trickled out on the night of the Eagles' preseason opener and became the biggest story in the NFL—and one of the biggest and most polarizing decisions of this 25-year period. Vick had not played at that point since 2006, but he was still only 29 years old and was one of the NFL's most dynamic players ever before he went to prison. He had been the league's highest-paid player and was a franchise quarterback, except the Eagles were bringing him in as a No. 3 quarterback. Donovan McNabb was established and Kevin Kolb was drafted in the second round to eventually be McNabb's successor. The Eagles saw a rare opportunity to add a high-level player.

Vick drove overnight from Virginia, as he explained in his book *Michael Vick: Finally Free* and stayed overnight at Jeffrey Lurie's home after meeting with Joe Banner. He played chess with Julian Lurie, Jeffrey's son and the eventual successor of franchise ownership.

"It wasn't so much a player evaluation decision as it was giving someone a second chance that we felt really would, from all indications, be great for Michael and also excellent for the Eagles," Lurie said more than a decade later. "I think we were all in awe of his physical ability.... I thought that was part of our identity."

The Eagles were prepared for the backlash that came from signing Vick—which even included protesters. Team officials, Reid chief among them, wanted to give Vick a second chance. There was also significant potential reward; it was not as if they were signing a long snapper. Vick was one of the most unique talents in football.

"We obviously did our homework on the background part," Reid said when Vick signed. "You're asking me the football side of it and the reward on the field. I think we know Michael Vick is, and I'm speaking in the past—a few years ago—was one of the greatest quarterbacks in the National Football League. He has tremendous athletic ability and I've always said to the people of Philadelphia that I would try to bring in the best players that could help our football team to achieve the highest goal and that's a Super Bowl. Michael will contribute."

It did not happen much in Vick's first season with the team. He attempted 13 passes. He rushed 24 times. He was inactive for the final two weeks of the season. The quarterback depth chart did not help—he was behind McNabb and Kolb—and it was understood that he needed to return to football, get in shape, and understand the offense.

"I've got to crawl before I walk," Vick said when he signed. "I can't imagine...after a two-year hiatus, going out and trying to be a starter for a football team, I just don't think it can happen. With as much God-given abilities as I have, I don't think that I would be able to do it. I think I could, but I wouldn't risk it. I just need time to get my feet wet and get acclimated. I thought this was the perfect situation, perfect scenario. I can come in and I can learn from Donovan, one of the premier quarterbacks in the game, one of the best at it. Everything that he's learned and the way he's been polished just comes from Coach Reid. I want to get with those two and do as much as I can to become a complete quarterback and I have time to do it."

The Eagles traded McNabb during the 2010 offseason, although the move was not made to open a starting spot for Vick. Kolb was the anointed successor. Vick would be the backup.

Teammates could see that summer that Vick had recaptured what made him special. Kolb didn't even last a game. He suffered a concussion in the second quarter of the season opener, and Vick relieved him for the second half. Vick was a sensation, throwing for 175 yards and a touchdown and rushing for 103 yards—all in one half.

It was not a fluke. One week later, when Vick started in place of Kolb in Detroit, he threw for 284 yards and two touchdowns and led the Eagles to a victory. Kolb did not get his job back. Reid decided to stay with Vick, seeing what the rest of the football world saw. When Reid made the change, he admitted he did not expect Vick to develop at such an accelerated pace. But it was clear to all—Reid, teammates, and the public—that Vick should be the quarterback.

"I think very few quarterbacks can go out and play the way he played the last couple of weeks and [do] some of the things that he did," Reid said at the time. "One of the questions we had about Michael Vick was, and has been a question throughout his career, 'Can he be a pocket passer?' I think you saw Michael Vick, under duress, was able to move, maintain his eyes down the field, and make throws down the field. He's one of the top third-down throwers in the National Football League right now and [he can] help this football team, obviously, win games."

Vick started 11 games at quarterback during the 2010 regular season. The Eagles won eight of them. He threw for 3,018 yards and 21 touchdowns and tallied only six interceptions. He rushed for 676 yards. He authored two of the most memorable games during this period—a sensational *Monday Night Football* performance against Washington that might have been the best quarterback spectacle during this era for the Eagles, and the Miracle at the New Meadowlands, when he led a miraculous comeback against the Giants. He finished second in Offensive Player of the Year voting and won Comeback Player of the Year.

Although the Eagles lost in their opening-round playoff game at home, Vick's season meant he had cast Kolb aside as next in line for the franchise quarterback role after McNabb. It's one of the items on Lurie's checklist. The Eagles rewarded Vick with a contract extension befitting a player of that status, giving him a six-year, $100 million deal. It was a crowning moment for Vick, who rebuilt his career and his image and returned to the top of the league.

"You never know what's going to happen," Vick said when he signed the contract extension. "You just live in the moment and take advantage of the opportunities you've been given. You know what type of talent you have, you know what you can do, you've just got to be patient, and that's something that I learned over the years unfortunately when I was away, but everything in life happens for a reason. That taught me patience, and I think that's part of the reason why I'm here today, being patient."

That season was the apex of Vick's time in Philadelphia. He could never recreate the 2010 magic. The Eagles underachieved in 2011—the "Dream Team" year—and turnovers became an issue for Vick. He won seven of his 13 starts that season, although only after the Eagles started 1–4 and Vick threw seven interceptions in the four losses. The Eagles rebounded with a four-game winning streak to finish the season, and the thinking was that the success could perhaps carry over to 2011. That was not the case. Injuries and inconsistencies slowed his season while playing behind a makeshift offensive line. He won three of his 10 starts and his performance declined. Andy Reid was fired, and Vick was not promised a starting job the following season when Chip Kelly became head coach.

The Eagles held a training camp competition between Vick and Nick Foles. It was clear that summer that Vick was the superior option, and he won the job in the preseason. But the fact that he was in a competition at all showed how his career with the Eagles had devolved.

"I had to come back and work for everything," Vick said in 2013 when he was named the starter. "It wasn't given to me."

Vick looked sensational in Kelly's debut before injuries again took a toll. When they did, Foles replaced him and kept throwing touchdowns and barely threw an interception. Just as Vick had overtaken Kolb, Foles had overtaken Vick. Such is the lifecycle in the NFL.

"It's hard to sum up my time here," Vick said when he cleaned out his locker in January 2013. "Everything has been so surreal and happened so abruptly."

It was like a shooting star, appearing so bright seemingly out of nowhere and then fading away. But when he was at his best, it was a sight to behold. Beyond football, he was revered by teammates. Jason Kelce still speaks about what kind of thrill it was to be a rookie snapping to Vick. The other featured players on the team at the time—LeSean McCoy and DeSean Jackson, for instance—seemed to take a backseat to Vick. He was the player they played with in video games, who had become an icon early in his NFL career.

Years later, Jalen Hurts speaks with reverence about Vick. And Vick's story also serves as one that Lurie points to as fulfilling the franchise's desired identity.

"If there was a case for a player that deserved the second chance...African Americans do not get many second chances," Lurie said. "And why shouldn't we be proactive and lead the way? I thought that was a good identity to have because it was genuine. It wasn't like we were trying to prove something that that was our identity. And so he was a wonderful locker room presence. Wonderful in the community. A pleasure to all of us to interact with an iconic figure for young players coming to the franchise. And I think it's signaled to the rest of the NFL players that the Eagles were not only a player-friendly culture that was extremely aggressive competitively, but that I'm open to things."

That's why Vick's tenure is viewed as a success, even if he was 20–20 in games he started behind center in an Eagles uniform. His presence always resonated beyond simply football. His signing will always be one of those remember-where-you-were moments.

10

Nick Foles

Nick Foles wanted to discuss failure. He had been named the Super Bowl LII Most Valuable Player, forever etching his name into NFL history by outdueling the Goliathan Tom Brady and New England Patriots while passing for three touchdowns and *catching* one, too.

Foles identified the lesson of his journey was what it took to be human—not superhuman.

"I think the big thing is don't be afraid to fail," Foles said the morning after Super Bowl LII in February 2018. "I think in our society today, Instagram, Twitter—it's a highlight reel. It's all the good things. And then when you look at it, you think 'Wow,' when you're having a rough day or your life is not as good as that, and you're failing. But failure's a part of life. That's a part of building character, growing. Without failure, who would you be? I wouldn't be up here if I hadn't fallen thousands of times, making mistakes. We're all human; we all have weaknesses."

It was a humble message. And it was true. His Eagles career could reveal as much.

Foles arrived in Philadelphia as a third-round pick in 2012. He was not the Eagles' first choice. The franchise actually had designs on taking Russell Wilson in the third round. When the Seattle Seahawks selected Wilson 13 picks before the Eagles were on the clock, they turned to Foles. Doug Pederson, who was then the Eagles' quarterbacks coach, put Foles through a private workout—the only position coach to do so. Andy Reid had final say on all football decisions—and was especially strong-minded when it came to quarterbacks. Foles did not have the athleticism of Michael Vick, who was the starter at the time, but Foles was not a plodder. In fact, Georgetown recruited Foles for basketball out of Westlake High School in Austin.

Although Foles was initially set to be the No. 3 quarterback, it was clear early in training camp that he had potential. He excelled in the preseason—Reid remarked then that he never had a rookie play like Foles in the preseason—and he became Vick's backup. When Vick sustained a concussion, Foles became the starter. The team was floundering and did not win much with Foles under center, but his poise earned him supporters in the team facility. Foles threw a game-winning touchdown to Jeremy Maclin in a December 2012 win over the Tampa Bay Buccaneers, and Maclin remarked that Foles' intangibles were "off the chart."

Reid was fired at the end of the 2012 season. Owner Jeffrey Lurie said the new coach would determine whether Foles or Vick—or someone else—would be the quarterback in 2013. When Chip Kelly was hired with an up-tempo, no-huddle offense, it seemed like a poor fit for Foles. Entering his second year, Foles said he would not have been kept by the Eagles' new regime if they didn't think he could function in their offense. There was ostensibly a quarterback competition, but it seemed clear early in training camp that Vick would be the starter. Vick struggled with injuries early that season, though, opening playing time for Foles. He was inconsistent, with a strong performance against Tampa Bay followed by a clunker against the Dallas Cowboys. Another Vick injury gave Foles another chance, though, and this time, he left no doubt. Foles tied an NFL record with a seven-touchdown performance against the Oakland Raiders in November 2012—he identified that game as the "a-ha" moment where the Eagles "took off"—and he was one of the best quarterbacks in the NFL for the remainder of the season. The Eagles won the NFC East with a Week 17 victory over the rival Cowboys, where Foles avenged his forgettable outing earlier in the season with a signature victory in his home state. Turns out you can recover from failure.

Foles threw 27 touchdowns to only two interceptions, which was the second-best touchdown-to-interception ratio in NFL history. His passer rating led the NFL. "He is the starting quarterback for the next thousand years here," Kelly said upon ongoing questions about whether Foles would become the Eagles' longterm quarterback. The Eagles hosted an opening-round postseason game against the New Orleans Saints, whose future Hall of Fame quarterback Drew Brees attended the same high school as Foles and set records that Foles shattered. Former Westlake coach Derek Long, who was Foles' head coach and Brees' defensive coordinator, said then he long saw "a lot of Drew in Nick." Foles left the field with a lead in that postseason game, but the Saints scored last to end Foles' second season. It was not the last time the Austin Westlake graduates would face each other in the playoffs.

After the sterling second season, it seemed Foles was on pace to take his place at the table with the great Eagles quarterbacks. I asked him before the 2014 summer what question he would raise if he happened to share a table with those quarterbacks—Donovan McNabb, Ron Jaworski, and Randall Cunningham.

His answer? How they responded to a bad game. In other words, Foles was always mindful of failure.

"If you have one bad game, it's really going to be talked about," Foles said. "I would ask them how they dealt with it when they had that bad game, when everybody was down on them, what they do. Because that's what I want to learn. That's what shows me a lot about people. When bad things happen in your life, how are you going to react?"

Foles tried his best to shield himself from the spotlight. After living with practice-squad quarterback G.J. Kinne in 2013, Foles got married to Tori in April 2014. He returned home from work and they cooked and played card games—"Speed" and "Palace" were the games of choice—to try to keep sanity in his life.

But the 2014 season was not as charmed as 2013, with more frequent turnovers (Foles threw 10 interceptions in eight games) and a completion percentage flirting at 60 percent. Foles broke his collarbone midway through the season and was replaced by Mark Sanchez, who had some early success in the system. When Kelly suggested at the end of the season that the Eagles would evaluate the position, there was speculation that Philadelphia would seek a change. The prevailing thought was that Kelly would try to land Oregon star Marcus Mariota. That never came to fruition, but before they could even try, Foles was traded to the St. Louis Rams for former No. 1 overall pick Sam Bradford. The oft-injured Bradford oozed with talent, although he had not been demonstrably better than Foles as a pro. That the Eagles attached a second-round pick to Foles in the trade showed that the Eagles were trying to move on from him—or perhaps did not negotiate well—even if the trade purportedly blindsided Foles.

The St. Louis honeymoon lasted nine games. The Rams benched him despite handing him a new contract, and they cut him after one season. The sharp decline in Foles' career left Foles disenchanted and pondering retirement. He went fly fishing with his brother-in-law to consider his future and admitted that "in my heart at that time, I was probably going to step away from the game." He prepared for civilian life, studying to become a pastor.

The person who rescued his career was the one who had started it: Reid. The Chiefs sought a backup quarterback to replace Chase Daniel, who had followed Pederson to Philadelphia in 2016. (The 2015 season went as well for Kelly as it did for Foles.) Foles reasoned that if he could fall in love with football again, it would be Reid who would squeeze it out of him.

It worked. Foles wanted to keep playing. The Chiefs were ready to draft a quarterback—that was Patrick Mahomes III, who would later factor into the Eagles' championship hopes—and Foles was a free agent again. Lurie, Roseman, and Pederson continued to think highly of their former starting quarterback, and Lurie was willing to absorb a $7 million salary cap hit when releasing Daniel to upgrade to Foles. Between Foles' contract and Daniel's cap charge, the Eagles were spending considerable resources on a backup quarterback. Then again, the franchise takes pride in how much it values backups.

For his part, Foles welcomed a return to Philadelphia. And he was more level-handed than when he left, unburdened by the expectations that came with being a young starting quarterback and benefiting from the perspective of nearly walking away from football. Plus, he learned that the grass is not necessarily greener away from Eagles green.

"I have nothing but great things to say about the city, the fans," Foles said upon re-signing. "I miss running out at the Linc and being part of that on game day. Crazy enough, you miss the boos from time to time. I laugh just thinking about playing and getting booed, and going back and throwing a touchdown and hearing the eruption. It's the only place that you get something like that."

Foles' first summer back with the team could not have foretold that he would become the Super Bowl MVP. He missed most of training camp and did not play in the preseason because of a sore elbow. He adjusted his pregame warm-up and wore a sleeve on his right arm to stimulate proper blood flow, and he had enough time to get healthy. Wentz played at an MVP level through much of the season, and Foles' job was to provide support in the quarterbacks room.

Then, everything changed—the Eagles' season and Foles' career. Wentz injured his knee in Week 14 game against the Los Angeles Rams and Foles helped the Eagles preserve the win and clinch the NFC East while the team awaited Wentz's diagnosis. A torn anterior cruciate ligament meant Wentz's MVP season was halted in December. If the Eagles were to fulfill the promise they showed through 14 weeks, Foles would need to be the quarterback to do so.

Leading up to the Eagles' Week 15 win over the New York Giants, Pederson made a deliberate effort to rally support for Foles. The fan base and locker room knew him, but they also knew he wasn't Wentz. Pederson did not harness the aggressiveness against the Giants when Foles threw four touchdowns and did not turn the ball over, showing flashbacks to 2013.

During Foles' career in Philadelphia, he earned the reputation for being a high-variance quarterback. There were weeks when he looked like a Hall of Famer and weeks when he looked like a journeyman. He seldom maintained consistency. That was evident in the final two games of the regular season, when Foles completed only 47 percent of his pass attempts in six quarters with one touchdown and two interceptions. The offense only scored 13 points.

Once again, Foles encountered failure with eyes open.

"If anyone's ever played a sport, you can't sit here and say, 'OK, that's what it is,'" Foles said. "I've had games like that, and I've come back and played at a higher level."

The bye week in the playoffs was Foles' chance to reset his mind. He spent time with his six-month-old daughter, reading to her during his morning coffee. (Foles, by the way, was known as the barista in the quarterback room.) The two weeks after the Rams game were a whirlwind, and the time off allowed Foles to process how life was changing. He did not process what was said about him. That was up to Pederson, who was even asked if he considered turning to little-known third-string quarterback Nate Sudfeld. Pederson emphasized to Foles that he needed to be himself, and the coaching staff (and Foles) made sure they knew who that was.

"Sometimes, the hardest things are the simplest things," Foles said. "Basically, get out of your own head and go play the game you know how to play."

The coaching staff and quarterback studied what he did best, including watching every pass completion of 15 yards or longer from 2013 to '14. The Eagles mixed in the quick-passing games and the run-pass options that allowed Foles to flourish under Kelly.

It was enough for the Eagles to escape the divisional round game against the Falcons to set up an NFC Championship Game against the Minnesota Vikings—a team whose opening day quarterback was Bradford, whom Foles was traded for in 2015. To add to the small-world, could-not-script-it-better subplots, the Vikings' starting quarterback in the playoffs was Case Keenum, the player who replaced Foles in St. Louis. Foles and Keenum were actually close friends, two Texas-bred backups maximizing their unexpected ascension into starting roles for postseason teams.

"I know this is what all you guys predicted back in the day—a Foles versus Keenum NFC Championship," Keenum joked with reporters.

Foles thrived in what was then the biggest stage of his career. He threw for 352 yards and three touchdowns and finished with the third-best quarterback rating in championship game history. He completed touchdowns of 53 and 41 yards—including one on a flea flicker—and played like a Super Bowl–caliber quarterback. The Eagles won because of him, not despite him.

"I'm so proud of you, bro!" veteran Chris Long told Foles. "I always believed in you."

The opposing quarterback in the Super Bowl wasn't a journeyman reserve. It was Tom Brady—the best quarterback in NFL history. Talk about being a second act. Foles emphasized the need to "live in the moment," which he found achievable based on his career arc. It was not that he played with the house money as much as he was unafraid to fail. He read the Bible and kept a journal on the morning of games. And you got the impression that if he was at home in Newport Beach, California, watching the game—or not watching at all—his life would not be any less fulfilled.

"A lot of people look at this moment and say, 'Wow, aren't you excited you [didn't retire] and are in the Super Bowl?'" Foles said. "I'm grateful to be up here.... But at the same time, if I would have made the other decision, my life wouldn't have been a loss."

It would have been a loss for the franchise—and Eagles fans around the world who were treated to one of the unforgettable performances in NFL history. Foles threw for 373 yards and three touchdowns and he *caught* a touchdown. And the amount of clutch passes was staggering. The Eagles would not have won the Super Bowl if Foles did not find Zach Ertz for a quick completion while falling backward on a fourth down on the decisive drive. He threw the game-winning touchdown to Ertz. He made smart decisions. He led the team.

"You've been playing your balls off, brother," Jason Kelce said to Foles. "I'm so happy for you."

When the clock struck zero, Foles held the brim of his hat and was reassured that the game was over and he had just won the Super Bowl. Jason Peters found him and called him "a legend." Wentz hugged him and told him he deserved it. "We're world champions forever!" Roseman told him. He stood onstage with Tori and his daughter, who wore headphones to block the noise, and Foles was named Super Bowl MVP.

Foles had slept for two and a half hours when he appeared at the morning-after press conference and discussed failure. He admitted in his book he was in no mood to share valuable insight. The answer was raw and from the heart, which made it resonate more. An assistant coach sent him a text message after the press conference and said the answer gave him chills.

"I could have talked about silencing the critics or proving all the doubters wrong. But what would have been gained by doing that?" Foles wrote in his book. "The truth is, I didn't want to discuss my victories, successes, or honors. I had no interest in dwelling on my own achievements. Everyone saw the game. They knew what happened. I wanted to talk about what they didn't get to see on the field that night—what nobody gets to see. The real secret of my success. So I highlighted my shortcomings and embraced failure as a tool for personal growth."

It was a powerful message, and a true summation of his career. Foles transferred from Michigan State. He had lost his starting job as an NFL quarterback. He had been traded. He had been cut. He played awful games. And he was a Super Bowl MVP. The way he would be viewed changed forever.

"I want to remember my core values," Foles said that summer.

The Eagles could have traded Foles that offseason, but they wanted to keep him as Wentz insurance. Backup quarterbacks matter in Philadelphia—and the Eagles would need him.

Foles returned to training camp in 2018 after an atypical summer for a No. 2. He went on a book tour to promote *Believe It*, which was a *New York Times* bestseller. He appeared at the ESPYs. And he needed to prepare for a season in which there was uncertainty about whether Wentz would be ready for Week 1. Wentz did not return until Week 3, leaving Foles to start the first two games. The Eagles split those games—Foles had his hero's welcome at Lincoln Financial Field in the opener—and Foles went back to the No. 2 spot. When the Eagles were 6–7 and Wentz's back injury was not improving, the Eagles decided to sit their franchise quarterback to let him heal. And that was when Foles added to his legend in Philadelphia.

The Eagles won their final three games of the season, including an upset over the Los Angeles Rams in the same venue where Foles relieved Wentz one year earlier. They went from 6–7 to 9–7 and earned a playoff spot. There was an identifiable confidence that the team demonstrated with Foles on the field, and teammates were happy to profligate the mystique. Long built a shrine in his locker for Foles with candles, a picture of Foles, and a copy of Foles' book. It was meant in good fun, but it also underscored Foles' popularity with teammates—and he kept validating their confidence.

In the home finale in Week 16, Foles set a franchise record with 471 passing yards and led the Eagles on a game-winning drive.

"It's Christmas. It's St. Nick," said Long, who joked that he thought the Texans were going to bury Foles next to the statue because of all the hits he endured. "You know [Foles] is going to put together a drive."

Foles waved to the crowd when he exited the tunnel. It was the last home game of the Eagles' season, and Foles knew he could be elsewhere in 2019.

"This city means a lot to me. This team means a lot to me. Wearing that jersey means a lot to me," Foles said that day.

One week later, Foles completed 28 of 33 pass attempts and tied an NFL record with 25 consecutive completions. The Eagles beat Washington and clinched a playoff bid. And Foles was not finished.

The Eagles traveled to Chicago in the opening round playoff game, where Foles once again led a game-winning drive. On a fourth down at the 2-yard line with 61 seconds remaining, Foles sprinted to his right and found Golden Tate in the corner of the end zone to tie the game. An extra point gave the Eagles a one-point lead, and when Chicago double-doinked a field goal at the end of regulation, the Foles era lived another week.

Once again, Foles had a postseason date with Brees. Foles was far more established than the first playoff meeting between Westlake graduates. Both had Super Bowl rings. Foles wore No. 9 because it was Brees' number, and now kids were wearing No. 9 because it was Foles' number.

"Playing against him [in 2013], I was a younger player," Foles said. "It's special getting a chance to play against someone you looked up to growing up. I still look up to him.... A lot's happened since then. Life's happened."

But like 2013, Brees bested Foles in a close game. Foles drove the Eagles downfield in the fourth quarter and almost put the Eagles ahead. A pass went through the hands of Alshon Jeffery and was intercepted. The Eagles' hopes of repeating were finished, and Foles faced the reality that his time in Philadelphia was finished.

Foles was set to become a free agent in 2019, and he deserved a chance to find a starting job. The Eagles were committed to Wentz. Foles knew it when he packed his locker on the day after the Saints loss. But he had a chance to leave on his own terms. In 2015, he was traded, so he could not say goodbye. This time, the fan base was sorry to see him go. There was a faction of fans who favored keeping Foles over Wentz. A healthy Wentz was the type of quarterback the Eagles would have designed in a lab, but there was no denying the team won games with Foles. He had the highest passing rating in franchise history, but even more, he won 24 of 31 games he started in an Eagles uniform. Wins are not quarterback stats, but they are often how a quarterback is judged.

"I think the big thing, what I always want to show, [is] you can't figure out a player by stats," Foles said. "The thing I've wanted to show is it's not about the quarterback. It really isn't. It's about how a team can come together at the end of the game. A quarterback is a piece of a puzzle, but it's how important that atmosphere is.... I've been able to show the league it takes a team."

Except Foles could never mimic his magic elsewhere. He signed a big contract in Jacksonville, started four games, suffered an injury, lost his job, and was traded to Chicago. He was released from the Bears and signed with Indianapolis. The Colts cut him, too. He finished his career as a journeyman. The journey did not bring him back to Philadelphia.

But he holds an indelible spot in franchise lore. He is part of the Philly Special statue outside the stadium. Lurie has not allowed another player to wear No. 9 since he left. He was a Super Bowl MVP in Philadelphia and the last pass he threw in an Eagles uniform was an interception. For someone who thought the lesson of his story was about confronting failure, that seems about right.

11

Carson Wentz

Carson Wentz's designation as the face of the franchise had been four years in the making when he became the highest-paid player in Eagles history in June 2019, before he had even started a postseason game in an Eagles uniform. It was formalized with the deal—and with the words of owner Jeffrey Lurie.

"Whether it's leadership, poise, the desire to be really, really good, if not great, attention to detail, smart, face of the franchise in so many ways," Lurie said when Wentz signed the $127 million contract. "It's how you draw it up."

That was the sentiment at the time. It was not the sentiment just two years later—before the contract formally commenced—when Wentz was benched, sought a trade, and the Eagles were willing to deal the player who once represented so much hope and pride for a franchise starving for the quarterback to be its face.

For as much joy as the Eagles have experienced during this 25-year period, one of the great frustrations was the decline of Wentz from the player who became a *bona fide* MVP candidate in his second season to one who looked lost and was eager to leave by the end of Year 5.

To understand the fall of Wentz, one must first realize how much the franchise had invested in Wentz's success.

After the Eagles fired Chip Kelly in December 2015 and gave Howie Roseman authority over football decisions again, there was a clear priority to acquire a franchise quarterback. Roseman had said that his gap year offered clairvoyance about the importance of finding stability—and top play—at that position, and there was an emphasis to do whatever it took to acquire him. The Eagles had tried to find a post–Donovan McNabb successor, but they had not spent significant draft capital to do it. The 2016 draft would be Roseman's chance. Team officials first watched Wentz at the Senior Bowl in Mobile, Alabama, one week after Doug Pederson was hired as coach. The Eagles realized upon watching Wentz and meeting him that they would not be able to draft him at No. 13, where they were originally supposed to pick. Through a series of trades that included veterans on the roster and multiple draft picks (including two first-round picks), the Eagles moved from No. 13 to No. 8 to No. 2 to land either Wentz or Jared Goff. Although the team met with both quarterbacks, the belief was that Goff would go No. 1 (the Los Angeles Rams had traded into the No. 1 spot) and Wentz would go No. 2 to Philadelphia.

The Eagles were smitten with Wentz, believing that he fit the market. Roseman compared his personality to that of Brent Celek. They thought Goff would fit in Southern California, while Wentz's flannels would go over well among the cold-weathered crowd. The Eagles brain trust visited Fargo, North Dakota, and

Wentz waited outside the facility to greet them. He marveled in the workout, in the classroom, and out to dinner. He was their highest-rated quarterback since Andrew Luck in 2012, giving them the face of the franchise they sought after the McNabb era.

"All I was thinking about today was when you were here in the building and the way we finished our meeting," Frank Reich said to Wentz on the phone when they drafted him, "and we were like, 'We'd love to have you in this room,' and you looked at us and said, 'Hey, make it happen!' So Mr. Lurie and Howie, they made it happen. So excited. So excited. Can't even tell you. And it's all in on your toughness and competitiveness. That's what it's all about!"

The trade for the Wentz pick did not sit well with Sam Bradford, a former No. 1 pick who was supposed to be the Eagles' starting quarterback. Bradford stopped attending workouts, but the Eagles planned to keep him and let Wentz spend his rookie year developing at his own pace. Pederson insisted Bradford would be the starter. And it was clear in training camp that Bradford would be the No. 1 quarterback while Wentz dazzled down the depth chart. Wentz suffered a hairline fracture in two of his ribs in his first preseason game, sidelining him for the rest of the summer. Before the third preseason game, Wentz underwent an on-field workout in front of Eagles executives. Wide receiver Jordan Matthews walked by Roseman and told the general manager Wentz was ready, an endorsement fresh in Roseman's mind a few days later when Minnesota Vikings quarterback Teddy Bridgewater suffered a season-ending injury. The Vikings were interested in Bradford to rescue their season, and the Eagles' depth chart question was solved by the Vikings' first-round pick. Wentz was hunting geese when the call came that he was the new starting quarterback. His unveiling would come in Week 1.

It added to the drama that the opponent was the Cleveland Browns, the franchise that traded the No. 2 overall pick rather than taking Wentz. Their rationale was that they needed more than just a quarterback, although had they deemed Wentz the type of prospect who would become an MVP candidate, they likely would not have traded the pick. (Think back to the Eagles' decision to hold onto the No. 2 pick in 1999 when Donovan McNabb was on the board and the Saints wanted to acquire the pick.) On that day, the franchise's future appeared in good hands. Wentz threw for 278 yards and two touchdowns in his debut victory, and he played well throughout the first month of the season. The Eagles won their first three games and Wentz did not throw an interception. Wentz's rookie season came with its inconsistencies, especially during a five-game losing streak late in the season, but there was overwhelming optimism by the end of the year. Wentz played all 16 games and showed flashes of excellence. His play earned admirers in the locker room and he developed a strong rapport with the coaching staff—so much so that the Eagles did not allow quarterbacks coach John DeFilippo to leave for a coordinator job after the season—and the Eagles were committed to improving the skill-position players around him for Year 2.

"We made this decision to trade up for the quarterback, [and] we're going to build around him," Roseman said at the end of the year.

The Eagles added Alshon Jeffery and Torrey Smith at the start of free agency, immediately giving Wentz established weapons. Less notable, but similarly important, was pursuing Nick Foles to be Wentz's backup quarterback. The thought was that Foles would be both a positive influence for Wentz behind the scenes and a capable backup should Wentz sustain an injury. They could not have projected that there would one day be sentiment that Foles should take Wentz's job.

That would have been nearly impossible to predict during the 2017 offseason, when Wentz's popularity soared. Part of the adjustment for Wentz was leaving his North Dakota cocoon—as popular as the North Dakota State Bison might be, it doesn't compare to the Eagles' fever pitch—and getting used to a new market and a new way of life. North Dakota is big in landmass, but it preserves a small-town feel. When I visited Wentz's hometown of Bismarck and his college town in Fargo, it was impossible to go anywhere without bumping into someone who had a Wentz connection. The attendant at the front desk of the hotel went to high school with him. I dropped into the office of a gubernatorial candidate, and Wentz's stepbrother worked the phones. Bring up Wentz's name, and there was some type of connection to him. Perhaps that could be suffocating, but it was also familiar.

In Philadelphia, there was suffocation without familiarity. He told a story of shopping at a mall in Deptford, New Jersey, chatting with a shopper and seeing a line of 20 more people waiting to speak with him. "Guys, I literally have to go," Wentz told them. "This isn't going to work." There's an expression called "North Dakota Nice," which takes on a different meaning in Philadelphia. Like the time Wentz went out to eat and a fan walked by and screamed, "You're the f—ing man," followed by the "E-A-G-L-E-S, Eagles!" cheer. Wentz bought a home in rural New Jersey, away from the Philadelphia hubbub and more comparable to his North Dakota upbringing than a condominium near the stadium. He could hunt and play with his dog. His brother lived nearby. He found his own ways to recognize his new home, including starting a foundation that fed the hungry with a food truck and hosting a charity softball event at the Phillies' stadium. But he also knew how to keep his distance—literally.

"It's just the things I like about North Dakota, that's who I am," Wentz explained then. "I'm not going to let the culture I live in and where I live change me. I'm just going to keep being me. If other people embrace it, that's cool. If they don't, I'm OK with it because I'm comfortable with who I am. Like the hunting and all that stuff, I'm fortunate enough that I can do that out in New Jersey. I can get that peace of mind [and] get away from the game."

The reality of criticism for a professional athlete can be explained in a scene during *Bull Durham*, when hotshot prospect Nuke LaLoosh had fungus in his shower shoes. "If you win 20 in the show, you can let the fungus grow back on the shower shoes and the press will think you're colorful," Crash Davis, the wise veteran, told LaLoosh. "Until you win 20 in the show, however, it means you are a slob." Roughly translated, one's quirks are only colorful when a player is playing well. And in 2017, Wentz played as well as anyone in the NFL.

It was apparent early in training camp that Wentz could be on the verge of a transcendent season in 2017. His early season performance showed that he had become a breakout player, with 13 touchdowns and three interceptions in his first six games. His signature moment came on *Monday Night Football* in Week 7 against Washington, whose coach at the time, Jay Gruden, said Wentz "progressed at a rate as fast as anybody I've seen" and that Wentz had "already proven...he's one of the top quarterbacks in the league." Wentz had played only 22 games to that point. He was only 24 years old. Wentz wowed viewers with a series of Houdini-esque plays. Jay Gruden's brother, former Super Bowl–winning coach (and Eagles assistant) and

ESPN commentator Jon Gruden watched from the booth and could not believe how Wentz emerged from a pack of defenders to run for a first down. And when a Wentz-designed play led to a touchdown on an odds-defying touchdown pass, Pederson called it "one of the best plays I've seen in a long, long time." Fans chanted "M-V-P," and it was not far-fetched. Wentz had a three-game stretch in November when he threw for nine touchdowns without an interception, and it looked like the Eagles had the best player on football. The Eagles' nine-game winning streak ended in Week 13 against Seattle, which was a notable loss because Wentz lost a costly fumble when he tried diving into the end zone for a touchdown and took a big hit. The turnover was an issue in the game, but the playing style was concerning when considering Wentz's career. His toughness was lauded, although when toughness turns into recklessness, and recklessness turns into injury, the entire franchise suffers.

That set the stage for the anticipated Week 14 game in Los Angeles—the team that picked Goff over Wentz in 2017. The Goff-Wentz angle was a major storyline that week, but so was Wentz's propensity for taking contact. Perhaps it was ominous. Wentz played one of the best games of his career in Los Angeles that day, throwing for four touchdowns. His fourth touchdown gave him the franchise's single-season record, breaking Sonny Jurgensen's mark from 1961. Yet Wentz did not even crack a smile—because he knew something was wrong.

One play before, Wentz scrambled to the end zone and lunged forward in an effort for points, just as he did in Seattle. The ball was not dislodged, but his knee ligaments shredded on the run when two defenders sandwiched him. (For the record, Wentz scored, except the play was nullified by a penalty.) He stayed in the game to somehow throw for the touchdown, but he immediately beelined toward the training tent. He walked off the field on his own power and into the locker room. After the examination, Wentz was declared out for the game. Zach Ertz, a close friend who was out for the game, went to the locker room to check out Wentz. They prayed together with their pastor on the phone.

"I figured I was of more use comforting him than [trying to] comfort the guys on the field," Ertz told *The Philadelphia Inquirer*. "I knew something wasn't right with his knee. He knew something wasn't right with his knee."

In a box above the stadium, Howie Roseman received word that an unofficial diagnosis was a torn anterior cruciate ligament, pending an MRI. He notified Jeffrey Lurie and retreated to the restroom, where he actually ran into FOX play-by-play announcer Joe Buck, who was unaware of the significance of the injury. Few people knew, even when Wentz greeted teammates on crutches after the Eagles escaped with the victory. Wentz rode a golf cart to the team bus wearing a bulky brace. The Eagles flew home, arriving in the early hours of the morning to a city in mourning.

Even in Los Angeles airport that night, when I waited for the redeye home surrounded by fans who just watched the Eagles win a pivotal game, the excitement at the gate was lacking. All anyone wanted to know about was Wentz.

Upon returning to Philadelphia, those fears were realized. The Eagles needed to try to win without him. Wentz walked off the field in the NFC Championship Game with a cane. Foles was the hero. Wentz wanted to be the one leading the team.

"As humans, we all want to be the competitors that we are and be out there on the field," Wentz said before the team departed for the Super Bowl. "Every time the offense runs out on the field on Sundays, it's tough. It hits me a little bit. But then I'm in it because I love these guys and I'm a part of this team just as much as anybody else."

Those were the public words. Behind the scenes, there seemed to be more to the story. ESPN reported in 2019 that there was a tense scene in the training room while Wentz was injured in 2017 when a teammate made clear that Wentz needed to lift his chin up and focus on the team.

Wentz still tried to maintain a behind-the-scenes role leading up to the Super Bowl, attending the 6 AM quarterback meetings. He was on the headset on the sideline and conferred with Foles between possessions. NFL Films caught him offering motivating words to Foles during the game. When the Eagles finally won, Wentz had tears in his eyes and embraced Foles while holding a newspaper with his backup on the cover.

"You deserve this, brother!" he said.

He was on the podium when the Lombardi Trophy was presented. He spoke at the Super Bowl parade. And there was belief that when it happened again for Philadelphia, Wentz would be the quarterback. Pederson dreamed of the Wentz-Pederson combination joining the lexicon of Tom Brady and Bill Belichick.

"Even in some of the quiet moments, I try to envision that," Pederson said at the Super Bowl. "In this league, if you have a quarterback and you do things right and you surround him with talented players and coaches, you can have a long career in this business and have the success those two gentlemen have had.... That's something myself and Carson and the guys we have around him could possibly have in Philadelphia."

That never came to fruition. The Eagles failed to even win a postseason game with Wentz as the starter.

Foles returned in 2018 while Wentz recovered from the torn ACL, a task that consumed Wentz—and even made him relatively reclusive, at least compared to what is expected of quarterbacks. Both offensive coordinator Frank Reich and quarterbacks coach John DeFilippo accepted jobs elsewhere, creating changes in the offensive infrastructure from Wentz's first two seasons. Foles started the first two games of the season before Wentz was ready to return. Wentz was productive—15 touchdowns and three interceptions while completing 71 percent of his pass attempts in his first seven games—but he was not the MVP version of himself. That's what he wanted to be and it's what Eagles fans so deeply expected. The team was not winning at the same rate as 2017, and surfacing behind the scenes, unbeknownst to the public, was a back injury that worsened. The Eagles sat Wentz in December because of his ailing back after the team dropped to 6–7. This set the stage for more Foles heroics, and the backup led the Eagles on a three-game winning streak and an unlikely postseason appearance. They even won a road playoff game in Chicago with Foles while Wentz was left watching from the sides, just like the year before. For someone with an exacting personality, operating in the shadows was abnormal.

"It hasn't been the easiest last year for me on the physical level, just battling the injuries, but then just personally going through it, sitting on the sideline and then playing and then sitting on the sideline again," Wentz said in a wide-ranging interview after the 2018 season. "So I realize I maybe wasn't the greatest teammate at times because I was emotionally kind of all over the place. To the outside world, I probably didn't show it much. But internally, you're definitely fighting some sort of emotions.... So there's things to learn just about how to handle myself in certain situations."

Even if there was Wentz versus Foles discussion on local talk radio stations, the franchise did not share in the debate. The

Eagles wanted to stay the course with Wentz and would allow Foles to leave in free agency. The commitment to Wentz was not only evident by allowing the Super Bowl MVP to leave; it was backed by a four-year, $128 million contract that surpassed Donovan McNabb's 12-year, $115 million contract from 2002 and Fletcher Cox's six-year, $103 million deal from 2016. The Eagles could have waited another year to prove that Wentz could remain healthy—or even win in the playoff—but it had always been the franchise's strategy to try to act sooner than later when securing a quarterback to a new contract. (This proved true four years later with Jalen Hurts.)

The Foles shadow was gone in 2019, and Wentz made efforts to improve his shortcomings. There were outreaches in the locker room to become more accessible, as the organization had pushed him to do. He altered his diet and was noticeably leaner. He was past the injuries that had mired his previous two seasons.

"I feel, obviously, in a different place," Wentz said before the 2019 season. "With just everything I've gone through the last couple of years, with the injuries. Especially from the mental side of it and just having peace of mind with everything. So... knowing that I'll be out there [Week 1] and everything with that, I feel like I'm just mentally in a much different place—and physically, I feel good, too. Little more relaxed, you could probably say."

But nobody would confuse the 2019 Eagles with the 2017 group. Wentz remained healthy throughout the regular season for the first time since he was a rookie, although his production waned, and the Eagles were a middling team with injuries elsewhere limiting their upside. Yet Wentz showed why the franchise was so bullish on him during a December rally when he led the Eagles on a four-game winning streak to win the

NFC East. He did not throw an interception during that stretch. He would finally have his postseason start, three years belated.

He lasted two drives and nine offensive snaps. On the first play of the second drive of the January 2020 game against the Seattle Seahawks, Wentz faked a handoff and scrambled to his right side when a Seahawks safety grabbed his legs. Wentz tried falling forward. Seahawks defensive end Jadeveon Clowney dove at Wentz from behind, with Clowney's shoulder driving Wentz's helmet into the winter turf.

"I knew something was wrong right away," Ertz said that night.

Wentz climbed up and remained in the game, just as he did when he tore his ACL in Los Angeles in 2017. After five plays, the Eagles punted, and Wentz returned to the sideline.

"Stay ready," Wentz told backup quarterback Josh McCown.

He knew, like Ertz did, that something was wrong. Wentz went into the makeshift blue medical tent for evaluation, and then was escorted to the locker room by two security officials. He did not return to the game because of a concussion.

"I feel for him," Pederson said after the game. "I feel bad for him."

Wentz never played in a full Lincoln Financial Field again.

In the days after the playoff loss, Pederson shuffled the coaching staff and tried to improve the Eagles' use of play-action. Meanwhile, the front office was evaluating quarterbacks in the draft. Wentz's contract made it more difficult to carry experienced, expensive backups like Foles, and the reality that Wentz had played nine snaps in six postseason games since he joined the organization served as an impetus to watch the position closely.

There had been whispers in the organization that the Eagles liked Hurts. But the second round? Roseman phoned Wentz on draft day to share that the Eagles were interested in Hurts. Sure enough, they drafted the Alabama-turned-Oklahoma quarterback whose intriguing talent was trumped by his off-the-chart intangibles. The Eagles made strong public-relations efforts to try to emphasize that Wentz maintained his status within the organization.

"Nobody is going to be looking at a rookie quarterback as somebody who's going to be taking over [for] a Pro Bowl quarterback, a guy who's been on the cusp of winning an MVP," Roseman said then.

"If I were to start questioning Howie and the management now, I'd really be questioning myself," Wentz said in May 2019. "Because when I signed the deal that I did, it was really my way of showing that I trust and believe in what we're doing in Philly, and they trust and believe in me."

What was said and what happened did not align. The COVID-19 pandemic created unusual circumstances as it was, with meetings conducted virtually and less time to adjust to the new system and new teammates. Those, of course, were mere excuses during a season that went awry and a franchise quarterback who bottomed out.

The Eagles opened the season 0–2–1, with Wentz turning into a reckless, turnover-prone quarterback. His improvisation drew raves when it yielded big third-down conversions in 2017, but it led to head-scratching mistakes in 2020. By Week 8, Wentz committed four turnovers against the rival Dallas Cowboys, and Pederson started to field questions about whether he would sit his starter. Injuries to the offensive line meant Wentz was often under duress. An unproductive group of receivers was led by someone who started the season on the practice squad. The offense was more inconsistent than innovative. The Eagles shuffled the depth chart elsewhere and tinkered with the play-calling, but the cold reality was that their franchise quarterback was part of the problem—not the solution. Had the stadium been full like it is in a non-pandemic year, Wentz would have heard the boos that he avoided for much of his Eagles tenure.

The exacting personality showed its other side, with sources telling *The Philadelphia Inquirer* that Wentz "had increasingly rebuffed advice, defied criticism, and clashed with...Pederson."

The breaking point came in Week 13 against the Green Bay Packers. The Eagles were 3–7–1 at the time and on a four-game losing streak, and the offense failed to score a touchdown in the first half. Pederson said he wanted a "spark," so he turned to Hurts. This was not a spark. This was an explosion. (Or perhaps an implosion.) The franchise quarterback was benched, and there was no way to rationalize what happened.

"I'm not the type to worry...and look over my shoulder," Wentz said after the game. "At the end of the day, I can play better. We can as a team, and as an offense, play better. There's always going to be different things going on in the building or different chatter. That's part of this business. It's what I signed up for, the scrutiny, the challenges, the adversity, all of it. I've got to handle it all—the good, the bad, and the ugly."

He never played in an Eagles uniform again. Pederson had often insisted that he was "married" to Wentz, since they came in together and had been linked throughout their tenure. That marriage was on the rocks. Wentz ran the scout team and worked with young players in practice, and reports of his displeasure were widespread.

In his comments after the season, Roseman compared Wentz to a finger on his hands and how "you can't even imagine that they are not part of you." As is often the case, what's revealed on the surface is different from what was happening behind the scenes. Wentz's disenchantment was well known, and Pederson did not want to change his coaching staff again.

Pederson was fired. Wentz demanded a trade—even with Pederson gone. The franchise quarterback no longer wanted to play for the franchise. Sirianni remained ambiguous at his opening news conference about the team's plans at quarterbacks, hardly the type of response if the team knew their $128 million quarterback would remain in Philadelphia.

A trade seemed to be a matter of when—not if. By February, the Eagles agreed to a deal with the Indianapolis Colts. The trade reunited Wentz with Frank Reich. The Eagles acquired significant draft capital and even though they took a league-record $33.8 million salary cap hit in 2021, the trade cleared their books of Wentz thereafter. That relief (and the draft picks) proved pivotal in rebuilding the team.

On one hand, it was an organizational failure for the Eagles to move on from a player they had invested so much hope and resources in to become the face of their franchise. But there also proved to be a benefit in cutting their losses when they did rather than compounding the problem. The Eagles rebounded quicker than Wentz did, which speaks to their decision. Wentz's decline continued elsewhere, and he went from Indianapolis to Washington to out of the league before signing with the Rams three months into the 2023 season. Meanwhile, the Eagles were back in the Super Bowl with a new franchise quarterback in two years.

But the way it ended should not totally obscure the reality that when Wentz was at his best in Philadelphia, he was a phenomenon in the city and for the franchise. The 2017 season remains historic. Who knows what would have happened had he never tore his ACL in Los Angeles in 2017, if injuries did not disrupt his career, and he remained on the trajectory he showed?

Or perhaps 2017 was the outlier, that he played beyond his level that year. Regardless, he is a part of the franchise's history—both the good and the bad.

"My time there was a whirlwind," Wentz told reporters before he played against the Eagles in 2022. "It was wild."

12
Jalen Hurts

On a March 2023 evening at a casino ballroom in Wilkes-Barre, Pennsylvania, Jalen Hurts closed his acceptance speech for the Maxwell Football Club Player of the Year award with a statement ostensibly about coming minutes short of winning the Super Bowl. But it could have been about other moments in his football career: making the national championship game as a freshman at Alabama, being benched at halftime in the national championship game as a sophomore, rebuilding his career at Oklahoma, outlasting a franchise quarterback after he was drafted as a backup in Philadelphia, or quieting trade rumors after his first year as a starter.

"I know I didn't walk through that fire just to smell that smoke," Hurts said that night.

Hurts does not stand outside the fire. He always walks through.

Hurts had been in the public spotlight since 2018 when he became the first freshman quarterback to start for Nick Saban. He opened his college career against Southern California in a 52–6 victory, and it was apparent that the fire was not too hot for Hurts. The Crimson Tide went undefeated that season until the national championship, when Hurts left the field with a lead before Clemson won on a last-second play. One year later, when he had a chance to avenge the national championship game, he again helped lead Alabama to the final game of the season. But when he was 3-of-8 at halftime, Saban benched Hurts for Tua Tagovailoa in hopes of sparking the offense with a more proficient passer. It worked—Alabama came from behind and won in overtime. What stood out to the Eagles years later was how Hurts responded. He did not sulk on the sideline. He supported Tagovailoa and reveled in the victory. And he didn't transfer that offseason, either. He competed with Tagovailoa to try to earn the starting job his junior year.

"The dude had to be the first into the weight room, had to be the first onto the field, sprints—he had to be first," Tagovailoa remembered in the summer of 2022. "It really tells you how he goes about his life. It tells you how he sees things and looks at things as a competitor."

Hurts did not win the job and spent his junior season as the No. 2. When Alabama needed him to enter the SEC Championship game later that season, Hurts stepped in and led Alabama to a win. Saban grew emotional discussing Hurts after the game. Hurts transferred to Oklahoma for his senior season, improved as a passer in Lincoln Riley's offense, and finished as a runner-up in the Heisman Trophy balloting. The way he handled his college career left an impression with Eagles' decision-makers. They met with Hurts for a formal interview at the 2020 scouting combine and asked the quarterback why they should draft him.

"I've been able to kind of cement myself in two prestigious programs," Hurts told them in the interview, as seen in a video released by the team. "I think people have found a way in both of these places to follow me. And I'm not going in and saying, 'Hey, come on, y'all gotta follow me.' That's earned, not given. People lead because their peers let them. For some odd reason, people follow me wherever I've been."

He told them he can make every throw. He told them he doesn't put a ceiling on his potential. He explained that he's a student of the game.

Shortly after the combine, COVID-19 kept players and executives at their homes. It was an atypical draft season, and teams did not have the same volume of reference points that they would use in a typical year. It also meant meetings were remote, and there was more mystery—even internally—about what teams would do in the draft. At the highest levels of the organization, though, there was interest in Hurts. Carson Wentz was supposedly entrenched as the franchise quarterback, although he had an extensive injury history, and his contract was about to swell to the point that the Eagles believed they needed a cost-controlled backup quarterback. That was part of the appeal of Hurts. There was also the reminder of missing on Russell Wilson a decade earlier, and the Eagles did not want to repeat that mistake of bypassing a quarterback who left some members of the organization smitten. When Hurts' name was announced in the second round of the draft, it was the stunner of the evening. Howie Roseman tried to explain the decision—and he gave Wentz notice it was coming—but the pick sent shockwaves around the league. Even Hurts was surprised.

"When I saw PA [on the phone], I thought it was Pittsburgh," Hurts told Jason Kelce on the New Heights podcast. "I had no idea I was coming.... From the interview, I didn't think I was going to be an Eagle."

The COVID restrictions kept the Eagles from having an in-person offseason program, and even during training camp, there were virtual meetings and restrictions that made it more challenging for players to build those relationships. For Wentz, who had just moved past the Nick Foles shadow, the presence of a high-profile second-round pick was different than when the Eagles had a non-threatening veteran quarterback. Teammates could tell early that Hurts showed promise—and that he had the aura that allowed him to take command of a locker room elsewhere. Like Hurts said, people lead because their peers let them lead. DeSean Jackson remembered Hurts "ripping the [starters] apart," and Jackson remarked to Roseman about Hurts' ability.

For most of Hurts' rookie season, he remained the backup who was used sparingly in running situations. It was not an ideal arrangement. The season was a disaster and Wentz regressed. It became clear by December that the quarterback was a problem. Doug Pederson had resisted making a change before it reached a breaking point in Green Bay in Week 13. The Eagles were on their way to losing their eighth game of the season, and Pederson said he wanted a "spark"—perhaps even like halftime of the national championship game. He turned to Hurts. Hurts threw a touchdown, giving the offense more vigor than it had displayed with Wentz, and Pederson stuck with Hurts the following week against New Orleans. The Saints entered the game with the best rushing defense in the NFL. Hurts gashed them for 106 rushing yards, becoming the first Eagles quarterback to reach 100 yards since Michael Vick. The offense looked different. So did the franchise. There was no turning back. Hurts finished the season. Even in defeats, his potential was clear. He topped 300 passing yards in back-to-back weeks, and the conversation around the quarterback of the future became more complicated than ever.

The Eagles made a coaching change, dismissing Pederson and hiring Nick Sirianni in January 2021. The change was not made with Jalen Hurts or his playing style in mind—in fact, Sirianni had not coached a quarterback with Hurts' mobility in the past—but Wentz's future remained a lingering question. When the Eagles traded Wentz, it was Hurts' team almost by default. The Eagles did not make any move to upgrade over him, only signing Joe Flacco as veteran insurance. They stocked draft inventory for the 2022 season, so if they were unconvinced of Hurts or sought an upgrade, they would have assets to do so. Hurts, then, had a year to prove his ability.

Philadelphia also became introduced to Jalen-isms. When he speaks, it can seem like he's reading a fortune cookie. He described a "so what, no what" mentality. He has shared that "10 percent of life is what happens to you; 90 percent is how you respond." He wants to "be a coffee bean," because when a coffee bean goes into water, it changes the water. (This compares to a carrot that wilts and an egg that hardens on the inside.) He wants you to know that "rent is due" daily, and for good measure, he does not intend to miss the payments. He tries to "keep the main thing the main thing," insists that the "lamp is never full," and wants to be the "thermostat and not the thermometer." Good luck finding much joy in victory, because "enough is never enough." He keeps the same face on the sideline—touchdown or interception, win or loss—and the equanimity has become a trademark default. There's a meme that makes him laugh that shows him with the same face after a touchdown, interception, fumble, and end of the world. He laughs because he knows it's true.

"I've just always been that way," Hurts said. "Same face."

That's all part of Hurts' charm, although it's considered motivating when the Eagles win. If they lose, it can be grating. Seven games into Hurts' first season as the starting quarterback, the Eagles were 2–5 and Hurts' production was inconsistent. His statistics might have seemed gaudy in a pass-heavy offense except the production was too often coming while the Eagles were trying to get back into games. It did not help that they had a leaky pass defense and needed an upgrade of pass-catching talent. Around midseason, the Eagles shifted the offense. Hurts' running ability was always a threat, and the Eagles leaned into an elite offensive line and the pressure that Hurts' legs put on the defense. This coincided with a shift in play calling from Sirianni to Shane Steichen, and quarterbacks coach Brian Johnson coming down from the coaching booth to the sideline to interact face-to-face with Hurts. The Eagles won seven of nine games to claw back into playoff contention. Hurts missed one of those starts because of an ankle injury that slowed him late in the season and required minor surgery after the season, but his value to the team was evident by the way teammates and coaches responded to him—and, to Hurts' credit, the way he responded to them. During a pivotal Week 15 win over Washington in Hurts' first game back from the ankle injury, the Eagles started with an interception on the opening drive and a fumble on the second drive. Sirianni, in his expressive manner, scolded his quarterback on the sideline. Hurts invited the coaching. "I've been telling him all year that I'm a coach's kid," Hurts said. "Basically, all the coaches' kids out there know what that means. It means they've been coached. They've heard everything." Sirianni and Hurts shared a kinship because of this similar childhood experience, and Hurts responded with one of the best games of his career—20-of-26 for 296 yards and one passing touchdown with 38 rushing yards and two touchdowns. It was an example of how Hurts did not want to be tiptoed around as a quarterback. He went to play for Nick Saban for a reason. The Eagles did not need to worry about offending him. They only needed to worry about improving him.

"In high school, I lived with the guy that was chewing me out," Hurts said. "I made it clear to [Sirianni] all year, 'You know, you can get on me a little bit.' So after the fumble, he came up to me and said what he had to say. Then later on in the game, he comes back and jokes with me and says, 'I guess I'm just going to start coaching you like your dad coached you.' So it was a funny moment. Whatever he said worked."

It was a credit to Hurts that he quarterbacked the Eagles to the playoffs in his first year as the starter. But his first postseason game left fans with more questions than answers about whether Hurts would be the team's long-term quarterback. It was one of the worst games Hurts had played in an Eagles uniform, appearing overmatched against the Tampa Bay Buccaneers. NFL Films caught the opposing coaching staff questioning Hurts' ability to read their defense. It was Hurts' postseason debut, and the Eagles were an inferior team compared to Tampa Bay (with Tom Brady at quarterback), but Hurts left the stadium that night with a walking boot on his left foot and an unknown offseason in front of him.

"I know we're all judged on the last game that we play—I understand that and fully get that," Sirianni said after the game. "But I felt like Jalen grew throughout the year, and he got better as a passer. And he got better reading the defenses, getting the ball to the right place. He developed so much in his ability to extend plays, not only making plays with his feet but also making plays downfield on the scramble.... I feel really good with what we have in place right here at the quarterback position. I thought he had a great year, and he came a long way, and that's what I expect from Jalen because of the type of football character he has, the toughness that he has, the love for football that he has."

Publicly, the Eagles offered messages of support at every touchpoint to start the offseason. Both Russell Wilson and Deshaun Watson were available via trade that offseason, and the belief was that the Eagles were interested. Neither player wanted to come to Philadelphia, though, so the speculation was moot. Franchises—and players, too—are often as loyal as their options. Hurts was the quarterback. And one of his biggest supporters happened to be Lurie, whose voice mattered most in the organization.

"We have a young, 23-year-old playoff quarterback who gets better every year in college and in the pros," Lurie said at the league meetings in March 2022. "He's had really one full year. No one knows where that's going to end up, but I think what you do know is you have a guy that is incredibly dedicated, [an] excellent leader of men. Players around him gravitate to him. He will do anything and everything to get better and work on every weakness he has to try to maximize every strength he has. And that's why we're committed to Jalen at age 23. Who knows what the future holds, right?"

Nobody did, but Hurts intended to write his history. He does not walk through fire to smell the smoke.

One refrain heard often—whether from Sirianni or others—is that whatever potential Hurts possessed, he would reach it because of his makeup. But in order for the Eagles to gain a full evaluation of Hurts, they sought to upgrade the talent around him. That included a blockbuster draft-day trade to land A.J.

Brown, who had named Hurts, a close friend, the godfather of his daughter. The two had envisioned pairing together and were on FaceTime shortly after the trade. They shared another FaceTime call during the summer of 2022 when a report came out about an uneven minicamp performance by Hurts. The description perturbed Brown, who went to social media to defend his friend. Hurts remained unfazed. So it was not a surprise that on the first day of training camp, Brown arrived wearing a baseball cap that read HURTS SZN. Sirianni wore a shirt with Hurts' face on it, too. The message was clear from day one that season—this was Hurts' team. The hope was that in addition to natural progression entering his second year as a starter, Hurts would benefit from continuity on the coaching staff. The 2021 season to the 2022 season was the first time Hurts had the same play-caller in back-to-back years since he was in high school. He did not need to learn a new system. He did not need to adjust to the proclivities of a new coach. They knew him, and he knew them.

From the start of the season, the improvement was obvious. Hurts turned into one of the NFL's finest quarterbacks. He threw for 243 yards and rushed for 90 yards in Week 1. He completed 84 percent of his pass attempts in Week 2 and stayed inbounds on a highlight-worthy touchdown when he avoided the sideline, bullied through a defender, and carried a would-be tackler into the end zone. It occurred on the *Monday Night Football* stage, and a national audience saw what teammates had been expecting that season. Hurts did not slow down, pushing the Eagles to an 8–0 start. At that point in the season, he had 18 total touchdowns and only three turnovers. The Eagles introduced the "Tush Push," when Hurts' strong lower body helped him push his way behind the offensive line for a quarterback sneak that made every drive a first-and-9. Yet it stood out how unimpressed Hurts was by the Eagles' undefeated start. Remember how he always had the same face? He even seemed peeved whenever the record was described to him. His obsession was reaching an impossible standard.

"It's an ongoing journey," Hurts said. "If you think one day you arrived, you won't. There is no arrival. There's only the journey."

In fact, Hurts said there was only one scenario when he would allow himself to leave the field with satisfaction: "Usually the last game."

So it seemed like a race to the last game. There were thrills along the way—Hurts won in his return to his hometown of Houston, playing in front of family and friends; he rushed for a game-winning touchdown in Indianapolis; he threw for 380 yards in Brown's revenge game against Tennessee. A convincing case could have been made for Hurts to win MVP. His arm and leg formed a potent combination. Hurts corrected any suggestion that he's a dual-threat quarterback. At the behest of Brian Johnson, Hurts explained that he's a "triple-threat quarterback." He can beat you with his arm, his legs, and his mind.

"I think it's something that is often overlooked when you talk about a quarterback's game, even in my game," Hurts said. "You have to understand what you're doing; you have to be consistent in your decision-making.... That's in addition to making throws, making the runs when I'm supposed to. And also the third threat of trying to be a coach on the field and knowing what I'm supposed to do and knowing everybody's job—it's something I definitely challenge myself to do. And it's not easy."

Then on a frigid afternoon in Chicago in Week 15, a 263-pound Bears defender crushed Hurts into the ground. His right shoulder, the one that would soon help him earn a quarter-billion-dollar contract, was stunned with pain. Jordan Mailata instructed Hurts to stay on the ground. "Pick me the f— up!" Hurts said, according to *The Philadelphia Inquirer*. But he knew there was a problem. Hurts returned to the sideline and told a team staffer, "My s—'s broke," according to a *Sports Illustrated* article, referencing his collarbone. (The diagnosis, he later learned, was a sprained SC joint.) Hurts insisted on staying in the game despite pain unlike he'd ever felt. But he couldn't fool the training staff once they knew the extent of the injury. Hurts missed two games. The Eagles lost both. They needed to win in Week 18 to clinch the top seed, so Hurts returned to do just enough to outlast the Giants. The victory gave Hurts more time to recover for the playoffs. And when he returned, teammates noticed the Eagles had their swagger back. In back-to-back postseason wins, Hurts totaled four touchdowns and did not turn the ball over.

"I know this is high praise, but to have him out there is like having—I shouldn't even go there—it's like having Michael Jordan out there," Sirianni said after the divisional round victory. "He's your leader. He's your guy. Hopefully that's the biggest respect I can pay to him, comparing his ability to being on the field to a Michael Jordan type. This guy leads. He brings this calmness to the entire team. He plays great football. He's as tough as they come."

This comparison carries weight with Hurts. He endorses the Jordan brand, wearing Jumpman cleats. When he retired from injury, he wore a T-shirt with a newspaper cover from Jordan's return that read I'M BACK. He changes every day in a locker stall that has a poster of Jordan with a Jordan quote: "Some people want it to happen, some wish it would happen, and others MAKE it happen."

Hurts also knew that, like Jordan, the best players are defined by championships. And he was on the doorstep of winning the Super Bowl.

"This is not a time for reflection," Hurts said after leading the Eagles to the NFC Championship Game. "It's really hard for me to do that. I try to enjoy the moment, but my joy comes in winning. I know the job isn't done. I never knew how far we would come, I never knew how far we'd go, but I never said it couldn't be done."

For someone marked by stoicism, Hurts appeared noticeably loose leading up to the Super Bowl. The brighter lights can blind some players. For Hurts, he operates as if the lights are brighter *because* he's on the stage. That became especially true on game day. It might have been Hurts' finest performance in an Eagles uniform. There were MVP ballots that would have had his name over Patrick Mahomes had the Eagles made one more defensive stop. He threw for 304 yards and a touchdown. He rushed for 70 yards and three touchdowns. He tied the game with a two-point conversion. The lone blemish was a fumble when the ball slipped from his hands and was recovered for a score by Kansas City. (Hurts tried apologizing to teammates for this miscue after the game; they didn't want him to bear that burden after the game he played.) Otherwise, it was a quarterback masterpiece that put his name in NFL record books—the most rushing yards by a quarterback and tied for the most rushing touchdowns by any player.

"To me, Jalen played the best game I've seen him play in the two years that we've been together," Sirianni said after the game. "You really look at the game and that was good for the NFL in the sense that the two best quarterbacks in the NFL played against each other on the biggest stage [under] the biggest lights."

Mahomes, who beat out Hurts for MVP that season, stood in the winner's circle. And he knew what the silver medalist had accomplished that night.

"If there was any doubters left [about Hurts], there shouldn't be now," Mahomes said. "The way he stepped on this stage, and ran, threw the ball, whatever it took for his team to win. It was a special performance. I don't want it to get lost in the loss that they had. Even whenever we got all the momentum in that game, and we went up eight points in the fourth quarter, for him to respond and move his team down the football field and run in himself on a two-point conversion, it was a special performance by him."

Hurts had been on the doorstep before. He climbed his way back. He went through the fire. And even that night, with the pain of the Super Bowl loss, there was confidence that Hurts would reach that stage again.

"You either win or you learn, that's how I feel," Hurts said that night. "You either win or you learn."

There was no longer any doubt or question. The Eagles had their franchise quarterback.

"The thing with Jalen I am so optimistic about is he has this incredible—and I'm not telling you anything you don't know here—but seeing him virtually every day he has an incredible passion for being phenomenal," Lurie said two months later at the league meetings, calling Hurts the most mature 24-year-old he had ever met. "And you see that in the great ones. We all know in other sports, and with certain quarterbacks in this league, you can define them by obsession with detail and work ethic. We always knew Jalen was talented, had a very live arm that we felt was discounted in college because he was such a great runner, and his character was always considered great. But maybe the advantage we had was we really respected his ability to throw the football, and that would improve based on tremendous work ethic. I think the future is so great for him."

Hurts was eligible for a contract extension after his third season, and the Eagles were prepared to sign him to a lucrative deal just as they signed McNabb and Wentz during Lurie's ownership. The franchise's history during this period was to try to sign their homegrown talent as soon as permitted. It was an organizational philosophy that dated back to Joe Banner's time as team president. In Hurts' case, his eligibility overlapped with other top quarterbacks in the NFL who could also sign big deals. But the Eagles did not wait to see the deals other quarterbacks would sign. Neither did Hurts, for that matter. The two sides agreed to a record-setting five-year, $255 million contract in April 2023. (The record lasted until the next quarterback signed.) It was a signature moment for the franchise. The "aura of commas," as Jason Kelce called it, was validation.

"Money is nice," Hurts said after signing his deal. "Championships are better."

Hurts emphasized that the contract was "not an arrival point," and that reaction was part of the appeal with Hurts. The Eagles were not just signing a player. They were investing in the person—and even the persona.

"It's crucial, no matter what, that you can find your quarterback for the present and the future," Lurie said, "and to have that person as sterling a character, as passionate about his craft, and as dedicated as this young 24-year-old is remarkable."

Of course, an Eagles historian might remember a similar sentiment four years ago when Wentz signed his contract extension. Hurts would tell you rent is due every day, although this allowed him to make a considerable down payment. Part of how Hurts earned the contract was with a playing style that involved using his legs and exposing himself to hits, and there were questions about whether the Eagles would try to protect their investment by calling fewer designed runs. If nothing else, the Wentz experience showed how injuries could take a toll on a quarterback.

"We didn't pay him more to do less," Sirianni said.

Hurts, who coined the phrase, "It's a Philly thing," explained that playing in Philadelphia was special because of "the fans, the culture, the enthusiasm, the passion, and love for the game." He also acknowledged that he surrendered anonymity and could not go anywhere in his new hometown. Hurts struck up a relationship with two former school principals who started FoodChasers' Kitchen, a restaurant on the outskirts of Philadelphia. He mentioned on national television and at a Super Bowl press conference that they made his favorite cheesesteak. He celebrated the NFC Championship Game at their restaurant, and they put the "Jalen Special" on the menu. The restaurant swelled in popularity because of Hurts' organic endorsement. He had a Philadelphia version of the Midas touch, and his mass-market appeal was apparent from national television commercials and his becoming a national magazine coverboy.

"Heavy is the head," Hurts acknowledged.

Entering the 2023 season, Hurts needed to again adjust to a new play-caller after Steichen's departure to Indianapolis. The Eagles promoted Johnson, and the close personal relationship between Hurts and Johnson was viewed as a benefit. When Hurts made a mistake in a training camp practice, Sirianni still hollered at his star quarterback. Hurts still responded with a self-imposed penalty of push-ups. There was curiosity about an encore, although given the way Hurts played in 2022, it was always going to be a difficult act to follow.

"I've never really reported to the opinions of others, the expectation of others, or the standards of others," Hurts said before the season. "So I won't start now."

Hurts' 2023 campaign appeared different from the previous season. Opposing defensive coaches had spent the offseason studying how the Eagles—and Hurts—excelled in 2022, and they were determined to at least present different defensive packages and play calls for the quarterback. The early portion of the schedule included a heavy dose of unscouted looks, with Hurts blitzed at a significantly greater rate than the previous season. His turnovers increased. His rushing production waned while dealing with a knee injury. He was still making winning plays—the Eagles opened the season 5–0 and won 10 of their first 11 games—but it was not at the standard that Hurts had set the previous season.

Then, the standard was all that mattered. In 2023, the message was different.

"When did winning not become the main thing?" Hurts asked. "Winning is the only thing that truly matters. You have important things, you have priorities. You have 1A and 1B. 1A is winning, 1B is playing to the standard. Now you can win, but not play to the standard, and you're still unfulfilled. You can play to the standard, and not win, and you're still unfulfilled. So what matters?"

Hurts was nonetheless considered an MVP favorite in November when the Eagles' wins outpaced the rest of the league. The high-water marks included a pair of 319-yard passing performances with six touchdowns in two wins against Washington. He rushed for a memorable game-winning touchdown on a sterling overtime drive in a win against Buffalo. Among the quarterbacks who were on the losing side of his wins were Mahomes, Josh Allen, Matthew Stafford, Dak Prescott—and even Tagovailoa. Hurts bested the Buccaneers in his first meeting since that ill-fated postseason game two years earlier. There was a reason for Hurts to strut. Yet he knew he needed to play better. He explained his conflicted emotions despite a 12-yard, walk-off touchdown run.

"I shake my head and I don't really know how to feel sometimes, because I just want to play to the standard at all times," Hurts said after the game. "That's why it's kind of weird for me.... It's [in] a sense manipulative to myself, because winning is the only thing that matters, but the standard is pretty darn important, too."

If only he knew what was coming. He experienced only one win in the final six games of the season, with the Eagles' collapse costing them the top seed and the division crown. Hurts became an afterthought on MVP balloting. Instead, he was left answering questions about what was wrong. In Week 15, Hurts threw an interception on the Eagles' final drive when they were trailing by three points. He freelanced on the play with A.J. Brown, changing the play call. After that game, Hurts suggested the team was not committed enough. (He later amended the comment to explain he was starting with himself.) And the season kept getting worse. He injured his thumb in a Week 18 loss to the New York Giants. And though he played in the postseason game against Tampa Bay, it did not go much better than two years earlier. For the second time in three years, the Eagles were knocked out in the opening round to the Buccaneers. This time, they were favored—and they were a major disappointment.

"It wasn't our turn," he said. "And I can accept that, knowing that the sun will rise tomorrow and there will be another opportunity to attack it.... We'll learn from it. I know I'll learn from it."

A few days later, standing by his locker, Hurts lamented the reality that someone else would win the Super Bowl. He spoke about the need to continue to evolve—as a player, as a leader, as a man. But he pushed back on the idea that he needed to change his personality, that keeping that same face was suddenly problematic. "There was a time where the things that you said make me great, make me unique, make a me a great leader—at least that's what was said—are now things that are a little different and interpreted in whatever type of way," Hurts said.

He was right. When the Eagles win, his steadiness is credited for keeping the fire ablaze. When they lose, he's charged with needing more fire. He surmised it's all based on the results. His career was evidence. He's lost his job and taken a job. He's held onto his role, and he became entrenched in his role. He's still smelling the smoke, and it has not stopped him from walking through fire.

PART 4

THE ICONS

13

Brian Dawkins

BRIAN DAWKINS DID NOT MERELY RUN ONTO THE FIELD before games. He crawled. He screamed. He pounded his chest. He waved to the crowd. He emerged from the smoke in the southwest corner of the stadium like a superhero. He became a different person—"Weapon X," as he would call it. Or maybe he became all those fans in that stadium who wore No. 20 jerseys and cheered for him. When Dawkins' jersey was retired in 2012, he posed that very question: What would those fans do if they could play one game?

"Would you do a flip? Would you crawl? Would you do those things?" Dawkins said. "Probably so. Because you're so excited to play those games."

Dawkins is one of the great players of this period and in the history of the franchise, and one of two who has already been enshrined in the Pro Football Hall of Fame. He was a nine-time Pro Bowler and four-time All-Pro who was named to the NFL's all-decade team in the 2000s. He finished his career with 37 interceptions and 26 sacks. But more important than honor or accolades, Dawkins was perhaps the most beloved player of this era.

"Brian embodied everything about a working-class city," Lurie said when Dawkins retired. "He was talented, worked hard. Appreciate who you are, be comfortable with yourself, look in the mirror and don't try to put on airs, just be hard, tough, and want to win. He loved the fans, and I think they knew it. With a lot of players, there's a barrier sometimes in being able to connect with the fans in terms of communicating from your heart. Brian always communicated from his heart. The way he'd run out onto the field and the way he played. It's one thing to be alive and energetic, but to play with that consistent intensity every game of his career was, for me, extremely special."

As Dawkins explained, he did not merely hear the fans. He listened. That is an important distinction. And he wanted to represent them.

"One of the things that I've been blessed with—or cursed with—is I played with all of my emotions on my sleeve, and you can read me pretty easily by the way I'm feeling on game day," Dawkins said when he retired. "I like to try my best to not disappoint people. I purposely try and go out and do my best to make sure my coaches, teammates, and fans know that I gave it my all on the football field. With me playing as long as I did in Philadelphia, I heard what they said. I didn't just hear it, I heard and listened to what they said. I felt the pain they had from past failures and the way they are treated sometimes in the media. I heard those things, and I took it to heart and I understood them. The thing that I always wanted to do is to go out and put a certain product on the field to have those certain entities proud of me when the game was over. Hopefully, I have poured everything emotionally and physically out on the field.

The last thing is I don't care what people say about me being exuberant. I don't care if you did or didn't like it. If you didn't like it, I didn't care about that because I'm going to be me. I'm going to play with my emotions on my sleeve."

Dawkins came into the NFL under former head coach and defensive coordinator Emmitt Thomas, who preceded the Andy Reid era. Thomas was a staunch advocate for bringing Dawkins to Philadelphia. But Dawkins' accolades started when Reid was hired and brought in famed defensive coordinator Jim Johnson, who utilized Dawkins as a versatile weapon in his blitz-heavy scheme. Dawkins could blitz like a linebacker and cover like a cornerback, and his thunderous hits made him a feared figure in the middle of the field. (Michael Vick, who later became Dawkins' teammate, said the hardest hit he ever took came from Dawkins.)

"I think the things that he saw in me were the same things that Emmitt [Thomas] and Ray saw in me, and they just used it in a different way," Dawkins said. "I was blessed to be able to run, and I was able to cover different receivers out in nickel packages. I had quick-twitch muscles and my hips weren't stiff, so I had a lot of cornerback attributes out in the safety position. That was not the norm when I came into the league: you had your big-guy strong safety and you had your smaller guy, maybe a little bit taller but smaller, free safety. He can roam and get the guy in the box. [Rhodes and Thomas] may have had me more covering, but when Jim got here, he saw that I could cover and he liked that part, but he would blitz me a couple times and he saw with the timing of the blitz that I was relentless. That's what Jim would always preach is the relentlessness. He wants you to be relentless and never to hold back. That's the way that I played, period. He began to throw more and more blitzes up for me. He would call me in the offseason just to see how I was doing and even on off days just to get into, 'I got a couple more things that I think you're going to like.' I was loving it because I'm being used in a different way. I wouldn't say or take this lightly, but I don't know if there would be a Weapon X or Wolverine personality on game day if Jim didn't believe in me to use me the way he used me."

That was the style that made Dawkins beloved in Philadelphia and feared around the league. When Dawkins signed a contract extension in 2003, Johnson was quoted as saying that if he were to build a football team, Dawkins would be his free safety. It was as if he was designed to play in Johnson's defense. That's why Dawkins is in an exclusive club of NFL defenders with at least 35 interceptions and 20 sacks. The ability to play everywhere from the deepest part of the secondary to in the quarterback's armpit made Dawkins a rare breed.

At the end of Dawkins' career in Philadelphia, he was in the franchise's record book for most games played, tied for the most interceptions, and was second in most seasons and most Pro Bowl selections. The fact that he did not finish his career with the Eagles remains an organizational regret. He played his final seasons in Denver, although he later returned to the organization and was hailed by Eagles fans when he was enshrined in the Hall of Fame.

"I know some of you drove all the way from Philly," Dawkins said during that August 2018 day in Canton, Ohio. "And listen, I have a good understanding that you don't have money just to waste. So that means that you put hard-earned money that you could be saving to come out here and celebrate with your boy! So thank you! Thank you for loving me the way that I love you. I love you back."

When Dawkins reflected on his finest moment with the Eagles, he returned to the day that many from his era pinpoint—when the Eagles finally reached the Super Bowl during the 2004 season after three consecutive losses in the NFC Championship Game.

He remembered "the exuberance, the joy, the feeling of a burden lifted off of your back" when he saw tears in Johnson's eyes. "Dawk, we did it, we did!" Johnson said to him.

"I'll never forget that, and that'll be something that will always stand out among so many great moments I had in Philadelphia," Dawkins said.

When Dawkins was honored in Philadelphia during his jersey retirement, he mimicked the introduction that he made famous. In those moments, Lurie felt the same emotion and excitement as his customers. It was a shared experience, which was Dawkins' goal. He didn't just want you to cheer for him. He wanted you to live through him.

"Every time Brian ran out, I'd get goosebumps," Lurie said. "It was uplifting—you're excited for every player on the team, and you're excited for the game to start, but when Brian went through the tunnel, it was like you felt physically different. You felt goosebumps, and it was like, let's get the game going and let's watch No. 20 out there. It was very, very special, and it's hard to explain. He was just a very special football player and person."

Players are often asked about their legacies. Dawkins' legacy remains clear. There are still fans who wear No. 20 jerseys more than a decade later. Dawkins has since left the front office and now devotes his time to his foundation and philanthropic endeavors. Watching him at a Philadelphia after-school program in 2021, it was striking to think that the kids in the room never saw Dawkins play. He is adding to his legacy that way, inspiring and helping kids who were like him as a teenager in Jacksonville.

But the adults in the room, those who watched him play, those who saw him crawl and scream and pound his chest? His legacy is entrenched—and everlasting.

"I just want it to be one where fans, teammates, coaches, whoever, and everyone that I've played with, played for, or in front of, that he gave everything that he had to the last drop, whether it's on game day, in preparation, with the media, or someone needed help off-the-field, that he was there for me with that, and that if he didn't know one of the answers, he wouldn't lie and he would help me find it," Dawkins said. "If my legacy is that, I can trust it."

14

LeSean McCoy

Before LeSean McCoy's first game back in Philadelphia in 2015 after he was unceremoniously traded earlier that year, McCoy crouched down at midfield in a Buffalo Bills jersey and kissed the Eagles logo. McCoy was only 27 years old, and he had rushed for more yards than any player to ever wear an Eagles uniform.

That record remains. So does a legacy of a brilliant career that ended in Philadelphia too soon—and not by his own choosing.

"I want to be remembered as the best running back to ever—*ever*—play as a Philadelphia Eagle," McCoy said when he officially retired as a member of the franchise in 2021. "I wish it lasted longer. I feel like the rushing yards record would be even bigger. I could have been there for the championship."

McCoy has called the phone call from Andy Reid in 2009 one of the highlights of his career. That's when Reid informed him that he would remain in Pennsylvania. He grew up in Harrisburg, just two hours outside Philadelphia. He played college football across the state in Pittsburgh. The Eagles played the Pittsburgh Steelers in an August 2008 preseason game, and Howie Roseman attended Pitt's practice before the game to scout their prospects. With the offense backed up on their 1-yard line, the sophomore running back took a handoff, reversed field, and raced 99 yards for a touchdown. He eluded defenders and outran defensive backs. Roseman asked an assistant coach if he had ever witnessed that type of running back.

"Tony Dorsett," Roseman was told.

"It was hard not to leave with a lasting impression," Roseman said in a 2012 interview.

A few days after Roseman offered the memory, McCoy was asked if he recalled the play. He offered confirmation, although he stopped short of suggesting that was a major factor in the Eagles keeping him home.

"I think it was the 21 touchdowns," McCoy said with a smile, referring to his final year in college.

Despite McCoy's college success, he slipped to the second round of the draft. McCoy was sick during the scouting combine, which kept him from working out. (Roseman told NFL Network that McCoy said he had a 103-degree temperature, and McCoy was sneezing throughout the interview in a cramped room at the Crowne Plaza.) As McCoy explained, he was said to have a "teenage body frame"—he was only 20—and there were questions about how he would transition to the NFL. He held grudges against running backs drafted ahead of him, notably offering cold words to Knowshon Moreno during the 2013 season.

On his first day of training camp, McCoy saw Donovan McNabb and Brian Westbrook and thought to himself, "Holy s—!"

These were the players whose posters were on his wall. He had watched McNabb in the Campbell's Chunky Soup commercial.

As a rookie in 2009, McCoy waited his turn behind Brian Westbrook while showing promise—enough that the Eagles released Westbrook and opened the top spot for McCoy. As a 22-year-old in 2010, McCoy rushed for 1,080 yards and caught 78 passes—the most by any running back in the NFL. By 2011, McCoy rushed for 1,309 yards and 17 touchdowns and was named first-team All-Pro. He had become a *bona fide* star—with a new five-year, $45 million contract to lock him down to a franchise he adored.

"I love this team, and I'm kind of a hometown kid from Harrisburg, which is like an hour and a half away," McCoy said when he signed. "Nothing could be better than being here for the long term."

By the end of the 2013 season, McCoy wore a champion belt.

Chip Kelly took over for Reid that year, bringing the Eagles an up-tempo offense (and a new philosophy). The off-field mix might have been initially combustible—from dress code to hydration to sleep, McCoy was at odds—but the on-field results were staggering. He was the NFL's best running back in 2013, with a career-high 1,607 yards, 268 yards better than the No. 2 rusher on the list. It was the most rushing yards in a season in franchise history, and McCoy finished second in the NFL's Offensive Player of the Year voting. The season included a franchise-record 217 rushing yards in the unforgettable Snow Bowl. McCoy was only 25, and it didn't take much imagination to see a path to Canton, Ohio.

Longtime Eagles running back coach Ted Williams said he looks for characteristics that cannot be taught, because there are fundamentals that can be developed. McCoy's quickness through the hole and stop-on-a-dime, make-defenders-miss elusiveness were the hallmarks.

"LeSean embodied what a running back was for me," Westbrook once said. "He's a guy who can make you miss, can make big plays, can make plays in an open field. He wasn't a great short-yardage back, but he wasn't 220 [pounds], either. But what I want if I was a coach, on my team, are playmakers. I want guys that you may lose two yards here and there, but if you can hit that hole and run for me, that's important to me. Because I know we have a chance in every single game."

In Week 14 of the 2014 season, McCoy rushed for a four-yard gain on a second down in the third quarter—one of the more unremarkable carries in his career. But that carry pushed him past 6,538 yards in his career, which was the mark set by Wilbert Montgomery for the most rushing yards in franchise history. McCoy was the new record-holder, and he added to that total in the final three games that season. He was only 26 and still had his career ahead of him, and so many meaningful records to his name: most yards in a game, season, and career.

That would be the last season he ever played for the Eagles. It was also the last time anyone wore No. 25 for the Eagles.

After the Eagles failed to make the playoffs following the 2014 season, there were questions about whether McCoy would return for 2015 due to his swelling contract. The unceremonious departure of DeSean Jackson showed that no one was off limits during the Kelly regime. But McCoy did not realistically expect to leave. And Eagles fans did not expect their top running back to get traded for a linebacker.

On March 3, 2015, Kelly was a scheduled speaker at the Jewish Community Center in Cherry Hill, New Jersey. Around 6:30 PM that night, while Kelly waited to speak, a buzz circulated through the gymnasium. Fans, some of whom wore

No. 25 jerseys and had attended the event 15 months earlier when McCoy spoke, were alerted on their smartphones to the breaking news from ESPN: the Eagles had traded McCoy to the Buffalo Bills for Kiko Alonso, who had played linebacker for Kelly at the University of Oregon. Kelly was not prepared for the trade to become public; he expected to finish it the next morning and had not even notified McCoy.

You could imagine how McCoy took the news of the deal. When his agent notified the star running back of the deal, McCoy needed to be assured it was not a joke. Kelly later cited salary as the biggest reason. McCoy said he was never informed about a money issue and was not approached about restructuring his contract. The bad blood between the running back and coach carried over to Buffalo, where he topped 1,000 yards in two of four seasons.

McCoy finished his career in Kansas City (with Reid) and Tampa Bay, winning Super Bowls in both seasons. Those rings were a fitting end to a career of a player who was one of the elite running backs of his era. But there was something missing.

"I do wish that, if I could have had a championship, I wish it would have been when I was an Eagle," McCoy said before winning his second Super Bowl. "I started there. And it means more to me—as far as my hometown being an hour away, being drafted, a lot of my friends are still my friends to share that with."

McCoy was close on different occasions to returning to the Eagles later in his career, whether by trade after Roseman returned to general manager or on the open market. It never materialized, and he eventually signed a one-day contract to retire with the franchise in 2021. He was honored when the Eagles played against Reid.

He walked through the bowels of the stadium and estimated that he could name 85 to 90 percent of the people that he passed. (He's known as "Shady," the nickname his mother gave him as a child.) Playing for the Eagles was not a workplace as much as a birthright for McCoy.

"All these things I thought about as a kid, they came true," McCoy said. "I've completed my dreams as a kid."

No player has ever been issued No. 25 since he left. That is not by coincidence, even if the number is not formally retired. He never won a Super Bowl in Philadelphia and he did not play past Year 6 with the franchise, but he's nonetheless one of the icons of the era. Yet the unfulfilled lingers in his mind.

"I have one regret," McCoy said when he retired. "[The] only regret I truly have is not being an Eagle in my prime. At the time I got traded, I felt I was probably—maybe second guy—other than Jason Peters.... That's one thing I regret. I should have always been an Eagle for my career and the majority of my prime years."

That might be true. He has 254 yards on Montgomery in career rushing yards. Nobody has approached the record since McCoy left. Maybe it remains that way, although he would have pushed that record a few thousand yards past where it stood when they traded him. It also would have added to his legacy. The Eagles have had great running backs, from Steve Van Buren to Montgomery. But McCoy is in the conversation—and perhaps atop it—for the legacy that he desired. He might be the best running back to ever play for the Eagles.

15

Fletcher Cox

FLETCHER COX LOOKED AT A SECTION OF THE EAGLES' auditorium reserved for his family and friends, a group of 20-plus who came to Philadelphia from his native Mississippi, and remembered 12 years earlier. Cox was age 21 at the NFL draft in New York City when the Eagles selected him, a self-described country boy preparing for an unfamiliar part of the country. Those family members were with him then. So on this day in the spring of 2024, when he announced his retirement after 12 seasons, he wanted them present.

"Hopefully one day, a few years from now, I'm putting on a gold jacket," Cox said. "And I'll have the same exact family here and they'll help me celebrate."

For other players, such a thought would seem farfetched. When it came to Cox on the football field, little seemed impossible.

Cox had only played four NFL seasons in the summer of 2016 when the team created a mural for its promotional video to hype fans for the upcoming season. It was revealed in the final cutaway during the closing credits. The mural showed iconic Eagles—the types who have spots in Canton, Ohio, not even to mention the franchise's Hall of Fame. Chuck Bednarik prayed above Frank Gifford after delivering an unforgettable hit in 1960. Reggie White, perhaps the greatest Eagles defender ever, was shown with a halo around his head. Brian Dawkins looked like a superhero while flexing his biceps. Jeremiah Trotter, perhaps the best Eagles linebacker of this era, swung an ax as part of his trademark celebration. And Cox, who was 25 and had never won a playoff game to that point, was featured as part of the quintet.

The implication was clear then, if it wasn't obvious when the Eagles made Cox the highest-paid player in franchise history months earlier. Cox was expected to be discussed in the category of the great defensive players in franchise history.

"I'm probably far from them," Cox said at the time. "But it is an honor, though, for the Eagles to even have me in that conversation. I've still got a lot of work to do to even get to where those guys are. They are the greats to be a part of this organization."

That comment was made after Cox signed a $103 million contract extension that showed with nine digits how he was a centerpiece of the organization. Howie Roseman, who at one point had a big poster of Cox hanging in his office, said after Cox signed that he had the chance to become "a great player in the history of the franchise." That's long been the kind of discussion surrounding Cox. Great talent begets great expectations. Cox's locker stall was next to Graham, who has been Cox's teammate throughout his entire career in Philadelphia.

It was posed to Graham in 2016 what was left for Cox to accomplish.

"To be a Hall of Famer," defensive end Brandon Graham said. "And win a championship, so we can be known forever in Philly."

Nearly a decade passed since that summer. Cox remained in Philadelphia. He won a Super Bowl on a team when he was perhaps the best player. He made six Pro Bowls. He had been an All-Pro. Cox's statistics were never eye-popping at the position—he had one season of double-digit sacks—but there were games when opponents created game plans by making sure they knew where No. 91 was on the field. At the Pro Bowl in January 2020, Jason Kelce identified Cox and Jason Peters as the two teammates whose brilliance defied scheme.

"You could have anybody coach them—and they've been fortunate to have great coaches," Kelce said. "You can have anybody playing next to them—and they've been fortunate to have great players next to them. But at the end of the day, those two would have been Hall of Fame talents, no matter what team they ended up on."

When this sentiment was shared with Cox, he explained a lesson he learned as a rookie from DeMeco Ryans, who later became an NFL head coach: "Don't let a scheme reflect what kind of player you are.... Great players find a way." That's what Cox did with multiple defensive coordinators and in multiple schemes.

Philadelphia witnessed the entire arc of Cox's career. There are some players who are only present for parts—the rise, the pinnacle, or the decline—but Cox has never left. Even in 2022 and 2023, when it appeared the Eagles could move on from Cox, he always found his way back. Part of that is because of how he values the franchise. It might not be with the same public outspokenness of Kelce or Graham, longtime teammates and fan favorites, but it's with a quiet loyalty that is evident when he takes the field with a "C" on his chest or has the option to leave and elects to stay.

"Being in Philadelphia," Cox said, "changed my entire life."

To understand why and how, take a trip to a town known as the gateway to the Mississippi Delta: Yazoo City, Mississippi. With a population of just more than 10,000, Yazoo City sits about an hour north of Jackson, which is the state capital. Cox takes pride in his hometown, even though the goal was always to leave. In fact, his high school guidance counselor hung a newspaper clipping from Cox's draft night in her office so students could see there is a way out of Yazoo City. When Cox introduced himself on *Sunday Night Football* during the 2018 season, he did not say Mississippi State. He said "Yazoo City High School"—whose football stadium now bears his name.

"A lot of these kids don't have a ticket out of here," the counselor, Christy Cader, said in 2012. "We all saw [football] as [Cox's] ticket out of here."

A similar message was shared by his high school football coach, who told a story of a "Two-Two"—a former football player at the high school who was said to measure 6'7", weigh 300 pounds, and run a 40-yard dash in 4.7 seconds. Embellished or reality, it was explained that Two-Two could have played at SEC schools such as Ole Miss or Mississippi State, and maybe be like Cox and play on Sundays. But Two-Two didn't finish school, and can often be found by a small bridge that forbids loitering on Martin Luther King Jr. Avenue in Yazoo City, near a three-room, single-high trailer where Cox was raised. The dichotomy was offered to Yazoo City high school players when Cox was in his rookie season. "He's a $10 million man. And Two-Two is on the bridge." Cox saw the world beyond Haley

Barbour Boulevard, even if he could still swear by the crawfish at P-Reaux's Cajun Mudbugs & Shrimp.

"A kid from Yazoo City, just being where I am now," Cox said in 2023, "allowed me to live my life and go back and give back to those kids, and let them believe that there's a way out of small towns, no matter who you are."

This is a big theme in conversations with Cox. He's been described as a "big ol' country boy" who likes to hunt and fish. He owns a ranch in Texas and a drag racing team. That pace of life required an adjustment when he moved to Philadelphia a few months after his 21st birthday.

"Just everything," Cox said about how his life changed. "I mean, lifestyle, the way you look at things, the way you approach things. The biggest thing I think, I was here...21 years old, so I became a grown-up fast. So this city taught me how to become a young man, about growing up and doing everything in a professional way."

In Doug Pederson's book *Fearless*, he told the story of how two veterans broke team rules by wearing tinted visors during practice. Cox asked his teammates what they were doing and sent them inside to take off the visitors. Pederson viewed this as leaders policing the locker room, which is better than when coaches must do so.

Cox's presence in the organization is well known, and he's been said to have a strong connection with Roseman. Even when there have been times when Cox's career obituary appeared ready to be printed, the Eagles have always brought him back. And the reason why speculation had existed is because that back part of Cox's career arc became apparent in later years.

When the Eagles drafted Cox No. 12 overall in 2012, former defensive line coach Jim Washburn said, "When God made him, he meant him to play in this system right here"—a reference to the rookie's ability to penetrate the line of scrimmage and pressure the quarterback. One year later, when the Eagles shifted to a 3-4 defensive scheme upon Chip Kelly's hire, defensive line coach Jerry Azzinaro said, "Big, strong, athletic guy that can play in any system God invented." The versatility was apparent when Cox flourished as a 3-4 defensive end, even tallying 9.5 sacks in 2015 as a 24-year-old, fourth-year lineman. NFL Films captured star Dallas Cowboys tight end Jason Witten remarking in the middle of a standout performance from Cox, "He's too f—ing big in there. Ninety-one is a man, dog!"

By 2016, the Eagles hired Jim Schwartz and switched Fletcher Cox to an attacking scheme that made stars out of defensive tackles. Cox, in the prime of his career, was a foundation player for the defense. That was most apparent during the Eagles' Super Bowl. In the divisional round playoff victory over the Atlanta Falcons, Cox played 90 percent of the defensive snaps. He sacked quarterback Matt Ryan while tallying two hits on the passer and two tackles for lost yardage. Graham said at the time it was the best Cox had ever played. Cox's instructions to himself were to "take over the game" and the rest of the team would follow. "A man on a mission," Pederson said. Cox earned a reputation from teammates that lingers to this day: "Playoff Fletch."

During the Super Bowl parade, Cox's attire was purposeful. He wore White's No. 92 Eagles jersey. That was the company with which Cox was expected to be associated in Philadelphia. (When Cox once explained why he wore No. 91, he noted that White briefly wore that number in Philadelphia before switching to No. 92.)

The best season of Cox's career came in 2018, when he opened the season with a stated goal of winning Defensive Player of the Year. He did not earn that designation, although he reached double-digit sacks for the first time (10.5) and was first-team All-Pro for the first (and only) time in his career. This was the type of player who was meant to be on that mural. In fact, the only defensive lineman who had reached more Pro Bowls by that point was White.

His production has never reached that point on a consistent basis ever since. Cox earned his fifth consecutive Pro Bowl appearance after the 2019 season, although that appeared to be based more on reputation than outstanding production. Offseason surgery caused him to start slowly, and he finished with only three and a half sacks. Cox was entering his age-30 season, but he insisted he had not hit his ceiling.

By 2021, Cox had grown frustrated. The Eagles switched to a new defensive scheme under first-year defensive coordinator Jonathan Gannon, and the top defensive lineman recorded only one sack in the first 13 games of the season. He questioned Gannon's scheme after a bad loss in Las Vegas, stewing about the calls and noting, "I don't get paid to play screens." There were rumors that the Eagles could trade Cox, which would have seemed unfathomable two years earlier. Cox did not make the Pro Bowl roster and insisted that he could still play to that level. The Eagles briefly cut him that offseason before bringing him back at a renegotiated contract number, and the thought was that it might be his last year in Philadelphia.

Except Cox did not look like a declining player. He had a renaissance during a seven-sack campaign—his most since 2018—and returned to his second Super Bowl. Even if he was no longer the headliner, he remained a respected player in the middle of the defense.

"Fletch making plays, obviously, in this city, that's what he does," Nick Sirianni said during the postseason run. "When the defense is going because Fletch is doing what he's doing, that's a really good thing.... Everybody is feeding off of that. He's a dominant football player. He's been a dominant football player in this league for a long time. Everything on the D-line can't always be judged on stats. I know that we do that at times, that's just the way it is. But he changes the game."

When the Eagles ran onto the field before Super Bowl LVII against the Kansas City Chiefs, Cox led the group. He flapped his arms like an eagle and wore his captain patch while playing for the only franchise he has ever known.

Maybe he never reached the level of White or Dawkins. But he's one of the faces of Eagles football during this era—an iconic player who will one day join the franchise's Hall of Fame and was a captain and key player on some of the best teams in franchise history. Canton is not out of the question.

"His legacy here will to be able to say that he's been around for a long time," Graham said, "and he was able to be dominant for all these years."

In the locker room after the final game of his career, Cox addressed teammates. He expressed appreciation. The gratitude continued when he announced his retirement. He could have kept playing, but he left while still among the best on the team. Philadelphia had never seen Cox as a reserve filling out a rotation. They only saw the player worthy of a mural. And that's how he wanted to leave it.

"I gave this game all I could give," Cox said, "and the game has given back."

16

Jason Kelce

LET'S START WITH THE SPEECH, BECAUSE WASN'T THAT DAY the essence of Jason Kelce? But which speech? There are now two epic oratory moments in Kelce's career that could be considered "the speech."

Kelce is one of the best players in franchise history—perhaps the best center of his era in the NFL—and there's so much to the Kelce story, from the way he emerged from sixth-round pick to day-one starter, to how he turned into an All-Pro midway through his career, to the way he can run 40 yards downfield on a screen, to how he is as a teammate and leader. Yet the most vivid Jason Kelce memories might not even be on the field. He wore a bejeweled Leprechaun suit reserved for Philadelphia's annual Mummers Parade on the Rocky Steps at the Philadelphia Museum of Art at the end of the Eagles' Super Bowl parade, offering perhaps the most famous parade speech in all of sports. That was once "the speech"—until he retired in the spring of 2024, when Kelce spoke for 41 minutes in an old sleeveless shirt, sweatpants, and flip-flops. He left an audience and fanbase in tears. Both speeches became a rallying cry for the city. They'll be part of Philadelphia lore.

The parade speech came after thoughts had been bubbling all season—and helped by some celebratory beers—and focused on the team and the city's underdog story. He singled out characterizations that teammates, coaches, and executives had overcome, and narratives they rewrote.

> It's the whole team! It's the whole team! This entire organization, with a bunch of driven men who accomplished something. We were a bunch of underdogs. And you know what an underdog is? It's a hungry dog. And Jeff Stoutland has had this in our building for five years—it's a quote in the O-line room that has stood on the wall for the last five years—"Hungry dogs run faster." And that's this team.

The retirement speech had been the culmination of notes accumulated throughout his career, striking on sentiments that were important for him to hit—football, family, and Philadelphia. Persistence and belief are themes Kelce has harped at different times in his career, and they came through that afternoon.

"So this all brings us here to today where I announce that I am retiring from the NFL, after 13 seasons with the Philadelphia Eagles," Kelce said. "And today, I must admit, I am officially overrated. Vastly overrated. It took a lot of hard work and determination getting here. I have been the underdog my entire career and I mean this when I say it, I wish I still was. Few things gave me more joy than proving someone wrong."

And to understand Kelce, you must understand persistence. His grandfather once gave him a card with a Calvin Coolidge quote that he carried in his wallet:

> Nothing in this world can take the place of persistence. Talent will not; nothing is more common than unsuccessful men with talent. Genius will not; unrewarded genius is almost a proverb. Education will not; the world is full of educated derelicts. Persistence and determination alone are omnipotent. The slogan "Press On!" has solved and always will solve the problems of the human race.

In fact, this is a message he delivers to teammates every year in a speech. Like before the 2021 season, when coach Nick Sirianni asked him to speak to the team. He explained how the quote "summarized what I believe in."

In that speech, with tears coming to his eyes, he gave a Cliffs Notes version of his career. He explained how he was a walk-on at Cincinnati who college coaches did not believe in before he developed into a starting offensive lineman. He described how he was a sixth-round pick who was "too small," and earned a starting spot as a rookie. He admitted how in 2016, "everyone in the city was ready to trade me…they'd trade me for a f—ing washing machine. They thought I was done. The only person who wanted me was [offensive line coach] Jeff Stoutland."

And what was the difference? Persistence. He pressed on.

After he won the Super Bowl, what came to mind? The characteristic that his career—and his iconic speech—exemplified.

"Persistence has summed up my whole career, summed up my whole life," Kelce said. "Just keep going, keep moving forward. No matter what obstacle is in the way, just keep moving forward."

"That's his motto, man," former Eagles offensive lineman Isaac Seumalo told The Athletic in 2022 of the "press on" message. "That's what he lives by. I think everybody kind of knew that about him. The actions kind of told us what he was, but the source and the quote and how much motivation it gives him, it just all kind of clicked and it makes a lot of sense."

Of course, there's more nuance to the story. Kelce's story is not only about persistence but rare talent that fit Howard Mudd's scheme. For the first 12 years of Andy Reid's tenure as head coach, Juan Castillo was the offensive line coach and sought size, length, and power. Howard Mudd took over in 2011 and looked for more athleticism, instincts, and vision on the field. A 280-pound converted linebacker might not have been appealing elsewhere in the NFL, but Mudd saw a player who reminded him of six-time Pro Bowler Jeff Saturday. It was also why Kelce was able to find playing time early in his career.

Kelce started 16 games as a rookie before a torn ACL halted his second season after two games. When Kelce returned in 2013, he was part of Chip Kelly's new offense that required an athletic offensive line. He was also linked with Stoutland, who has been his position coach ever since. They've been together longer than some marriages, and each has been pivotal for the other. Both are former linebackers who show the solution when the right mix of intelligence and intensity are combined. Stoutland considers Kelce a quarterback at center.

This period was when Kelce first emerged into a Pro Bowler and signed a lucrative contract extension. He proved to be a foundational player for the Eagles throughout Kelly's tenure, and appeared to be one of the key players when Doug Pederson took over in 2016. Even though Kelce was named to the Pro Bowl that season, he would likely admit it was based more on reputation. He had a down season by his standards, and the next offseason included trade rumors. If not for Stoutland's belief in him, Kelce speculated he would have played elsewhere.

"He was adamant my problems could be fixed with proper technique, fundamentals, and work. And work we did," Kelce said. "That offseason and training camp, I focused on using my hands better, playing with leverage, proper footwork, and prepared with an edge to prove to myself that I was good enough. The following season in 2017 I enjoyed the finest season of my 13-year career not only as a player, but as a team. And it meant more because of the struggles and work we had been through. Without him, I doubt any of this would have been possible, or that I'd still be here. Since that offseason, I have amassed six All-Pros, five Pro Bowls, and I'm recognized by some as one of the best centers to ever play the game. I am very proud knowing where I once was and the legacy I have left behind and the man we can all thank is Jeff Stoutland."

That's part of what made 2017 so special. When the Eagles won their postseason games that season, Kelce returned home, sat in the shower, reflected on his career, and burst into tears. The victory was the culmination of his career—no scholarship, sixth-round pick, injury, almost traded.

"My father and mother told me to stay after my dream," he said with tears in his eyes after winning the Super Bowl. "And I've officially accomplished the best thing in this sport with a group of guys who mean the world to me."

He does not conceal emotion. Lane Johnson's perseverance brought him to tears. He said country music can do the same. The passion is real. The parade speech was evident. And sometimes, it's manifested with anger.

"It wasn't always the right way, but it was the Jason Kelce way of leading, right?" said former Eagles offensive lineman Matt Tobin, who played with Tom Brady and Russell Wilson and considers Kelce "just as good, if not better" as a leader. "It's the only way he knew how. It might have had anger involved at times; it might not have."

The Kelce scouting report when he came out of Cincinnati included a note on his temper. And teammates share stories of times when that temper is exacerbated, such as when his car was spray-painted as a prank when he was younger and he stormed around the meeting rooms trying to find out who did it. Or when he kicked the chalk in the weight room. Or when he kicked the trash can at practice.

Throughout the years, Kelce has been identified as a favorite teammate. He's earned respect in the locker room from players on both sides of the ball, of all ages and backgrounds. When Jalen Hurts was asked what he thought of the Eagles' 2023 offseason moves in their attempt to return to the Super Bowl, the quarterback identified only one move: "Kelce's back. That stood out." Of all the titles Kelce holds, "teammate" might be near the top.

"The cafeteria and the locker room," Kelce explained in 2021, "is the only reason I'm still playing football."

The operative word might be *playing.* Kelce does not miss games. He entered the 2023 season with 139 consecutive starts. He had not missed a game since 2014 despite ailments to almost every part of his body. In 2018, he played through an MCL tear, a torn elbow, an injured knee, and a broken toe. He remarked that he had a brace on the entire left side of his body. But come Sunday, he's on the field. Pederson said he's "never really been around a player, an offensive lineman of his caliber, that does what he does day in and day out."

"A lot of luck, to be honest with you," Kelce said of staying healthy enough to play.

Kelce contemplated retirement after his last few seasons. He came close, taking time at the end of each season to decide whether it's worth playing. Stoutland told him that he will know it's time to retire when he does not want to play anymore. Kelce countered that will never happen. Stoutland assured him it will. Mudd once told him, "When in doubt, don't." So he kept playing football, with his career obituary seemingly on ice each year. By the end of his 13th season, Kelce knew his time was finished. His body had not failed on him yet, but he knew if he kept playing, he would not maintain the level he expected of himself. Plus, as he explained in his retirement speech, his wife and three daughters gave him "a life that increasingly brings me more fulfillment off the field than it does on."

He planned for what's next. He started a podcast with his brother, Kansas City Chiefs star tight end Travis Kelce, that tops listening charts and is reportedly worth nine figures. A documentary that chronicled his penultimate season became Amazon's most-watched documentary. He organized a Christmas music album for charity. He created an apparel line and foundation to help support children in Philadelphia. He invested in cattle ranching. He spent three days in Los Angeles during the 2023 offseason at the NFL's Broadcasting and Media Workshop, wowing network executives with his command in front of the camera and microphone. Kelce was never a free agent as a player, but he was the top media free agent upon retirement.

"[Football] is the thing I've done the most with my life and it's the one thing that I'm really truly an expert at," Kelce said at the media workshop. "So I think it would be a disservice to step away from that completely. I think however I utilize that—whether it's coaching high school, coaching in the NFL, doing media—there's only so many things that you get an opportunity to do to use that expertise once you're done playing."

However wide his brand spreads—and the Q rating reached new heights in 2023—it will never be bigger than in Philadelphia. During the 2021 season, when basketball player Ben Simmons sat out during a staredown with Philadelphia 76ers management, Kelce used his pulpit to dismiss the notion that Philadelphia is a difficult market for a professional athlete.

"I think it's pretty f—g easy, to be honest with you," Kelce said. "You just go out there and play hard. Want to be loved in this city as a baseball player? Run to first base. They're going to f—g love you. That's what it comes down to. If you go up here and make a bunch of excuses, if you come here and try to lie to them and act like they don't know what they're talking about—which sometimes they don't—when you really act that way or when you aren't accountable when you're making mistakes or not getting better or anything like that, they're going to crush you."

Kelce speculated that a difficult place to play would be Jacksonville, which does not have the same type of fan engagement as Philadelphia. And if the fans are emotionally invested, the athlete must make a similar emotional investment.

"Growing up in Cleveland, I watched all of my favorite athletes leave the city. Hell, a whole team left the city," Kelce said when he retired. "It has always been a goal of mine to play my whole career in one city and I couldn't have dreamt a better one and a better fit if I tried. I don't know what's next, but I look forward to the new challenges and opportunities that await and I know that I carry with me the lessons from my time here and that forever, we shall all share the bond of being Philadelphians."

Of course, it helped for Kelce to say this as one of the best players in franchise history. Jalen Reagor, a failed first-round pick, might have a different perspective. Then again, Kelce explained that every player gets "crushed" at some point in their careers, and Kelce felt that in the middle. It's up to the athlete to determine how he lets that affect him. He said if they "stick to it and fight through it"—persistence, remember?—the fans will "respect the hell out of you."

"You have to realize this is a blip in time. And over the course of my career, *I* write the narrative," Kelce said. "I'm the one who decides what this is.... That's how you control everything. If I just do this better, if I go out there and ball, if I go out there and play really good, nobody's going to have any choice but to love you and appreciate you. That's what I tell the guys. You write your own narrative."

Kelce wrote his own narrative. He's beloved, a franchise Hall of Famer and a Philadelphia icon.

"At times, you hate it as an athlete, especially those new to our city," Kelce said when he retired. "But when you've been through it enough, you learn to appreciate it. No one celebrates their own like the City of Philadelphia. Athletes become demigods in the city, even ones whose deeds span decades before. The Eagles are the No. 1 ticket in town, the most talked about thing at nearly every moment. But that amount of attention, you better be ready to overcome the lows that will happen and be ready to persevere in the face of the criticism. Yes, they will let you know when you are not performing well, every time, but they will also love you if you show effort, aggression, desire, the will to fight.

"They will love you in this city, if you love *it* the way you love your brother. You will be loved by going above and beyond to show that you care because they care. They've been caring for generations in this town about this team and they aren't about to except a bunch of excuses and soft-ass nonsense representing the name of the front of the jersey, something they've invested their entire lives in. If you don't like what the fans and media are saying, as a player, it's very easy. Love them. Treat them like your brothers, and go out and play your balls off. Wear your heart on your sleeve and I guarantee you change those narratives."

That's how he became a franchise icon in Philadelphia.

17

Jason Peters

To understand the brilliance of Jason Peters, consider this: when venerable Eagles offensive line coach Jeff Stoutland was hired in 2013 after three decades coaching college football, one of his linemen from Alabama sent him a message and asked if he would show Jason Peters the same Peters film he used to teach the college linemen.

"Ask any of the players I coached," Stoutland told reporters, "I teach the left tackle off of what [Peters] did."

Peters played in Philadelphia from 2009 to 2020. During that period, he made seven Pro Bowls—tied with Brian Dawkins and Reggie White for most in franchise history—and was twice named first-team All-Pro. His presence in the locker room and throughout the facility loomed large; he was someone who had the ear of everyone from an offensive tackle trying to make the roster to Jeffrey Lurie atop the organization. The Eagles' decision-makers did not simply consider Peters the best left tackle in the NFL while playing for the Eagles. They thought that about him *before* he played in Philadelphia. It was why they traded a first-round pick to acquire him as Tra Thomas' replacement.

"Jason Peters is the best left tackle in football," Andy Reid said in the press release announcing the trade for Peters.

Peters had been a tight end at Arkansas who was undrafted by the Buffalo Bills and learned offensive tackle at the behest of then coach Mike Mularkey while adjusting to the NFL. He was on the Bills' practice squad and became a special teams contributor before emerging as a starter in his second season. By Year 4, he was a Pro Bowler. By Year 6, the Eagles made him a franchise left tackle to replace Thomas, who held the position for more than a decade.

"We needed to replace Tra, and we tried to seek out the best left tackle in football," Reid said at the time. "That's how we went about it."

Peters lived up to the billing with the Eagles. He was a force for the Eagles in his first three seasons with the franchise, earning Pro Bowl honors each season and first-team All-Pro in 2011. When he tore his Achilles tendon in the spring of 2012, the Eagles could never recover from his absence. The team cratered, and a regime change came the following season. That was when Stoutland first coached Peters—and Chip Kelly saw the physical marvel that had amazed teammates and staffers.

"I don't think there is a player like him in the world, to be honest with you, someone that big, that fast, that athletic," Kelly said. "I catch myself in practice just going, 'Wow.' He's 350 pounds, and he runs like he's a tight end."

He earned the nickname "the Bodyguard." In a memorable 2014 game against Washington, Peters seemed to fight the entire opposing roster after a hit he deemed unnecessary on quarterback Nick Foles. Peters was ejected and fined. His teammates loved him for it.

"The guy just cheap-shotted Nick Foles, and I reacted," Peters said. "I shouldn't have done what I did, but I was just trying to protect my quarterback."

He also defied the typical age curve. The Eagles drafted Lane Johnson in 2013 to eventually replace Peters, who had already turned 30. Johnson played with Peters for nine seasons. The Eagles gave Peters a third contract extension before the 2017 season, when he was already 35.

"Do you want to win a Super Bowl, or do you want to save money?" Peters asked. "It's their decision. I give us a good chance on a line to help all the other guys and get where we want to go."

As it turned out, the Eagles won the Super Bowl without Peters. In Week 7 of the 2017 campaign, Peters clutched his knee early in the third quarter. The entire Eagles sideline—and the opponents' sideline—cleared to support Peters, who was carted off the field and eventually diagnosed with a torn anterior cruciate ligament. The Philadelphia crowd chanted his name. Peters barked instructions to Halapoulivaati Vaitai, his eventual replacement. And throughout the remainder of the season, Peters remained a presence in Vaitai's ear and around the team. When the Eagles won the Lombardi Trophy that Peters was so determined to keep playing to win, he walked out of the stadium holding the hardware. He had not played, but the respect was clear.

Even with a ring, Peters would not retire. He needed to prove that he could return from another major injury. Stoutland marveled at his recovery, claiming he would never count out Peters and believed Peters thrived on the idea that outsiders thought he was too old.

"Since I've been here, since 2013, all I've ever heard, 'Ahh, he's too old, he can't do it, he's not going to make it,' and he's proved everybody wrong, every single year," Stoutland said. "This is unbelievable...you might never see another Jason Peters again! I'm being honest with you now. This man is an absolute incredible, incredible player, who still shows...before he got hurt, OK, and he actually played a little bit while he was hurt, playing at an extremely high level."

But Peters never returned to his pre-injury level. The Eagles drafted Andre Dillard in 2019 with the plan to eventually take over for Peters, and the idea was for the transition to occur in 2020. Late in the 2019 season, when it seemed Peters was playing his final games in Philadelphia, he pushed back on the suggestion that he was in the twilight of his time in green.

"You're counting my opportunities. Not me," Peters said. "I roll. You tell me somebody better than me, and I'll walk away from the game."

After a beat, he asked: "You got somebody?"

You try being the one to tell Peters he's about to be replaced.

"OK then," he said. "I'm going to keep rolling."

Peters lingered on the market during the 2020 offseason with the Eagles set to turn to Dillard. When Brandon Brooks suffered a season-ending injury, the Eagles re-engaged with Peters...to play right guard. He agreed. Sure enough, Dillard was injured during training camp that season. Peters moved to left tackle after his contract was adjusted, although he could not stay healthy. He played eight games and finished the year on injured reserve.

Even if he might have outstayed his excellence, it did not tarnish his career with the Eagles. Until Peters' final season, he maintained an iconic—almost mythical—reputation with the Eagles. He called Lurie his best friend. He also would stay after practice and work with a rookie pass rusher or an undrafted lineman. He gave tips on finances—from 401(k) to NFL Players Association benefits—and always looked out for younger players in a quiet, behind-the-scenes way that did not often earn headlines but was understood around the locker room. I once asked Peters who served as *his* Peters when he came into the league. One of the answers was Jonas Jennings, a starter on the Bills at the time.

"Jason was a special kid. He worked hard. He didn't mind the extra work. And he wanted it," Jennings said in a 2019 interview. "I was a guy who stayed after practice a lot. So to see him jump onto my coattails and start to do those things, and [he] wanted to learn from a guy like myself, who was only [a] third-round pick making the league minimum? It was good to reach one, teach one. And [who] was a better guy than Jason?"

When it comes to playing left tackle for the Eagles, the answer is nobody.

PART 5

THE STANDOUTS

18

Jeremiah Trotter

During training camp in 2006, as a 29-year-old in his second of three stints with the Eagles, Jeremiah Trotter found the training room quiet one morning at Lehigh University.

"Listen," he told his younger teammates. "I've been cut before. It ain't a good feeling. You have to be excited to be here and take advantage of the opportunity to get better. Every chance you can be out here, you have to look at it as an opportunity to get better. You don't want to be sitting at home wishing you did something different."

This context is relevant when reflecting on Trotter's career, the best linebacker during this era with the Eagles who left, came back, left again, and came back again. He now has a spot in the franchise's Hall of Fame, which is especially noteworthy considering how contentious his departure once was.

"I want to thank Jeffrey Lurie and the Eagles organization for giving a small-town young kid the opportunity to play the game that he loves," Trotter said at midfield in 2016 when he was honored by the team with induction into the Eagles Hall of Fame.

That happened before the timeframe of this book—in 1998, when Ray Rhodes was still the coach, and Trotter slipped to the third round out of Stephen F. Austin because of a knee injury. He became a full-time starter in 1999, thriving under new defensive coordinator Jim Johnson. By 2000, he was a Pro Bowler and first-team All-Pro patrolling the middle of the Eagles defense. He celebrated a big play by mimicking the swinging of an ax, which became his trademark celebration and earned him the nickname "Axeman." It derived from his father chopping wood back home in Texas.

He could have—and perhaps should have—been one of those Eagles who played for a decade. However, he engaged in a bitter contract dispute in 2002 that resulted in the organization rescinding the franchise tag. Trotter felt disrespected and left for Washington and spent two seasons playing for an NFC East rival.

"It was tough because I wanted to be in Philly and my heart was here," Trotter told *Philadelphia Magazine* in a 2016 interview. "Negotiations fell through, and I had to make a decision for my family. For me, the toughest thing was leaving the city where I made my name. I really was one of those guys who bled green. I wore my heart on my sleeve and felt like I was as much a part of the city as the fans. I think it hurt me most that I just wasn't wearing the Philadelphia Eagles green and playing in front of the Philadelphia Eagles fans. It was great to come back; I felt like I was coming home. I remember I used to go home from Stephen F. Austin and visit my parents. I knew how my parents felt because that's how I felt coming back."

It didn't work in Washington. He injured his knee in his first season with the team and received an unexpected phone call—from Andy Reid, who was in charge of personnel during that bitter exit.

"I couldn't believe it," Trotter said in a 2004 *Washington Post* article. "It was an unexpected phone call from an unexpected person at a much-needed time. I was mentally down as well as physically down at the time. He called me and lifted my spirits."

Trotter was not the same player in 2003 and was released by Washington. This time, Trotter sought to make amends. He phoned Reid when Reid was on a fishing trip in a remote part of Utah, but somehow he connected with the coach. He wanted to return to Philadelphia. Trotter came back on a minimum contract. The plan was for him to play special teams and be a reserve linebacker.

Midway through the season, Johnson made a change and re-inserted Trotter into the starting lineup. It propelled the defense. He even made the Pro Bowl again—from only nine starts. The mid-career renaissance helped push the Eagles to the Super Bowl, with Trotter even recording a sack and an interception in the first postseason game before leading the team in tackles in the NFC Championship Game.

Trotter spent the next two seasons with the Eagles, even bypassing opportunities elsewhere because he had found the right fit. But in 2007, at age 30, the Eagles released him before the season when he no longer possessed the speed needed for the position. The departure was less acrimonious. In fact, Trotter even met with reporters at the team facility after the decision—an uncustomary gesture.

"I agree with his decision, too," Trotter said, according to the *Philadelphia Daily News*. "Obviously, I want to be here, but he's making a decision that he feels is best for the team. That's what this league is about; the turnover ratio is big every year.

They're always bringing in someone to try to better the team. Who knows what the future holds, but...now it's my time."

Surprisingly, the future held one more stint with the Eagles when he returned to the team in 2009. He played 13 games and one postseason game. It did not happen the way it was scripted, but he finished his career where it started.

There was no more ax to grind.

19

Brian Westbrook

BRIAN WESTBROOK CAN STAND WITH THE GREAT RUNNING backs of his era—but not necessarily back-to-back.

"I see Eddie George a lot," Westbrook explained over the phone during the summer of 2023, referencing the 6'3", 235-pound four-time Pro Bowler. "And when I stand next to Eddie George, he looks like a linebacker, a defensive end. And I look like a little kid."

He tells his kids they played the same position, and his children are in disbelief.

Westbrook was listed at 5'10" and 203 pounds. Nearly two decades later, running backs look more like Westbrook than George. And they certainly play more like him. Westbrook is one of the "all-time great Philadelphia Eagles"—words said by Andy Reid—and is in the franchise's Hall of Fame. Yet he only once topped 1,000 rushing yards in a season. Westbrook's brilliance lay in how many ways he could affect the game.

"In my mind, there has not been a more versatile running back that the NFL has seen," Reid said in 2010 when the team released Westbrook after eight seasons with the team.

Westbrook finished his Eagles career with more yards from scrimmage than any player in franchise history—9,785—and was only behind Wilbert Montgomery in rushing yards when he retired. But he also was ranked third in receptions at that time, which shows the different ways he was used. In some ways, Westbrook was ahead of time. He helped change the game.

"We were in an era of football where running backs got 25 carries in the game. They would do that for 16 weeks," Westbrook said. "And then I come along, and Andy said, 'OK, we're not going to give you 25 carries a game. We're going to give you 25 *touches* a game and you're gonna get it in a lot of different ways. And because of the different ways that you're going to touch the ball, we're going to keep the defense so off balance that they're not going to expect the deep ball down the field. They're not going to expect you lining up and running the corner route, running a post route, running across or catching the ball across the middle and then using the same skills that you have as a running back to exploit a defense. They're not going to expect that because they're not close back there. They're going to have three linebackers, at least, in the game. And now we're going to take advantage of that. 'Different mentality. Andy Reid was before his time that way because there was only one other team in the league doing that, and that was the Rams with Marshall Faulk.'"

Westbrook noted how running backs two decades later such as Christian McCaffrey and Alvin Kamara are used this way. And it's not a stretch to say there's a cause and effect. Ever use Westbrook in a video game? Ever have Westbrook on your team in a fantasy football league? (If it was the latter, you surely were not happy when Westbrook famously stopped short of the end zone in 2007 before it was en vogue.)

"I think part of that was brought by some of the things I was able to do at the position," Westbrook said. "Just a realistic view. Some of the guys that are coaching now, they were playing video games with me as a kid. And they were able to capitalize on some of the things I was able to do as a running back as a kid while playing video games.... They're using so many of those things to their advantage at this point. And clearly, some of that came from some of the things that we did offensively."

Westbrook was a college star at nearby Villanova, where he first came on Reid's radar. His versatility was apparent even then, topping 1,000 rushing yards and 1,000 receiving yards as a sophomore. He set an NCAA record during his college career with 9,885 all-purpose yards. His contributions with the Eagles started as part of a committee backfield and special teams standout, but he eventually became the lead running back. His ability to move around the formation left defenses flummoxed, and his ability to help as a runner and receiver made him a threat on any down. In 2007, Westbrook led the NFL with 2,104 yards from scrimmage in 15 games.

In a certain way, he helped change the game. When his children watch football, they see more running backs who look like their father than those who look like George.

"The era of football we're in now is much closer to [that than] what it was with Eddie George," Westbrook said. "Now you can't have a conversation about what's going on with the running backs without mentioning their ability to catch the ball out of the backfield."

Westbrook is one of the reasons.

20

DeSean Jackson

In 2018, while DeSean Jackson played for the Tampa Bay Buccaneers, he burned the Eagles for a 75-yard touchdown on the first play of the game in a fashion that had become too familiar—and vexing—for Eagles fans. Jackson later passed Eagles coach Doug Pederson on the sideline.

"You should have never let me go!" Jackson told him.

"I wasn't even there!" Pederson responded.

The reference was to 2014 when, in one of the most polarizing decisions during recent franchise history, the Eagles unceremoniously cut Jackson at the urging of then coach Chip Kelly.

At the time, Jackson was 27 and had just finished the best season of his career with 82 catches, 1,332 yards, and nine touchdowns. He was on pace to become one of the best players in franchise history. From 2008 when he was a second-round pick by the Eagles through 2013, Jackson totaled 6,117 yards (1,223 yards per season) and 39 total touchdowns. He had made the Pro Bowl three times and authored some of the most memorable moments, including the walk-off touchdown in the Miracle at the New Meadowlands in December 2010. Perhaps that career could have been even better had Jackson stayed healthier.

"At a young age, you don't have to look at how I'm taking care of my body, how I'm resting, how much I'm partying," Jackson said in 2019. "As you get older, you mature, you wake up and say, 'My body's hurting a little more,' maybe I need to sit in the hot tub longer, maybe I need to get to work earlier, get on the field and go stretch. Little things like that. As a young kid, when I was 24, I could wake up out of my bed and go run. I used to always say, 'Cheetahs don't stretch.' I looked at myself as a cheetah. But now I'm a little older, these joints hurt a little more."

There were non-football questions surrounding Jackson in the 2008 draft, which was part of the reason he slipped to the second round. Andy Reid wanted him and became an important figure in Jackson's life—a "father-son relationship," as Jackson termed it, which is a meaningful comment considering Jackson lost his father during his Eagles career.

Jackson was an instant star, which he admitted he did not handle as well as he could have. His desire for a new contract in 2011 affected his effort and production, and he was benched for a game after skipping a meeting.

When Kelly took over, Jackson thrived in the new offense, although there was an apparent personality clash. Kelly suggested it was a football decision precipitated by the salary cap—an NJ.com report had come out before the release linking Jackson to gang connections, so the timing was suspicious—but the end result was the Eagles lost one of their most dynamic players during the prime years of his career. During the next five seasons, Jackson made the Eagles pay. In six games against the Eagles, he surpassed 100 yards four times and scored three touchdowns. His teams beat the Eagles in five of those six games.

"There's no hard feelings. I understand this is a business. Things happen in this business," he said. "As a young kid, coming from Los Angeles, California, honestly, if I can sit here and tell you I was going to write out this story for it to be this way, I probably wouldn't have told you that. The best I can say is that you move forward in your life. After every step you take, you can't go backward."

In 2019, Howie Roseman sought to rectify the 2014 release by reacquiring Jackson. At that point in his career, Jackson was still a feared deep threat. But he was not the same player at age 33, and he could not stay healthy. He played in only eight games during two seasons, and the Eagles released him in February 2021 when the nostalgia had run its course and the bloated salary was more of an understandable rationale than it had been seven years earlier.

At the time of his (second) release, Jackson was No. 3 in franchise history in receiving yards, No. 4 in yards per catch, No. 6 in receptions, No. 9 in receiving yards, and tied for first in punt return touchdowns. He was truly one of the great players in franchise history. The sad part was wondering what those numbers could have been and how the record book would have looked had his Eagles career not been halted at age 27 when he still had more to offer.

21

Malcolm Jenkins

Malcolm Jenkins did not arrive in Philadelphia in 2014 with anything near the reputation he built when he left in 2020. The idea that Jenkins would be considered one of the most important Eagles of this era and that he would become an important figure in the city with a lasting legacy would not have been considered ambitious when he signed as a free agent—it might have been considered preposterous.

In a heralded class of free-agent safeties when the Eagles had a clear need at the position, Jenkins seemed like a fallback option. He was inexpensive and far from a headliner. The New Orleans Saints did not want him back. They replaced him with the top safety on the market, Jairus Byrd—the one who many Eagles fans wanted and who actually overlapped at Oregon with Chip Kelly, then the Eagles' head coach. But the Eagles were drawn to Jenkins' versatility and leadership. And Jenkins saw Philadelphia as a place where he could rescue his career.

"Personally, I was in a place where I felt like I was against the wall," Jenkins said during an interview in the fall of 2023. "I had just been let go by a team where I had envisioned playing for my whole career. I was a first-round draft pick, I was starting to feel like a bust, and so my drive and focus when I got to Philly was at an all-time high. Because in my mind, I signed a three-year deal. I figured I had two years to prove myself and I'd either be out of the league, or I [would] get an extension. That was my mentality every single day."

He came to Philadelphia with Darren Sproles. One day during his first spring, Sproles told him that others in the building thought he did not like being with the Eagles. When Jenkins asked why, the answer was that he walked around with his hood on and did not engage often.

"Hold on, I'm just focused!" Jenkins told him. "I love it here!"

Because in Jenkins' mind, this was his last chance to prove he was an NFL player. By the time he said farewell to Philadelphia after six seasons, he helped deliver the Eagles their first Super Bowl, earned three Pro Bowl invitations, barely missed a snap in games or practices, became one of the most important leaders in the organization, developed into a powerful voice for social justice, and built an enduring presence in the Philadelphia community.

As Jenkins explained, what he demands from himself "naturally spreads throughout the room." He wanted to lift weights next to the defensive linemen. When he pulled the weights they did, he wondered who was slacking.

"It's hard for you to slack if the person next to you is going hard every day," Jenkins said. "And I'm not quiet about it."

This was partly inherent to his personality. He earned a scholarship at Ohio State when his parents enrolled him at a football camp during a summer visit to Columbus, Ohio.

Jenkins' family paid for him to attend—he was not a top recruit with an invitation. But the other top defensive backs did not want to defend the best receivers in the Midwest. Jenkins did not mind. He runs toward challenges, not away from them. He kept going to the front of the line. He did not back down. The Ohio State coaches noticed.

When he was drafted by New Orleans, he learned from leaders such as Roman Harper, Jonathan Vilma, and Drew Brees. So when he came to Philadelphia, the way he was wired became infectious—to some, at least.

"It makes people either not like me or they buy in," Jenkins said, "and most of the time when you have people who want to win and want to be great, they buy in."

In Jenkins' first home game with the Eagles, the team started slow against Jacksonville. Fans shared their frustration. Jenkins loved it. He was with his people. This passion was what he wanted. It helped fuel him.

When Jenkins intercepted passes in three of his first four games with the Eagles, it became clear that he was a prize for the franchise. Saints coach Sean Payton later said that his biggest regret was letting Jenkins leave in free agency. Jenkins made sure to credit Kelly and defensive coordinator Bill Davis for valuing his versatility and allowing him to play a role "complementary" to his skill set. In New Orleans, he was mostly a free safety. But in Philadelphia, he played all over the field—including the slot, linebacker, and both safety spots.

However, Jenkins was not convinced it would be the perfect match in Philadelphia until 2015—a forgettable year for the organization—when the Eagles were mired in losing. He made comments on the radio about team accountability. The coaching staff did not like that he was publicly outspoken about it. Jenkins backed up his words by scoring a touchdown in an upset of the New England Patriots. At the time, Kelly did not have captains on the Eagles. Jenkins thought the way he played—and led—that week helped improve his reputation in the organization. The Eagles rewarded him with a contract extension that offseason, ensuring he remained a core player with the team. He won the back-against-the-wall bet on himself he made two years earlier.

"I never played for the money. It let me know they valued me," Jenkins said. "I was thinking when I got there, [that] I might be two years from being at home.... And in those two years, I had solidified myself as somebody that not only the team but the city wanted to keep around."

After the coaching change in 2016, Jenkins continued to flourish under Doug Pederson and new defensive coordinator Jim Schwartz. With Schwartz, Jenkins found a similarly competitive person who valued Jenkins' game and his mind. Jenkins' best seasons came under Schwartz, and the Pro Bowl honors started to follow. Jenkins used to walk through a corridor in the team facility and knock on the wall that featured photos of the organization's Pro Bowlers. He wanted his picture in that space. Walk in that space now, and you will see No. 27.

Schwartz said Jenkins played seven of the 11 different positions in his defense—and "knew all 11 like a coach." Whereas other players might make a couple of mistakes per game, Jenkins' mistakes happened maybe once a season.

"I've thought a lot over the years about all the great players I've coached, and Malcolm goes right up there," Schwartz said in 2020. "He's probably the smartest player I ever coached, and leadership-wise you take all those players, if he was on that [team] he would probably be elected team captain.... I don't think I've ever been around a smarter player. We were playing Seattle [during the 2019 season], and he heard the offensive line say something about a look that we had, and it's the only time I remember him doing this in four years. He came to the sideline and said, 'Schwartz, next third down call, I guarantee we're going to get a sack.' I had so much trust in him that next third down I called it, and it happened exactly the way that he said, and we got the sack. But it was all just because of what he heard. He heard the offensive line talking about, 'Hey, next time we get this look, this is what we have to do.' That is rare in a player. That's rare that a player can understand what the offense is doing so well and can decipher things like that."

During the 2017 season, Jenkins helped lead the Eagles to their first Super Bowl. He was productive on the field and instrumental in the locker room. When Carson Wentz tore his ACL in December that season, Jenkins offered a stirring locker room speech to energize—and direct—a team that could have been dispirited. He was the one who brought the team together before games. He wore a "C" on his chest for a reason.

But that season was similarly marked by Jenkins' activism. He was leading the Players Coalition during a turbulent period that included President Donald Trump publicly rebuking those who took a knee during the national anthem. Jenkins did not take a knee, but he raised his fist. Among players, there were disagreements about the coalition accepting the league's pledge for social causes. In his free time, Jenkins met with lawmakers and community officials.

Jenkins also had turbulence in his personal life. He met with a therapist and admitted in his 2023 book, *What Winners Won't Tell You*, that he had suicidal thoughts. When the Eagles finally won the Super Bowl, Jenkins described the moment as a relief.

Not joy—relief. For someone who was always mindful of his words, this was selective syntax.

"It was the highest amount of stress I ever had in my life," Jenkins said. "When it was over, that's all I felt. It was a release. I could breathe now."

Jenkins explained that he became "really good at compartmentalizing" while in Philadelphia, almost to his own detriment. The way he framed it, he learned how to "be where my feet were." When it was practice, he practiced. (And the only time he missed practice was during a concussion recovery, when the league forbade him from being a full participant.) In the film room, he watched film. In the weight room, he would look across the street from the NovaCare Complex and see the stadium as a reminder of why he was putting in all the work. He would not allow his mind to drift away from football while playing football, and he tried to avoid worrying about football while away from work.

When Jenkins reflected on his Eagles career, he was actually most proud of the 2018 and 2019 seasons. In those years, the Eagles were ransacked by injuries and still rallied to make the playoffs. Jenkins did not miss a game. He said the team survived on "sheer will" and didn't fracture—a reality that he felt partly responsible for upholding.

"It took the most effort as a leader, as a player," Jenkins said. "I knew I couldn't miss a game. I couldn't miss a snap. I knew I had to adjust my playing style in the game, in the scheme that we ran, so that we could execute and give ourselves a chance with a little bit less talent than we wanted. And we just went off togetherness."

By the end of the 2019 season, Jenkins knew his career in Philadelphia was finished. The franchise did not offer him a contract before the season. He felt the organization did not value him as much as he valued himself. He does not have regrets about his time with the Eagles, although he wishes he could have acknowledged the finality before he played in the January 2020 postseason game.

The ending seemed to come with bitterness, as is often the case when a marquee player is forced to finish his career elsewhere. But it ended up working out well for Jenkins. He had finalized a divorce and his ex-wife and children relocated to New Orleans. Free agency allowed him to sign with the Saints and remain near his children.

Even though he finished his career elsewhere, Jenkins is most remembered for his time in Philadelphia. He considers the city home, and the franchise formally honored him during the 2023 season. Before games, Jenkins would glance to the top of Lincoln Financial Field. He wanted to be recognized in the stadium's rafters on both sides—with the team honors and the individual honors. There's a Super Bowl banner hanging that he helped deliver. And he might one day enter the franchise's Hall of Fame. That thought might have been considered preposterous in 2014.

One decade later, his imprint on the organization and city is undeniable.

"I want to be remembered as someone who led with love in every aspect of life," Jenkins said. "I want somebody to watch my games or talk about me as a player [and say], 'He loved this game. He loved his teammates. He loved to compete. He loved the city.' I want them to see me in the communities, that he loved people. I want them to see me as a family man, and so he loved his family and friends. That's how I try to live my life. And I hope that part is recognized in everything I do."

22

Lane Johnson

By Lane Johnson's second decade in the NFL, an opinion about him became accepted as conventional wisdom. It was not hyperbole. It was not a hot take for ratings. It was the type of observation that could be stated as fact.

"Lane to me is one of the best tackles in the world," Nick Sirianni said in 2022 before Johnson's 11th NFL season. "He is the best right tackle in the world."

Chris Long, Johnson's former teammate and a close friend, called Johnson a "future Hall of Famer" on his *Green Light* podcast a few months later. And Long also wondered if Johnson did not get the appreciation that he deserved. Because Johnson has become one of the great players of his generation, an iconic Eagle whose dominance is realized when considering what some of the top pass-rushers don't do against him. He went on a two-year stretch without allowing a sack. He stonewalled the Defensive Player of the Year in the NFC Championship Game.

The Eagles build game plans knowing they can leave Johnson on an island on the right side of the line of scrimmage, almost like putting a bill on automatic payment and knowing it will post each month.

Johnson was not always viewed with such reverence—at least by the public. There was a time earlier in his career when he was so infuriated about a Pro Bowl snub that he drove to the team facility at 2:30 AM after he was left off the roster and slept in the locker room. Another snub a few years later continued to leave him incensed. He played the position as well as anyone, but because he was on the right side and not the left side, he was not given the same type of respect.

"The whole thing was you could play good at right tackle, I had really good early years, but it was always left tackle/right tackle dilemma," Johnson explained in the summer of 2023. "Maybe I would have had more accolades if I was a right tackle all along. But sometimes things take time to develop.... When I came in, the right tackle/left tackle dilemma was [not] what it was now."

In fact, Eagles general manager Howie Roseman believes that Johnson changed the NFL because he was the face of the transformation of how left tackles and right tackles were viewed. The league had traditionally viewed the left tackle as the superior offensive lineman because he protected a right-handed quarterback's blindside. Michael Lewis wrote a best-selling book with this premise, and it was turned into a feature film. Contracts reflected as much. Pro Bowl voting, too.

"I think what it changed for me was this perception that right tackle is different than left tackle," Roseman said during the spring of 2023. "He really changed the game."

Johnson did not grow up as a right tackle. He did not even grow up as an offensive tackle. He was a high school quarterback in Groveton, Texas, with a graduating class of 33 students. At 6'6" and 200 pounds, he wanted to be Brett Favre. No major college saw him as Favre. He went to junior college at Kilgore College, trying to earn attention as a quarterback that way. He learned he was not a quarterback. It was a difficult season for Johnson, who moved to tight end. He added 50 pounds and his athleticism was apparent. Major colleges noticed—including Oklahoma. Johnson went to the powerhouse and became a defensive end. Sooners coach Bob Stoops needed offensive linemen and wondered what it would take for Johnson, then 270 pounds, to reach 300 pounds. "A cheeseburger and a week," the strength coach said.

It took only a couple of weeks at Johnson's new position for Stoops to think he could become a first- or second-round pick in the NFL. Johnson played two seasons as an offensive tackle at Oklahoma, and his draft stock ascended to the point that he earned an invitation to the Senior Bowl. At that point in the draft process, the thought was that Johnson would go within the first three rounds. Johnson had his sights set higher. In fact, Johnson and his agent, Ken Sarnoff, chatted with the Indianapolis Colts general manager in the lobby of a hotel in Mobile, Alabama, and the executive paid the compliment that Johnson reminded him of the offensive tackle the Colts drafted two years earlier. Sarnoff appreciated the compliment. Johnson fumed. He did not think that lineman could "hold my f—n' jock." Johnson was named the Senior Bowl's Most Outstanding Lineman that week and his draft stock continued to skyrocket. He was viewed as a potential first-round pick, although Johnson was ready to show he was one of the best prospects in the draft. On the night before his athletic testing at the scouting combine, he dined with Sarnoff at Ruth's Chris Steak House in downtown Indianapolis and looked Sarnoff in the eyes while making this declaration: "I'm going to rip this f—ing combine to such a level that these motherf—s have never seen anything like it. And when it's all said and done, I'm gonna go top five."

Johnson's pledge could be taken to the bank. (It was a lucrative pledge, too.) He measured 6'6" and 303 pounds and his 40-yard dash finished in the 99th percentile, his broad jump finished in the 98th percentile, his vertical jump finished in the 96th percentile, and his three-cone drill finished in the 94th percentile. It was the type of workout that remains a part of combine lore. The top two offensive tackles were considered Eric Fisher and Luke Joeckel. Johnson had pushed his name into their category.

"You have a 6'6"-plus, 310-pound guy that runs a 4.7 40; that's faster than Anquan Boldin did," then NFL Network analyst Mike Mayock and future Raiders general manager said before the 2013 draft. "He's jumped 34 inches, that's the same as A.J. Green. He broad jumps 9'10", the same as Stevan Ridley. So you have a 300-pounder who is putting up numbers at the combine like a skill position player. And everybody around the league and around the country now is starting to realize, wait a minute, we have this unbelievably freakish athlete who has only played a year and a half at left tackle, and every game you put on gets a little better. And how good could he get? That's what's fueling all this. Fisher might be safer and Joeckel might be the safest. But this kid's ceiling is unlimited, and you might have a perennial All-Pro for 10 years, and I think that's what's happening."

The Eagles drafted No. 4 overall in the first year under Chip Kelly. It was their highest draft pick since taking Donovan McNabb in 1999. However, this was not considered a particularly strong class of quarterbacks. So when the Eagles would typically look at a quarterback to reset the franchise, the top position in this draft was offensive tackle. Fisher and Joeckel went Nos. 1 and 2 that season. New Eagles offensive line coach Jeff Stoutland had traveled to Texas to put Johnson through a private workout and left smitten with the prospect. Johnson might not have been the most refined at the time, but his upside was the highest—as Mayock alluded to in the pre-draft comments.

"I remember [Stoutland] said to Howie, he said to me, he said to the room, 'This player is not the best tackle day one, but if we just look at who is going to be the best tackle in the draft in two years, three years, this guy is going to be so much better than the other two tackles,'" Lurie said in 2022. "From that, I'm thinking, 'Gosh, if we're in a position where we're choosing between two players or Lane is [there], we really need to elevate Lane to a position to where we have a chance to have him.' He was right, and Stout's been right a lot more than he's been wrong ever since."

When Dion Jordan—a potential Eagles target—went No. 3 in a trade to Miami, the Eagles took Johnson. However, they had a franchise left tackle. Jason Peters was returning from an injury, but he was entrenched in the position.

The thinking was that Johnson would play right tackle until Peters retired, considering Peters was already 31. But Peters played in Philadelphia for nearly a decade longer! Johnson settled in at right tackle, and he did not want to move. Plus, the NFL changed, too. The top pass rushers no longer rushed entirely from the quarterback's blind side. (And for what it's worth, the left-handed Michael Vick was the first quarterback Johnson protected, so Johnson technically protected the blind side.) Johnson saw the NFL's top pass rushers coming from the defensive left. It became imperative for teams to have athletic tackles on the right side, too.

Johnson's run as the Eagles right tackle has been mostly top-level play, interrupted by notable absences. Early in his career, Johnson missed four games in his second season due to suspension for a performance-enhancing substance. In 2016, he was suspended 10 games as a second-time offender. Johnson blasted the NFL Players Association, suggesting that the supplement he took had been approved by the union, although there were unlisted ingredients that caused him to fail the test. Nonetheless, the suspension was upheld, and Johnson's reputation was tainted. The Eagles went 2–8 without him. "I failed the team," Johnson said. He returned in 2017 vowing to avoid anything that could cause a test, and that he was "pissed off" with the plan to take it out on the league.

"All last year, ever since I left the building, I had a long time to think," Johnson said. "When I got back on the field, I was going to make it count. I was going to make my opponents remember who I am. So whenever you game-plan the Eagles, you better know who I am. That's been my whole mentality."

He weighed 325 pounds, adhering to a new diet and trying to prove any doubters wrong. When one defender that season called him "'roid boy," Johnson took it personally. There was a stretch during the Super Bowl season in which Johnson played Pro Bowlers each week, and he blocked them better than anyone else. Then Denver Broncos edge rusher Von Miller, one of the NFL's stars, told the *Denver Post* that Johnson was the NFL's premier right tackle. Johnson maintained that title, and in 2019, the Eagles gave him a contract that made him the highest-paid tackle in the NFL—regardless of side. It was validation that it did not matter whether he played on the left or right. He was perhaps the best in the league. Except he only made the Pro Bowl as a replacement player. And he knew that five of the six offensive tackles voted into the All-Star Game on the initial ballot played on the left side.

"I'm just trying to validate right tackles—that's really it," Johnson said at the Pro Bowl that year. "It's still seen as a left tackle's game. I'm trying to change that."

In 2020, Johnson's lingering ankle injury required surgery. And in 2021, Johnson left the team after three games. There was concern about his wellbeing. He eventually returned and explained that he had been dealing with anxiety and depression. He cycled off his SSRI antidepressant medication and had reached a breaking point. He drove 22 hours back home to Oklahoma. The Eagles remained mum on his whereabouts and his status. In his time away, team security chief Dom DiSandro and right guard and close friend Brandon Brooks were confidants. He vowed to try to destigmatize mental health, a pledge that he maintained in the subsequent seasons.

"Lane Johnson and what he's openly come back from this year and to think...the amount of people that he's given hope to," Jason Kelce said in 2021 with tears in his eyes. "And that's the business we're in.... We're in the business of hope. What we do every day, what we do every game inspires millions of people. What we do off the field hopefully inspires people."

On the field, Johnson might never have been better. He did not allow a sack throughout the remainder of the 2021 season and during the 2022 campaign, when he was named first-team All-Pro. And any discussions about him often mentioned that he might be the best offensive tackle in the NFL—no matter the side. Because Johnson is finally on the right side of history.

23

Zach Ertz

Zach Ertz learned that he would be traded before his final game in an Eagles uniform in 2021. He still wanted to play—and the Eagles were willing to let him, injury risk and all—because of the significance of the moment for Ertz. Even with a rocky end to his nine-year career with the franchise, Ertz wanted to run out of the tunnel one more time in an Eagles uniform. He wanted to experience the emotion of scoring a touchdown and hearing the fight song (which he did) and the adulation of a crowd that he came to adore.

Had his exit occurred one season earlier, which Ertz expected, he would not have had that moment because the stadium was empty due to COVID-19. This was a chance for Ertz to say farewell, even if the details of the trade were not yet known to the public.

"This is home," Ertz said after he was traded to Arizona. "Philadelphia is home."

Ertz could not imagine the city would steal his heart when he arrived in 2013 from a cross-country flight tired and nervous. He was a 22-year-old lifelong Californian brimming with talent. He became hardened by early-career criticism and left as someone who loved Philadelphia—the fans, the city, the franchise. As he explained it, he grew up in Philadelphia. His mother and one of his brothers made the city his home. It's where he became a husband and started a foundation committed to making lives better for kids who knew him only as No. 86.

He wanted to stay and finish his playing days wearing that number in Eagles green, just like his favorite athletes who spent their careers in one place such as Kobe Bryant, his favorite basketball player, and Jason Witten, his favorite tight end. He arrived with the Eagles as an understudy for Brent Celek, who played only in Philadelphia. But it did not make sense for either side in the end, and anything that ends usually does not end well. Nary a player writes his own farewell. That did not obscure the reality that Ertz was one of the great players in franchise history. He caught the game-winning touchdown in Super Bowl 52, offering him immortality in Philadelphia. He rewrote record books, setting the NFL record for most receptions by a tight end in the season and leaving just shy of Harold Carmichael's franchise career record. Howie Roseman called Ertz an "Eagles Hall of Famer"—that seems to be a lock—and a potential Pro Football Hall of Famer.

"I'm not the greatest Eagle by any means, but I think just in today's world, just handling this city, I would say for you young players, [this] city's tough. But [the fans] are honest," Ertz said in January 2021. "Whether you had a great day or a terrible day, they don't want any excuses, and I don't think I ever made an excuse.... I think this city is the best city to play for, and I couldn't have asked for a better experience. The city means a lot to me, it means a lot to my family, and I'm thankful."

Ertz's early seasons with the Eagles included tantalizing talent, but there was an ongoing belief that Ertz could be better. Fantasy football players became fatigued by the annual storyline of an upcoming "breakout" season. A low point might have been in 2016, when Ertz failed to block a defender chasing after Carson Wentz along the sideline in a loss to Cincinnati. Ertz's toughness was questioned.

"I was in the dumps a little bit," Ertz said. "That definitely puts things in perspective."

That sparked a turnaround in 2017, when Ertz reached the Pro Bowl for the first time and was entrenched among the NFL's top tight ends. He supplanted Celek as the top tight end in Philly. He reworked his body to try to avoid soft-tissue injuries—he even appeared in *ESPN The Magazine*'s body issue with his wife, soccer star Julie Johnson (née). He became more spiritual after observing the way teammates dealt with criticism and adversity.

The go-ahead touchdown in the Super Bowl seemingly responded to any charge levied against him. One was that he does not gain yards after the catch. On the decisive score, Ertz caught the ball around the 5-yard line and pushed through contact to reach the end zone. There was a belief that he padded stats in meaningless moments of insignificant games. A third-down in the red zone with the game on the line in the Super Bowl is a sufficient answer; there was not a more significant moment in his career.

"The fans never gave up on me," Ertz said. "I told them at the time that they would never question my effort again, and I am lucky to be in this situation playing for this city. I will never take it for granted."

The Super Bowl parade also signaled Ertz's personal growth. Few might remember his speech. (They remember the man he followed: Jason Kelce.) But for Ertz, who stuttered and needed speech therapy as a kid and had his opening press conference cut short because of the nerves of the moment, a short speech in front of 700,000 at the parade was evidence of the strides he had made.

"I'm not going to be perfect on the field, I'm not going to be perfect in my postgame answers or any media session," Ertz said. "I just focus on taking a deep breath, staying calm, and trying not to make the situation bigger than it is."

There were plenty of big moments left for him. In 2018, he set an NFL record for tight ends with 116 receptions to go along with 1,163 yards—making him the only 1,000-yard pass-catcher of the Doug Pederson era. In 2019, Ertz gave an emotional speech to his teammates about "burning the ships" on the night before a critical win over Dallas to keep their postseason hopes alive. Ertz suffered a cracked rib and lacerated kidney in the game and still returned for the postseason.

Talk about toughness.

His final season and a half in Philadelphia were less memorable. The Eagles were ready to turn the position over to Dallas Goedert and were not prepared to pay Ertz a big contract. Ertz said he wanted to stay and did not feel as if that was a mutual sentiment. Ertz thought he would be traded during the 2021 offseason, but the Eagles resisted while seeking better compensation. When they could not find the price they sought, they carried him into the season. Ertz did not take a scorched-Earth approach, instructing his agent against leaks or trying to ruffle feathers to force his way out of Philadelphia.

"I love this city too much to burn it down, like some people wanted me to do at times," Ertz said.

He dyed his hair as part of a bet with Kelce about how long he would last with the team. But he also found joy in the process—at a random training camp session, on another mundane route on another mundane day. When Bryant spoke to the Eagles during their 2017 trip to the West Coast, Ertz asked the NBA superstar for his favorite book. Bryant said it was *Jonathan Livingston Seagull* by Richard Bach, and Ertz bought it the next day. Ertz has worn the book out, learning that he must embrace being "lonely in your pursuit of greatness."

"I don't think you show up 16 times a [season] and go into the Eagles Hall of Fame," Ertz said. "You've got to show up each and every day. I love to practice.... I love the process of going to work on a Wednesday morning. I love the process of going to training camp practice on a Thursday when I don't feel like practicing, my body's telling me you really can't practice today, but mentally just preparing myself for when things are going poorly. Because I know they are going to go poorly at some point in the season, so telling my mind and my body that it's time to go. So I love the process. I love this game. And I think that's what [being] a Philadelphia Eagle is all about. Showing up all the time, doing your best, living with the results and then improving from there."

That is someone who knew Philadelphia. That's someone who loved Philadelphia. And even if his career brought him to Arizona, he still considered Philadelphia home.

"If you told me coming into the league that I'd be second all-time in this organization's history, it would be an unbelievable achievement," Ertz said. "Who knows? Maybe I'll come back to this organization and get 12 catches and Harold would go to No. 2."

24
Brandon Graham

THE MERE SUGGESTION THAT BRANDON GRAHAM WOULD BE included in "The Standouts" would have seemed outrageous 10 years ago. If there was a section reserved for draft busts, Graham would have expected to read his name there early in his career. That's how he was viewed—or at least what he was told.

The fact that Graham still played in Philadelphia for his 15th season, is ascending in different sections of franchise record books, is beloved in Philadelphia, and is responsible for the most important sack in franchise history shows the extraordinary turn his story took during his Eagles career.

"A little bit of my attitude and a little bit of luck," Graham said, "got me to this place."

The Eagles drafted Graham No. 13 overall in 2010—famously ahead of safety Earl Thomas, who could have replaced Brian Dawkins at safety. Graham's early seasons were stalled by injury and scheme changes. His enthusiasm radiated in abundance, but there was far less patience for it when he was not sacking the quarterback and Thomas was making Pro Bowls.

In fact, Graham feared the Eagles would cut him before the 2014 season. He was a reserve outside linebacker entering his fifth NFL season, long enough past the built-in time cushion allotted to high draft picks. The Eagles were intrigued by a little-known edge rusher named Travis Long who had spent the previous season on the practice squad. They were in a training camp competition and Graham suspected that he would be the odd man out.

"For sure, I knew I was gone," Graham remembered.

Long tore his ACL in the final preseason game, preserving a roster spot for Graham. Graham responded with 5.5 sacks while playing fewer than half of the defensive snaps. That turnaround season prompted the Eagles to sign him to a new contract the following offseason, and Graham found a second life for the Eagles. The narrative about him changed.

"I started focusing on myself and not worrying about what people [were] saying—that he's not living up to [being a] first-rounder," Graham said in 2014. "I mean, I got hurt. I was starting to feel real good and then I got hurt and I had to work from the ground up."

By 2016, he was a second-team All-Pro. By 2017, Graham was one of the best players on the Eagles. The signature movement of his career came on the grandest stage, when Graham sacked Tom Brady and dislodged the football to help clinch the Eagles' victory in Super Bowl LII.

If Graham retired that day, it would still qualify as a storied career. But Graham became a football version of fine wine, saving his best work for his thirties. In 2019 and 2020, which were his 10th and 11th seasons in the NFL, he combined for 16.5 sacks. He made his first Pro Bowl in 2020.

In 2021, Graham tore his Achilles tendon in the second game of the season. It was the type of injury that could end a career at that age. He returned in 2022, accepted a reduced role, and had the most productive season of his career. His 11 sacks were the first time he reached double-digits. He was elected as the Eagles' candidate for Man of the Year. He reached his second Super Bowl as a venerable team captain.

Graham's legacy in Philadelphia will not only be a well-rounded playing style that has put him among the franchise leaders in sacks and made him a reliable run defender on the edge. It will not just be a career turnaround that ranks as one of the most improbable in Eagles history, considering what he used to read when searching his Twitter replies as a 25-year-old.

Rather, ask teammates and coaches about Graham, and it is his unending enthusiasm that sticks out. He talks all game, from the coin toss to the handshakes. He's loud in the locker room and on the practice field. (Some would argue too loud. Jason Kelce jokes that Graham doesn't have to block the defensive players he instigates.) He calls it "good juju," and even if it is not fake, it can at times be manufactured.

"I don't know what the hell he's doing," Lane Johnson said, "but he ain't never had a bad day."

"That's a choice," Graham said. "Sometimes you need it, sometimes you need to fake it until you get the real energy."

Because it's contagious. A sports locker room can be like any office, where an employee can bring energy or sap it. And the NovaCare Complex is a better place because Graham is there.

"Brandon Graham is in my all-time favorite people to coach," Eagles assistant coach Jeremiah Washburn said. "He's Mr. Eagle. But even behind closed doors—and I say this, I'll be careful with comparison—I was in Baltimore as a young guy with Ray Lewis, and Ray Lewis was Ray Lewis behind the closed doors as much as in front of the cameras. And that's what Brandon Graham is. Brandon Graham in the meeting room, the locker rooms, one-on-one, all those things, he's always in tune, his energy's palpable. [Those are] the things he does for the rookie free agents, the people around the building. And he's a productive player that shows up the same way."

He is the random teammate's favorite teammate, which says something. Graham is not the 15-year veteran who's only confiding with the 30-somethings. He's not just keeping in touch with the franchise icons. Everyone from Chris Long to Travis Long—yes, Travis Long—would gush about Graham. In fact, Graham exchanged messages with Travis Long upon reaching the Pro Bowl in 2020.

It is good juju, and it's not a stretch to say it helped him last so long. He said it's a little bit of attitude and a little bit of luck, but it's been more than a "little bit" of attitude. It makes sense for Graham to be loud, because the one with the last laugh can laugh loudest.

"To go from 'he's a bust' to Super Bowl champions," Graham once said of his story. "Don't ever give up. No matter what people say, no matter how things seem to be going at that time, there's always light at the end of the tunnel. Even if it's a light speck, just open it up and keep on believing."

25

Brandon Brooks

The mortality inherent in a professional football career was apparent on January 26, 2022, when Brandon Brooks retired at age 32. He had missed 32 of his past 34 games at that point because of injuries, and with accumulating rehab periods putting his playing days peril, he said farewell to football.

"At what point do you listen to your body?" Brooks asked.

Two years earlier, he had been perhaps the best player at his position. Football has a way of making you go from the highest-paid guard in the NFL to applying to business school in 27 months.

Then again, Brooks had no problem appearing human. Good luck finding great athletes who appeared more vulnerable than Brooks. One of his lasting legacies as a professional athlete is honesty about mental health and his struggles with anxiety.

"It has always been a part of me, it will always be a part of me," Brooks said when he retired. "I want to be known as a person who was transparent, somebody who really wanted to help others by sharing my story. It will always be a part of my story."

Brooks signed with the Eagles in 2016 after four years in Houston. Offensive line coach Jeff Stoutland met with him when he arrived and offered a Staten Island version of a compliment. He had good tape, but if he could just keep his hands inside.... Oh, and also, he needed to do X, Y, and Z better. Brooks knew then he could reach another gear in Philadelphia.

Except Brooks missed two games during his first year in Philadelphia. It was first thought to be stomach problems, which had been explained as the reasons for absences in Houston. Brooks later learned he had an anxiety condition. He wanted to be perfect on every snap—as he described it, if he had 79 great plays in a game, he would only focus on the 80th that went wrong—and this tendency had debilitating effects.

"It's a double-edged sword," Brooks said. "It pushes you to be great, but sooner or later it will bubble to the surface."

He vomited before every game. This was the first time he learned why.

Then Brooks made a decision that changed his public perception—and changed his life. He decided to share what happened and take whatever scrutiny followed. He compared walking to his corner locker past teammates, microphones, and cameras "like walking down death row." The public reaction was overwhelmingly supportive, although initially, Brooks found internal resistance.

"I think back in '16, it wasn't talked about a lot," Brooks said when reflecting a few years later. "I was new to the team. At the same time, I have to put myself in my teammates' [shoes]. There's a guy from a different squad, he comes in, has an anxiety deal, X, Y, and Z. Now I've proven myself, they know what type of guy I am, people are familiar with me, things like that. So people are a lot more understanding as far as what's going on. And even back then, you had people say it's not real. But after having been with me for years, people see me go through it daily, guys know it's something I deal with every day."

Brooks started meeting weekly with a therapist. He found ways to accept anxiety as part of his life. It also helped that Brooks excelled when he returned to the field. It did not take long for Brooks to be considered among the best offensive guards in the NFL. He earned Pro Bowl invitations from 2017 to 2019, and the reverence with which teammates viewed him validated that he was an elite player. Even when he tore his Achilles tendon in the postseason following the 2018 season, he returned the next year even better. He did not even miss a game.

"The biggest thing everybody's forgetting is I tore my Achilles before, and when I came back, I was the best. *Period,*" Brooks said.

"The way he just embraced that whole situation and fought through all adversity and came back with such a positive attitude, I never once saw him down in the tank, worrying about him or 'Why me?' or any of that," Stoutland said.

Brooks was so good in 2019 that the Eagles rewarded him with another contract that was set to pay him $56.2 million through four years, giving him the highest average annual salary among offensive guards at the time. This could have been viewed as further validation during a career that did not need any more validation.

But the contract—and associated expectations—exacerbated the anxiety conditions. He reminded himself why he earned the money, which made sense as a rationalization but not as a coping mechanism. In Week 12 of the 2019 season, the nausea that was usually limited to mornings for Brooks extended to the pregame preparation. He was set to play without Lane Johnson, his partner on the right side of the offensive line. During pregame introductions, Brooks stayed behind, exhausted and dehydrated. He received fluids from an IV, but it could not improve his mental state. He played two drives before leaving the game, vomiting between the drives and having what he described as an "out-of-body" experience.

"I wanted to...show my teammates, when I say I'll do whatever it takes to be out there, I will do whatever it takes to be out there," Brooks said. "No matter what type of state I was in. So if I felt I was able to go in my weakened state or dehydrated or whatever, I was going to try to go. That probably was the first time that, no matter what was happening, I still came out and tried and played. I think it was also the first time that the team, as a majority, was able to see it live, happening, during an actual game."

A few days later, he went public again. This time, he knew what to expect. Brooks managed the anxiety, but his physical health became the problem. Injuries mounted later that season, that offseason, and the next year. He played in only 32 of his final 34 games with the Eagles. That prompted his retirement.

"He has been dealt adversity time and time again. From anxiety to injuries...it can break a person," Stoutland told the team website upon Brooks' retirement. "But it didn't break him, it made him stronger. It's a lesson to everyone in that room, that building, the city."

The way it ended did not overshadow the way it went. His time in Philadelphia was relatively short—six seasons, two of which were mired by injury. But his first four years, and the 2017–19 window in particular, gave him a lasting legacy in Philadelphia. It's hard to play offensive guard much better.

"You can't have joy without sadness," Brooks said. "The first four years, I wouldn't trade for the two if I had to weather these last two."

Even more, he'll be remembered for a courage that goes beyond returning from a torn Achilles tendon. It's become common for athletes to appear vulnerable with mental health challenges. Brooks helped pave the way. Soon after his first announcement, a note was tucked under his door in his Center City Philadelphia apartment. *Don't worry about being perfect. Our imperfections are what make us who we are.*

It was this sentiment that encouraged him to become a face, and perhaps even inspiration, for those who needed to leap the same hurdles he did. It is hard to play football as well as Brooks and be remembered for something different. His vulnerability allowed him to achieve immortality in the franchise's history.

PART 6

THE SUPER BOWL SEASON

26

2017

"Do you understand what we just did, bro?" Eagles linebacker Mychal Kendricks asked in a quiet moment in the Minneapolis locker room on February 4, 2018, minutes after the Eagles won the first Super Bowl in franchise history. "First time in Philly history!"

On that night, the players knew what has since come to bear. The 2017 Eagles are forever beloved. Before Game 6 of the 1974 Stanley Cup Final, Philadelphia Flyers coach Fred Shero wrote on the chalkboard, Win today and we walk together forever. That sentiment could be shared by the 2017 Eagles. They won that night in Minnesota over the New England Patriots, and they will walk together forever. As Malcolm Jenkins said in his postgame speech, "Be legendary! That s— is etched in stone!"

It's always special when a team wins a Super Bowl, no matter the circumstances. It matters more when it's the *first* time, and

Eagles fans will forever remember the first team of the Super Bowl era to finally bring a parade to Broad Street. But another part of a team's charm is when the winning is not necessarily expected—when it's a storm that ignites a fan base and the team is not burdened by expectations that can become weighty in Philadelphia.

That was the 2017 Eagles. The dog masks were won in January, but they would have been applicable in September. The Eagles entered Week 1 with 40-to-1 odds to win the Super Bowl, although the roster appeared stronger than prognosticators realized. Carson Wentz entered his second season as the starting quarterback and Doug Pederson was in his second season as the head coach. The coach-quarterback continuity was valuable. General manager Howie Roseman bolstered the talent around Wentz, including wide receivers Alshon Jeffery and Torrey Smith. Respected veterans were added to the roster, including Chris Long, Patrick Robinson, and LeGarrette Blount. And the Eagles made a concerted effort to upgrade at backup quarterback, bringing Nick Foles back to Philadelphia (at a considerable cost) to ensure they had a No. 2 they felt could win games if Wentz went down.

"I look back on my time in Green Bay as a player when we were making those playoff runs, those Super Bowl runs there. And do we have as much talent on this team [as] we did then? We probably have more talent," Pederson said during the summer of 2017. "But we also had a lot of talent in 2010 here, and where did that get us?"

Expectations, even internally, were not for a Super Bowl season. It was Year 2 of rebuilding. Progress was expected—competing for the division title and a playoff push. But the first Super Bowl in franchise history? Even those defending Pederson when an analyst called him the least-qualified coach in the NFL would not have reserved a hotel block in Minneapolis for the first weekend in February 2018.

"The key is that we have the opportunity to compete strongly now, and that's what I expect," Lurie said in the week before the season. "I see us as a team with an excellent blueprint, great opportunity, terrific direction, but we're in year two of the plan."

In the locker room, they liked that outside expectations were not putting them among the NFC's heavyweights. *Just wait,* they thought. *Wait until outsiders see the way Wentz has developed and will benefit from upgraded receivers. Wait until they see Nelson Agholor's move to the slot. Look at that offensive line. Look at that pass rush.*

"If we get this thing rolling and we start looking good on paper," Jenkins said then, "we'll be hearing praises."

The Eagles signaled it could be a special season from their opening drive in Week 1 against Washington, when Wentz eluded pressure, broke away from a strike, and heaved a deep 58-yard touchdown pass to Agholor—a former first-round pick who had endured criticism through his first two years in the NFL. When the Eagles clinched the victory with a Brandon Graham strip sack that Fletcher Cox returned for a touchdown—yes, a Graham strip sack—the Eagles celebrated by showering Pederson with Gatorade. That was an abnormal way to celebrate a Week 1 win, although it showed how aware the team had been of the criticism Pederson endured.

"That's Philly. Second-year head coach—pressure's on him, pressure's on us," left tackle Jason Peters told *The Philadelphia Inquirer* after the game. "Doug is kind of like an Andy Reid guy. He mentored under Andy Reid, and he's more of a players' coach, and when you have a players' coach, you tend to play harder for that guy."

That might have been a not-so-veiled contrast to Chip Kelly, although it also foretold what awaited the Eagles in Week 2—a trip to Kansas City to play against Reid and the Chiefs. Only eight players remained from the Reid era in 2017. They were key players who were mostly culture-setters under Pederson and maintained reverence for Reid, who was ever popular with his players. It was also the first time Pederson coached on the opposite sideline of his coaching mentor.

Pederson seemed to channel his inner-Reid—or at least adhere to an oft-cited Reid criticism—when the Eagles eschewed the run in a 27–20 loss to the Chiefs. The coach called running plays on only 19 percent of the plays in the game, which he admitted needed to improve. But the loss nonetheless provided a dose of long-term optimism for Pederson. The Chiefs had beaten the New England Patriots 10 days earlier, and New England was the defending Super Bowl champions and were the odds-on favorites to repeat.

"The takeaway is you're right there," said Pederson, who referenced the way the Chiefs played against the Patriots.

And if the Eagles were "right there" against a team that beat New England, then perhaps they, too, could play at New England's level?

Even the most hardened (or skeptical) Eagles fans might have suspected something special was brewing in Week 3, when little-known rookie kicker Jake Elliott nailed a 61-yard field goal as the clock expired to outlast the rival New York Giants. That game came two days after President Donald Trump attacked the NFL and said he would fire any player who did not stand during the national anthem. Jenkins had been holding his fist in the air during the national anthem dating back to the 2016 season, and the Eagles were described during the Super Bowl week as "the NFL's wokest team" by Bleacher Report. An undeniable part of the 2017 team's legacy was the way they were unafraid to confront social justice issues during a high-spotlight time in American history.

"I think telling our story and opening up will change a lot of people's perspective," Jenkins said. "We have that unique opportunity to bring people to the table and point to those issues, give people solutions, and educate people." (The Eagles found themselves a topic on non-sports programming a few months after the Super Bowl when the White House rescinded their invitation for the customary visit.)

The victory over the Giants started a nine-game winning streak. The Eagles reached 10–1, announcing their presence as one of the NFL's top teams. Each game stood out for different reasons, but there were two that most resonate years later: the Week 6 win over the Carolina Panthers and the Week 7 win over Washington.

The Week 6 win stood out because that was the night when it seemed the Eagles were legitimate heavyweights. They entered the game 4–1, although the four teams they beat had a combined record of 5–14. Meanwhile, the Panthers were 4–1 and hosted the Eagles on a short week. The Eagles missed key starters due to injury, including right tackle Lane Johnson. Carolina was a three-point favorite that night. The Eagles were the superior team, outlasting the Panthers with a 28–23 victory in which Wentz threw three touchdowns and Panthers quarterback Cam Newton, a former MVP, threw three interceptions.

"We just put the league on notice," Eagles safety Rodney McLeod said after the game.

If Week 6 was the Eagles' signature win on national television, then Week 7 proved to be Wentz's signature game on national television. Playing against Washington on *Monday Night Football*, Wentz cemented his status as an MVP candidate.

He finished 17-of-25 for 268 yards and four touchdowns, and he also led the Eagles with 63 rushing yards. Wentz showed his escapability in the fourth quarter when he emerged from a committee meeting of four Washington defenders ready to pulverize it. On the broadcast, play-by-play announcer Sean McDonough spoke on behalf of the audience when he asked, "How in the world did that happen?"

"That was ridiculous," tight end Zach Ertz said. "I don't know how you stop that as a defense."

And that wasn't even the only play that caused that type of reaction. Wentz also threw a touchdown pass when he stayed upright despite defenders converging on him and he completed a touchdown pass to rookie running back Corey Clement, who was the last progression in his read.

One of the reasons Wentz knew where to go? He convinced the coaching staff to add the play to the game plan, and it was inspired by one he ran in North Dakota State. In fact, the Eagles even called the play "Bison."

The winning continued and Wentz kept excelling throughout November. Roseman made a major in-season trade by acquiring running back Jay Ajayi, a move that signaled that the Eagles were ensuring they had the reinforcements needed to make a postseason run. The Eagles had endured injuries throughout the season—from Peters to Jordan Hicks, Darren Sproles to Chris Maragos—and showed the type of resilience that often mark championship teams. They even survived a game against Dallas when Elliott was injured, prompting linebacker Kamu Grugier-Hill to take on kicking duties. It seemed as long as they had Wentz, they could find a way.

That theory was soon tested.

The Eagles' second loss of the season came in Week 13 against the Seattle Seahawks, when an uncharacteristic error by

Wentz should have served as a warning. Wentz sprinted to the end zone from six yards away, sacrificing his body while diving toward the end zone with Seahawks defenders approaching. They pummeled Wentz and dislodged the ball. He watched it trickle out of the end zone. Wentz's propensity for inviting contact carried the risk of turnovers. Pederson always tried navigating the push-pull of coaching intelligent decisions without taking away his aggression. But anyone who watched Wentz feared that the risk was far costlier than a fumble.

"We've got to continue to educate and talk to him about sliding and protecting himself, getting down, all of that—the longevity of the season and his well-being," Pederson said after the game.

The Eagles stayed on the West Coast, spending a week in Southern California before a Week 14 game against the Los Angeles Rams to avoid back-to-back cross-country trips and also benefit from team bonding. Kobe Bryant, a devoted Eagles fan, met with the team while they stayed in Orange County. They practiced at the Los Angeles Angels' stadium, where baseball star and Eagles season-ticket holder Mike Trout left them gifts. A few Eagles employees even appeared as extras in the television program *The Goldbergs,* which was fictionally depicted in Philadelphia. Beyond the extracurricular storylines were lingering questions about how—or if—Wentz would protect himself.

Wentz played one of his finest games ever against the Rams. The Eagles faced a top opponent on the road with a chance to clinch the NFC East title, and Wentz threw four touchdowns through three quarters. It was the fourth touchdown, which actually set a new Eagles single-season record, that will live in infamy in Philadelphia.

Wentz rolled to his right at the 2-yard line and lunged forward toward the goal line, just as he had done against Seattle.

Two Rams defenders sandwiched the Eagles quarterback, who still pushed past the goal line.

"He gotta stop doing that," Ajayi said on the sideline, as captured by NFL Films.

A penalty flag nullified the score, and Wentz finished the drive—and threw his fourth touchdown—but there was clearly a problem. He barely moved, and he limped when he did. He did not celebrate the touchdown, instead retreating directly to the sideline. After a few minutes of evaluation, the medical staff escorted Wentz to the locker room. He prayed with teammate Zach Ertz. The initial diagnosis was a torn ACL, which was confirmed the next day when the team returned to Philadelphia.

The Eagles still needed to win the game. Foles relieved Wentz and did just enough for the Eagles to escape with a division crown, creating a conflicted postgame locker room. Wentz greeted teammates in crutches. The Eagles were one of the best teams in football and just clinched the NFC East, but they lost their franchise quarterback. Jenkins offered an impassioned speech in the cramped Los Angeles Coliseum visitor's locker room that set the tone for what was to come.

"Let's get this s— out of the way, man: Carson being out of this s—, bro, that s— sucks," Jenkins said. "But dig this... whoever's in this room, that's who we ride with, man! We said it: 'We all we got, we all we need.' Believe that.... Celebrate that s—, know where we're at. But at the end of the day, man, we have bigger goals. So we get back to work, man. You know what's in our minds, bro—championships, and that's it. Nothing short of that. No excuses. Don't f—ing blink."

The messaging continued from Pederson when the Eagles returned to Philadelphia, albeit in different language. The team pledged confidence in Foles, who was popular in the locker room and who some teammates had seen play at a Pro Bowl level with the Eagles. But the results at the end of the regular season were mixed and certainly not encouraging of a Super Bowl–caliber team. Foles particularly struggled on a Christmas night win over the Oakland Raiders when the Eagles clinched the No. 1 seed despite Foles throwing for only 163 yards. The Eagles did not enter the postseason looking like heavyweights—even with a 13–3 record.

The top seed in the postseason receives a bye week, and the Eagles did not use that to rest. There were two factors that were especially important during the time off. The coaching staff had not changed much with the offense when Foles took over for Wentz during the regular season, but the extra time gave them a chance to implement what Foles does best—and for Foles to remember what he does best. And the Eagles' leaders wanted to make clear that their team was more than the quarterback position.

"We still won 13 games. Number-one seed," Jenkins said. "Everyone's got to come through Philly. I don't care if *you* were starting at quarterback. We should be confident in that.... We win one game, we're in the NFC Championship at home at Philly. So yeah, I don't care who we have at quarterback, who we have at offense, we'd take those odds."

(The *you* Jenkins was referring to was this writer. It's a good thing Jenkins never tested his theory; it would not have worked.)

The Eagles' leadership committee asked Pederson if they could have padded practices—a rare occurrence at that point in the season—to raise the intensity entering the postseason. The first-team offense practiced against the first-team defense instead of against the top units facing scout teams. The message was clear.

"Guys didn't want to be off for the whole week," Jenkins said. "We wanted to get better."

Oddsmakers did not believe in the Foles-led Eagles. They were underdogs in the divisional round postseason game against the Falcons, who had won the NFC championship during the previous year. A few nights before the game, Johnson ordered German shepherd masks while perusing Amazon.com after discussing the gimmick with Chris Long at lunch. The entertaining—and confident—duo planned to show off the masks and conduct postgame interviews as underdogs after an Eagles victory.

The Eagles did not necessarily look like juggernauts against the Falcons, but all that was required to advance was to be one point better than the opponent. They benefited from early luck when a potential Foles interception ricocheted off the knee of a Falcons defender and into the opportunistic hands of Torrey Smith. That allowed the Eagles to enter halftime trailing by one point. Elliott connected on two field goals in the second half to extend the Eagles' lead to five points, enough that the Falcons needed a touchdown and not a field goal on their final drive to try to escape Philadelphia with a victory. The Falcons' combination of former MVP quarterback Matt Ryan, a Philadelphia-area native, and top wide receiver Julio Jones had a fourth-and-goal at the 2-yard line with 65 seconds remaining in the game. They could have dashed the Eagles' underdog story before it started.

Before the play, the Eagles defenders noticed a tell in the formation that they had discovered on tape. This allowed them to anticipate the play, sell out on the pass, pressure Ryan, and harass his receivers. But throwing the ball to Jones is often a good idea, and the Eagles' uber-confident cornerback Jalen Mills needed to hold up in coverage. The pass sailed through Jones' outstretched hands with Mills close enough to sniff his deodorant. The Eagles survived—and the masks were revealed and became an overnight sensation. A city that embraces underdogs (and even has a statue of Rocky Balboa as one of its beacons of culture) was personified by its football team.

"I think we embody what our city is," Jenkins said. "We're a bunch of guys [that] don't care about the glitz and glamor. Very blue collar. We enjoy a fight. We talk a little trash. And we fly around and hit people. We don't really care about the big plays. We enjoy the scrap. We don't want everyone to hype us up. We want to prove it every time we step on the field."

You can imagine the response one week later when the Eagles were underdogs again to the Minnesota Vikings—a team, by the way, that was playing with a backup quarterback. (Coincidentally, their Week 1 starter had been Sam Bradford, who was traded by the Eagles to open the starting spot for Wentz.) Philadelphia hosted the NFC Championship Game for the first time since 2004, and the crowd responded accordingly. Pregame warmups were a frenzy, with Meek Mill's "Dreams and Nightmares" providing the necessary mood. Jonathan Gannon, who would later become the Eagles' defensive coordinator, was an assistant coach on the Vikings at the time. He turned to star safety before the game and simply said, "Whoa."

"Best environment I've ever been at or a part of," he said years later.

The Vikings took a quick lead and almost added to it when Long and veteran cornerback Patrick Robinson made a play that should not be taken for granted in Eagles history. On a third-and-8 from the Vikings' 41-yard line, Long sped around the right tackle and nudged Case Keenum's right arm when the quarterback released the ball, which floated in the air short of the intended target and into the welcoming hands of Robinson for an interception that was returned for a touchdown. The Vikings never scored again. The Eagles scored 31 more points—including a deep 47-yard touchdown pass to Jeffery and a flea flicker to start the second half to Smith. The crowd chanted "Super Bowl!" The Eagles beat Minnesota, and they were going to Minnesota.

"The resilience this group of men has is unequaled," Lurie told the crowd—which seemed to remain standing the whole game—over the stadium's speakers. "What we've gone through, I've never seen anything like it. This group of men wants to win so badly for Philadelphia. These fans are the most passionate fans in sports. And by the way, we're not only going to Minneapolis—we have something to do in Minneapolis. One more win!"

It would come against the New England Patriots—the NFL's version of Goliath, Lurie's childhood team, and the franchise that beat the Eagles in their last Super Bowl. That memory might have stung in Philadelphia, but it was one of five Super Bowls Bill Belichick and Tom Brady had won together at that point. One of Pederson's tasks during the two weeks leading into the Super Bowl was to dispel the Patriots mystique and maintain the "faceless opponent" message he had tried to preach throughout the season. There was a healthy respect for New England, but they could not allow the Patriots to have an advantage even before the game started.

"If I make this all about them, we're in trouble," Pederson said in his first news conference after the meeting was set. "Everything is going to be written about it. Everything has been written about it, talked about it, discussed, debated. And it's about us. And I'll keep saying that. It's what we do and how well we execute. I can't worry about that."

Both teams stayed in hotels in the Mall of America in Bloomington, Minnesota, during the week before the Super Bowl, with frigid temperatures keeping them indoors and a number of players fighting seasonal colds. The Eagles practiced at the University of Minnesota's practice facility, although most of their game-planning and installation occurred during the Super Bowl week when the team was still in Philadelphia. Pederson made a few modifications specifically for the Super Bowl, including halting one practice session midway through—silencing the Nirvana and James Brown melodies from the speakers—and instructing the team to depart to the locker room to simulate the extended halftime that would come the following Sunday. But the Eagles didn't practice *all* of their plays on the practice field. Some were saved for walkthroughs in a hotel ballroom, including the Philly Special.

Game day finally arrived after a long wait, and Belichick and Pederson chatted for a few moments before the game. Belichick remarked how he could not find many games when the Eagles were behind—a compliment that Pederson tried to deflect.

"I'll tell you what, you get through this week, you're like, 'Finally!'" Pederson said. "There's a game somewhere in here."

In Jenkins' pregame speech, he reinforced what was at stake during the next three hours.

> You all want to be world champs? You all want to be world champs?.... Well, guess what? All it takes is to give everything you've got! Everything that you've got for 60 minutes! That's all that stands between you and immortality. We've been the best team in the league from start to finish. They're just finding out! So show the whole world today, man.

What followed was an unforgettable offensive performance. The Eagles scored on their first two possessions, including a leaping touchdown by Jeffery over cornerback Eric Rowe (ironically, a former Kelly draft pick in 2015 who Roseman quickly traded away upon regaining personnel control in 2016). The Patriots could not generate much offensive momentum early in the game, and they failed to convert a trick play when Brady ran a route and could not haul in a catch. It was the perils of throwing to the quarterback in a big moment. The Eagles never received the memo. Because on a fourth-and-goal at the 1-yard line with 38 seconds remaining before halftime and the Eagles holding a three-point lead, Pederson kept the offense on the field and approved a trick play—the Philly Special—in which reserve tight end Trey Burton threw to Nick Foles in the corner of the end zone. The Patriots were stunned. So was the viewing public. It is one of the most memorable plays in NFL history, and it gave the Eagles a 22–12 lead entering the extended halftime.

While Justin Timberlake played for the fans, both teams made adjustments. The Patriots focused on better incorporating star tight end Rob Gronkowski, and the Eagles had no answer for the Brady-to-Gronkowski connection in the second half. The tight end caught four passes (including a touchdown) on the opening possession of the third quarter, and there was legitimate reason for concern. The Eagles kept pace when Foles connected with running back Corey Clement in the back of the end zone on a controversial catch. In New England, fans thought Clement did not maintain possession. In Philadelphia, there was not enough evidence to overturn.

In the end, the officials kept the points on the board. (Want to impress a friend? Ask who the Eagles' leading receiver was in the Super Bowl. The answer is Clement, who caught four passes for 100 yards.)

The Eagles offense needed those touchdowns, because the Patriots appeared unstoppable. They reached the end zone on their first three drives in the second half to take a lead, and the pressure shifted to Pederson and the Eagles. For all of the memories that came from the Super Bowl, the most important might have been a simple two-yard pass to Ertz. It will not lead any highlight reels, but Pederson showed his fearlessness when he did not punt on fourth-and-1 at the Eagles' 45-yard line while trailing by one point with 5:39 remaining in the game. Data supported the decision, although conventional wisdom would have been geared toward a more conservative approach. Had the Eagles failed to convert, the Patriots would have had a short field and a chance to ice the game. Pederson was aggressive all season—and all game—and this decision highlighted that approach. The conversion allowed the Eagles to drive downfield to set up the decisive touchdown on a third-and-seven from the 11-yard line with 2:25 remaining. The Eagles called "Gun trey left, open buster star motion…383 X follow Y slant," a play that was added to the game plan for the Super Bowl, according to *Sports Illustrated*. Ertz was split wide and isolated against a safety in one-on-one coverage. Ertz cut inside after three yards, gaining inside leverage and catching the ball at the 6-yard line with the momentum to dive into the end zone.

With a five-point lead and 2:33 remaining in the game, the Eagles needed to do something that had been an arduous proposition through two decades in the NFL: stop Tom Brady. Schwartz told Pederson on the sideline that he was going to be aggressive and either make a play or get the ball back for the offense, implying that they would give up a play but the offense would have the ball last.

"Somebody on defense is about to be a superhero," Jenkins said to Darren Sproles on the sideline.

On the second play of the drive, that superhero was Brandon Graham. The Eagles' veteran, who had been maligned earlier in his career, rushed from the interior, dove at Brady with his left arm, and knocked the ball loose from the Hall of Fame quarterback. Derek Barnett recovered, and the Eagles regained possession in Patriots territory with 2:16 remaining in the game.

The offense took 70 seconds off the clock to set up a 46-yard field goal by Elliott, who continued a season of clutch kicks by giving the Eagles an eight-point lead. The Patriots had 58 seconds and no timeouts, and Brady brought them to the 49-yard line. His attempt at a Hail Mary on the final play was knocked to the ground by Robinson. The clock struck zero. The scoreboard read Eagles 41, Patriots 33.

"Eagles fans everywhere—this is for you! Let the celebration begin!" famed play-by-play announcer Merrill Reese said on radio in a spontaneous call he had waited to make his entire career.

The celebration began—in Minnesota and in Philadelphia.

"If there's a word called 'everything,' that's what it means to Eagles fans everywhere," Lurie said on the field in the trophy celebration. "For Eagles fans everywhere, this is for them."

In the locker room, Pederson brought his team together around him under a purple banner that declared the Eagles champions. The Lombardi Trophy was passed around between spraying champagne and indulging in Johnny Walker Blue. After each game during the Eagles' run, Pederson had told the team they were not done yet. Finally, they were.

> We're done, baby! I'm so happy for every one of you—coaches, players, Mr. Lurie, the organization—for everything you guys have put yourself through from day one... [and battling] through the injuries. Guys, I can't tell you how happy I am. I really am. You're world champions, men! World champions! Just look around! Look around. OK? This is what you guys have done. This is what you've accomplished. You guys get on me a lot about dress code

> and the way we practice and do things. Well, guess what? It's for this moment right here. For this moment! Because [that's] the discipline it takes to win this game. And this is a team game. We said before: an individual can make a difference. But... [Players: "A team makes a miracle!"] Tonight, you did it. We did it! Against a fine football team. When you're asked, you're complimentary. But at the same time, we're going to party!

It did not take much prompting. Light posts were greased back in Philadelphia, and that was nothing compared to the parade three days later. Pederson called it the "new normal." Kelce delivered the most memorable speech in parade history that remains a rallying cry in Philadelphia.

Do you understand what they just did? Even though they were on buses for parades, the adage proved true. The 2017 team will walk together forever.

PART 7

THE MOMENTS

27

Miracle at the New Meadowlands

DeSean Jackson did not expect to return the punt. There were 14 seconds remaining in a game that was improbably tied at 31, and the New York Giants were backed up to punt at their own 29-yard line. Giants rookie punter Matt Dodge was told to punt the ball out of bounds. Why would he not? Jackson was one of the most electric players in football. The Giants had already lost a 21-point lead during the previous eight minutes, and at that point, their hope was to simply get the game to overtime.

"I didn't think I was gonna get the kick," Jackson recalled with a smile more than a decade later.

Except Dodge somehow punted the ball inbounds after rushing the boot following a high snap—much to the dismay of Giants coach Tom Coughlin, whose ire was apparent from the time the ball left Dodge's foot. The low line drive was bobbled by Jackson, who actually used to bobble to let the Giants coverage unit overrun him. After a few steps backward, Jackson put on his accelerators. He described it as his cat-like instincts. The Giants could not keep pace with him. A ferocious block by Jason Avant against long snapper Zak DeOssie pancaked the last line of defense for the Giants, and the Eagles' second Miracle at the Meadowlands—albeit this one in a new facility—was about to take place.

In the video perch above the stadium, the Eagles' video director who witnessed Herman Edwards pick up a fumble on a kneel-down in the Meadowlands 32 years earlier shouted, "Oh my, God!" How often does a miracle happen twice?

When Jackson approached the end zone, though, he did not immediately cross the plane. It would not be like Jackson to score without flair, although this was also football intelligence. He ran along the goal line, with the intended effect draining the clock and the residual effect sticking it to the rival Giants.

"I really wanted to do something crazy," Jackson told *The Philadelphia Inquirer* after the game. "I know everybody wants to give me a hard time: 'He does this. He's arrogant. He's a showboat....' I'm not going to change."

"It was the equivalent of a walk-off, grand-slam home run," said longtime Eagles play-by-play man Merrill Reese, who in a 2020 interview called the play his favorite moment as a broadcaster *other* than the Super Bowl.

In fact, it was the first walk-off punt return in NFL history at that point. And what made it even more memorable was that it punctuated an unforgettable fourth quarter that made the punt return even more dramatic—and, to use a variation on a term often associated with it, miraculous.

Reese's radio call that day painted the picture. At halftime, Reese said the score was "Giants 24, the Eagles are still at their hotel." If you want to know how the defense had been playing, Reese said Giants quarterback Eli Manning operated with "enough time to read *War and Peace*."

The Giants took a 31–10 lead with just more than eight minutes remaining in the fourth quarter, and any Eagles fan at the stadium that day could not have been blamed for starting their drive back down the New Jersey Turnpike. Who comes back from a 21-point deficit in the final eight minutes of the game?

The answer is Michael Vick.

In a year full of sterling performances from the rejuvenated quarterback, these eight minutes were among his finest. In three drives, he went 6-for-10 for 131 yards and two touchdowns while also rushing for 96 yards and one touchdown. The Giants had no answer for him—and could not hold onto the ball long enough to keep Vick off the field. Reese called the sequence one of the finest quarterback performances he's ever seen.

Vick tied the game, but Jackson won it. The Giants were forced to punt when they went three-and-out, and Jackson was not the Eagles' regular punt returner. Consider him their home-run threat. Andy Reid whistled toward Jackson and told him to "get your butt back there," per *The Philadelphia Inquirer* story from that day. Reid kept whistling toward him. Jackson was unworried—and unstoppable.

In 2013, the play was voted by NFL.com readers as the greatest in NFL history. Even if that is debatable, it's undoubtedly the most memorable non–Super Bowl play of this period in Eagles history. As Eagles icon Mike Quick said to Reese on the radio broadcast when Jackson crossed the goal line into the end zone, "This is Miracle at the Meadowlands No. 2!"

28

Philly Special

"You want Philly Philly?" Nick Foles asked.

"Yeah, let's do it," Doug Pederson said.

That exchange changed Eagles history—and on a larger scale, NFL history—when the Eagles quarterback suggested to the head coach that the Eagles run a trick play at the goal line on fourth down in the Super Bowl. The play, which was actually called "Philly Special," became one of the most iconic moments in a Super Bowl and will forever be part of Eagles lore.

The Eagles clung to a 15–12 lead during a two-minute drill and brought the ball all the way to the 1-yard line. Foles attempted a pass to Alshon Jeffery on third down that fell incomplete, leaving the Eagles with a fourth down.

"That's a no-brainer," Patriots running back Dion Lewis said on the sideline, as captured by NFL Films. "He ain't going for it."

Maybe for other coaches. Pederson took pride in his aggressiveness, and the Eagles knew they needed touchdowns and not field goals to outpace the Patriots. It is easy to think that. It's harder to actually keep the offense on the field when a chip shot field goal would give the underdog Eagles a six-point lead.

"Hold on, hold on," Pederson said. "We're going for it right here!"

That's when Foles and Pederson shared the exchange that is now immortalized with a statue outside Lincoln Financial Field.

Pederson called No. 122, which was the Philly Special on Foles' wristband. "Philly Special. Philly Special," Foles said in the huddle to the 10 players on the field. The Eagles lined up in the shotgun formation with running back Corey Clement next to Foles. This was not going to be a short-yardage handoff to power back LeGarrette Blount, who stood on the sideline by Pederson and asked the head coach for the call.

Only wide receiver Alshon Jeffery split wide. The other pass-catchers—Torrey Smith, Zach Ertz, and Trey Burton—lined up tight on the formation's left side. This was a tense moment and there was a rabid Eagles fan base filling the neutral U.S. Bank Stadium, so Foles waved his hands to quiet the crowd. At Foles' urging, Clement slid one yard behind Foles. The quarterback started his cadence, then he stepped toward the line.

"Easy, easy! Kill, Kill!" he shouted. It seemed as if the Eagles were changing the play at the line of scrimmage, when it was actually subterfuge to confuse the Patriots. Foles took a step to Lane Johnson and patted the right tackle on his rear end, as if he was trying to adjust Johnson's position. What only those on the field and Eagles sideline knew was that Foles' call to Johnson was actually directed to center Jason Kelce, signaling for him to snap the ball to Clement.

The running back took three steps to his left and pitched it to Burton, who had run toward the quarterback. Burton was the Eagles' third tight end, but he entered the league as a Swiss-Army-knife-type player who started his college career at Florida as a quarterback. Foles froze at the snap behind Johnson and then leaked into the side of the end zone when no one covered him. Once Burton took the pitch, he saw Foles unguarded. Burton shifted his right fingers over the laces of the football and did not bother to set his feet, lofting the pass while still on the run. Foles turned to the ball and easily hauled in the catch with his gloved left hand under the pigskin and bare right hand atop. Foles' momentum carried him on a few long strides into the end zone, but he remained speechless until he turned around and saw his teammates running over to celebrate.

"Let's go!" he shouted while Johnson hugged him.

"That's as aggressive as you could possibly be, go for it on fourth down with the all-time trick play," NBC play-by-play announcer Al Michaels said on the broadcast.

"This play call has a chance to be remembered as one of the all-time greats," analyst Cris Collinsworth said.

On the sideline, the Eagles celebrated while some others were in disbelief. Malcolm Jenkins pumped his fist and remarked how incredible that they brought out that play in the Super Bowl.

"Hell of a call!" running backs coach Duce Staley said to Pederson.

"That was a dime, baby!" tight end Brent Celek said to Burton.

"Everything today!" Blount told Foles. "Catch them and throw them!"

"We talked about that play!" running back Kenjon Barner said to Foles.

"Hey, Foles, why were you so open?" Burton asked Foles in an exchange between passer and receiver.

"I sold it!" Foles said. "I did some acting!"

"You have more catches than Tom does!" an Eagles staffer said to Foles on the sideline, a reference to Tom Brady dropping a pass on a similar play earlier in the game. Foles actually catches passes before every game because it allows him to "be a kid for a little bit."

"A quarterback going out on a route?" Foles said after the Super Bowl. "That's probably the best it has looked. So we hit it at the right time."

That Brady was an intended receiver illustrates how the Philly Special is famous for the result more than the play design. It was added to the Eagles' playbook by Press Taylor, who was then a quality control coach and later became the Eagles' quarterbacks coach and passing game coordinator. As a quality control coach, he was tasked with studying film from around football at all levels to identify interesting play designs. He had stored a play from the Chicago Bears one year earlier, when wide receivers coach Mike Groh was actually part of the Bears staff. That play had been run by Clemson in 2012 and was also a version of what was used elsewhere, including at Oklahoma. The best coaches in sports are often thieves, stealing concepts they find elsewhere and adding their own twist.

"That's the play that's going to win us a game," Pederson said when he saw the play, according to *Fearless.*

The Eagles installed the play during the playoffs, and there was a belief that they would call it against Minnesota in the NFC Championship Game. When Burton first threw to Foles in practice, the ball came out too hard. Pederson wanted Burton to float it—not fire it. The next pass went over Foles' head, but the Eagles still had confidence in the play. However, the opportunity never came to bear. It remained in the playbook leading into the Super Bowl. This time, the Eagles did not practice it on the practice field. Rather, they limited it to the walkthrough in the ballroom at the Radisson in the Mall of America.

"As coaches we are often paranoid, especially when we are being watched as closely as we were during Super Bowl week," Pederson explained in *Fearless*. "You never know who is watching practice, and we didn't want it to be talked about publicly."

The play has become famous because of Foles catching it. But it should also be remembered that Burton was the one who threw it. The Eagles had been trying to find ways to get Burton to attempt a pass at some point that season, and they pulled it out on the biggest stage.

"I've been dreaming of throwing a touchdown pass since college," Burton said after the game. "I still don't believe it. Guys said, 'You just threw a touchdown pass in the Super Bowl.' It's something that I'll never forget and my kids will never forget. It's special."

But the play followed Burton—and it weighed on him. He signed a lucrative contract with the Bears one month after the Super Bowl. The Bears installed a similar play to the Philly Special to use during the 2018 season, and Burton was supposed to be the passer. He could not go through with the play because it brought so much anxiety.

"It just seemed too soon," Burton told *The Philadelphia Inquirer* in February 2023. "It was an important play and an important time in my life that was really special.... Why would I do it again? I did it in the Super Bowl. If you can give me another reason why I would do it again, then maybe I'd reconsider it. One time is good enough for me. I'm not a greedy guy. It happened, and I'm cool with it."

Pederson said the Eagles would retire the play. But that did not mean they would retire *similar* plays. On the final day of the 2018 mandatory minicamp, hours before the Eagles were given their Super Bowl rings during a raucous party, the Eagles ran a play that looked comparable to the Philly Special. Greg Ward, a wide receiver who was a converted quarterback, threw to Foles along the right sideline. The difference with this play was it was not a direct snap. Foles handed the ball to the running back. The Eagles actually stole it from the Patriots because it was the play they ran when the pass was attempted to Brady in the Super Bowl.

Sure enough, in Week 1 of the 2018 season when the franchise unveiled the Super Bowl banner, the Eagles needed life while trailing by three points in the third quarter. On a third-and-5, Foles handed the ball to Clement. This time, Clement pitched it to a reversing Nelson Agholor. Agholor completed a pass to Foles for a 15-yard gain. The Eagles gained momentum and eventually won the game. Burton watched the game from Chicago and sent a message to Agholor's account: "Nice throw."

The name of that play? Philly Philly.

Foles did not need to ask Pederson this time. They both wanted it and knew how it would turn out.

29

The Strip Sack

Brandon Graham is not coy about the moment that changed his life. He's watched the strip sack on Tom Brady that helped the Eagles clinch Super Bowl LII countless times since February 2018. The video gets sent to him. He has signed photos of the play. It is on his phone, reserved to cheer him up on a bad day. It is the most famous sack in Eagles history and the moment in the Super Bowl that brought the most joy to Philadelphia.

"It's definitely life-changing. It changed my life. Can't nobody take that away," Graham said in February 2023. "Going against Brady in the Super Bowl, somebody who puts daggers in people's hearts in those drives—especially that last drive.... I'm happy I was able to do that in my career, especially with how it went in the beginning. To be able to make a play like that in a town that never had a championship, it finally brought us one. It changed my trajectory of how people view me as a player."

Graham had already turned around his reputation by 2017, when he transformed from the bust label to a steady starter who was one of the top players on the team. But Graham did not have icon status in Philadelphia until the fourth quarter of the Super Bowl.

By that point, Brady was on the way to a historic performance. The future Hall of Famer had 465 of his 505 yards, the most he had ever thrown in a postseason game. He had led touchdown drives on all three possessions in the second half. The Eagles had not sacked him all game. So when Brady regained possession with 2:21 remaining in the game while trailing by five points, the prevailing thought was that Brady had too much time. One year earlier, he led a Super Bowl comeback while trailing by 25 points in the second half. He's known for his game-winning drives in big games, which included 11 in the postseason and five in the Super Bowl alone. This could add to his legacy—unless the Eagles disrupted.

On the sideline, the Eagles kept the rallying cry of, "One more stop."

"Funny thing is, somebody on defense is about to be a superhero," Eagles safety Malcolm Jenkins said to Darren Sproles on the sideline. "Whoever makes the play, somebody's going to be a hero."

"If the Eagles could come up with their one turnover of the game right here," Merrill Reese said on the play-by-play call.

Nick Foles passed Chris Long with an ambitious request: "Strip him!" Doug Pederson asked Graham for "everything you've got," because this possession would determine the game. On the second play of the drive, Graham lined up inside at defensive tackle in the Turbo package. That was how the Eagles used him on passing downs throughout the season, and it was a spot Graham was uniquely qualified to play in defensive coordinator Jim Schwartz's system because of his combination of power, speed, and leverage.

"I think when it's all said and done, when I'm in a rocking chair somewhere and I think of Brandon Graham, I'm still going to think of the forced fumble in the Super Bowl, and that was from a defensive tackle position," Schwartz said in May 2019.

Graham knew Fletcher Cox would be double-teamed on the play, meaning he would be one-on-one against right guard Shaq Mason. He did not even keep track of the down and distance (second-and-2). He simply knew pass, and in Schwartz's defense, pass meant attack. He told Chris Long he would shoot in the B gap—the gap between the guard and tackle.

Graham raced around Mason, and Graham's acceleration was such that Mason could only get his hands on Graham when Graham had already penetrated the pocket. Graham was able to stay upright against the tackle. Brady stepped up to pass, and Graham stretched his 32¼-inch left arm to punch at Brady and drive through the ball in Brady's grip. Graham closed his eyes while pushing the ball away. The ball popped from Brady's grasp and bounced on the ground. Defensive end Derek Barnett scooped the loose ball, which popped right into his arms.

"We got the ball!" Pederson shouted.

"They finally hit Tom Brady!" radio analyst Mike Quick said to Reese.

Teammates swarmed Graham on the sideline. The Eagles kicked a field goal to take an eight-point lead, and the defense was able to make one more stop to keep Brady from tying the game in the final seconds. Graham actually came close to sacking Brady on the Hail Mary, which would have been a double clincher, but Brady was able to slide in the pocket to avoid Graham and release the ball.

"If I wake up in a sweat at four in the morning," Schwartz said, "a lot of the time it's Brandon Graham missing him in the Super Bowl on the last play."

But Graham made the play that mattered most. He has since totaled double-digit sacks in a season for the first time, earned a Pro Bowl nod, and reached another Super Bowl. Nobody calls him a bust anymore—only an Eagles icon. And it comes with an iconic play. It changed his life. It changed the lives of Eagles fans. It changed the franchise.

In 2022, The Athletic's Bo Wulf spent a game day with Graham's wife, Carlyne, and Graham's family. After the game, they visited owner Jeffrey Lurie's private box. They were shown a photo prominently featured on the wall. It was Graham's strip sack of Brady.

"Daddy knocked it out of the quarterback's hand," Carlyne told her son, "and that's how we won the game."

How's that for a legacy?

30

Seven Touchdowns

Nick Foles' iconic status in Philadelphia might have come from his Super Bowl heroics, but Foles' undeniable spot in Eagles history might not have materialized without his unforgettable seven-touchdown performance against the Oakland Raiders on November 3, 2013.

"By the end of the game," Foles wrote in his 2018 biography, "I was more stunned than anyone by all that had transpired."

This was before the Super Bowl MVP. This was even before the finish of the 27-touchdown, two-interception, Pro Bowl campaign that first made Foles part of Philly lore. In fact, this might have been the start.

He had been an inconsistent quarterback to that point, unable to beat out Michael Vick for the starting job during training camp and showing flashes of QB1 potential mixed with bouts of backup material. Hence the high-variance label that later became an accurate descriptor.

An injury to Vick one week prior opened the door for Foles to rejoin the starting lineup for a team that had lost consecutive games and five of seven. Foles had started one of those losses, including a dreadful outing against the Dallas Cowboys two weeks earlier when he totaled only 80 passing yards on 29 attempts. The way he played against Dallas created doubts about the second-year quarterback, and a bad performance by Foles in Oakland might have rendered him a reserve.

Foles opened the game by leading the Eagles on a 10-play, 84-yard drive during which the ball only hit the ground once. He found Brent Celek for a two-yard touchdown to give the Eagles an early lead. And then he kept throwing touchdowns. At that point in Foles' career, his career high was three touchdown passes. He matched that total four minutes into the second quarter on a deep 63-yard touchdown pass down the middle of the field to Riley Cooper—Cooper's second of the game. He surpassed that total when he connected with Zach Ertz for a 15-yard touchdown late in the second quarter.

It was a perfect start to the half—four drives, four touchdowns. The half was a marvel for Chip Kelly's offense, considering the pass catchers were barely touched on all four touchdowns.

"I didn't do anything except run some routes," Cooper said. "He threw it right where it needed to be."

It also was an indictment of a Raiders defense that finished the season ranked No. 28 against the pass. But they had not seen anything like what happened that day. Neither had Foles.

When 16-year veteran defensive back Charles Woodson was asked after the game if he had witnessed any indication on film that Foles could have this type of performance, the future Hall of Famer offered a dose of reality.

"I don't think Nick Foles had seen anything on film that would give him any indication that he'd throw for seven touchdowns," Woodson told reporters. To that point, Foles said the only time he had ever thrown seven touchdowns in a game came while playing video games in his native Austin, Texas.

He did not slow down in the second half. He played even better. Foles needed only four official plays—five, when including a penalty—to complete his fifth touchdown. This one was to LeSean McCoy on a short pass that McCoy ran 25 yards for the score. The onslaught continued when he needed only three plays for his sixth touchdown, a deep 46-yard pass to DeSean Jackson. His seventh touchdown came before the quarter ended.

At that point, Foles was chasing history. He became the seventh quarterback in NFL history to pass for seven touchdowns. No quarterback had eight, and Foles was unstoppable that afternoon. Except his coach could stop him; Kelly relieved Foles after one drive in the fourth quarter.

"I know what the record is," Kelly said after that game in a press conference that took place in a weight room in the bowels of the O.com Coliseum. "But this isn't about records, it's about going out and getting a win. If I put Nick out there to try to get a record and he gets hurt, that's being silly. Records are meant to be broken when they're supposed to be broken."

Foles finished 22 of 28 for 406 yards and seven touchdowns, meaning the ball reached the end zone more than it touched the ground. Jason Kelce saw "a little bit of a different look" in Foles' eyes before the game.

"He just seemed so focused this game, like he had something to prove today," McCoy said in the locker room.

As Foles later revealed in his biography, he was "struggling emotionally and spiritually" going into that game. Foles' wife (then girlfriend) had been diagnosed with postural orthostatic tachycardia syndrome, a condition that affects the autonomic nervous system. The two lived apart at the time, with the separation weighing on Foles. "I couldn't fix Tori's health problems, and to be perfectly honest, I wasn't entirely convinced I could fix our offense," Foles wrote.

He pondered questions that went beyond where to pass the ball on third-and-eight—Should he be with Tori? Should he be playing football? What was his identity beyond football? Foles prayed by his locker before the game against the Raiders, seeking clarity about whether football is what he should even do with his life. The answer came with the historic performance. His cleats from that game were sent to the Pro Football Hall of Fame. It was not the last time he was commemorated in Canton.

After that game, there were no more questions about who would quarterback the Eagles. Foles remained atop the depth chart and led the Eagles to the playoffs, earned a Pro Bowl bid, and formed meaningful relationships in the organization that proved significant when the team brought him back to Philadelphia. He called the game the "turning point" in his career—a fortuitous sentiment considering what happened four years later.

"I look back at that day as the day we put everything together," Foles said in 2017. "Sort of that 'a-ha' moment.... 'We can do this, we know who we are, we can be explosive.' And we sort of took off from that point."

So did Foles.

31

The Monday Night Massacre

THE MICHAEL VICK ERA NEVER APPEARED BRIGHTER THAN on the night of November 15, 2010—even if Vick could not see it that way at first. The best game of Vick's career, and one of the best moments of the past 25 years of Eagles history, required an equipment change early in the game for Vick to actually see what he was doing. Then Vick could see clearly what was apparent to a national audience that night: the Eagles had found Donovan McNabb's successor.

McNabb, on the other sideline, could see it, too.

The Eagles played a *Monday Night Football* game against the rival Washington Redskins. Vick did not enter the 2010 season as the Eagles' starting quarterback in the first year after Donovan McNabb was traded to Washington. A concussion to

Kevin Kolb during the season opener created a spot for Vick, who teased with glimpses of the Vick of old during his first four starts of the season. It was cemented in front of a national audience on *Monday Night Football* in a game that earned the nickname "Monday Night Massacre," when Vick finished 20 of 28 for 333 yards and four passing touchdowns, with 80 rushing yards and two rushing downs. The Eagles won 59–28. It was the most points scored during the era covered in this book. You would need to go back to 1934 to find a better scoring performance.

"That game," Vick said in an interview 10 years later, "showed the world, showed me, I could still play."

A primetime NFC East game will always draw eyeballs, although this one carried extra drama. McNabb had beaten the Eagles one month earlier in his first game back to Philadelphia and called the trade a mistake for the Eagles. Two hours before kickoff in Landover, Maryland, news surfaced that McNabb agreed to a $78 million contract extension. Then during pregame warm-ups, Washington safety LaRon Landry and Eagles receiver DeSean Jackson scuffled. Teammates joined and officials needed to intervene. That was additional motivation for the Eagles, and Vick knew what Andy Reid had designed for the offensive play in his opening script.

"Those two things really got me going," Vick said.

It did not take long for Vick to become the story. The Eagles opened with the ball, although a muffed kickoff return pushed them back to their own 12-yard on the opening possession. The left-handed quarterback lined up under center and faked a handoff to running back LeSean McCoy, then turned his body and rolled to his left 10 yards. He planted his back foot at the 2-yard line, took a step, and hurled a pass as deep as he could—more than 60 yards in the air.

"I thought I threw it too far," he said.

Except who was on the other end? Jackson. And there's no such thing as throwing it too far to Jackson.

The defender chasing Jackson? Landry, who was the instigator in the pregame kerfuffle. Jackson accelerated past Landry around the 35-yard line, where he stretched his arms to catch the pass while Landry dove to stop him. The pass somehow hit Jackson in stride. Jackson stayed on his feet, and as he is wont to do, turned toward the defense and danced into the end zone for the 88-yard touchdown.

"When he put two hands on it, I knew DeSean doesn't drop balls, so I knew he wasn't going to let go," Vick said. "It was an amazing moment."

After the Eagles defense forced a three-and-out, Vick needed only five plays to bring the Eagles back into the end zone. He scrambled seven yards—juking a Washington defender in the process—and dove past the goal line to give the Eagles a two-score lead less than five minutes into the game. One decade later, Vick called this drive "just as important or even more important" than the unforgettable 88-yard touchdown to begin the game because it allowed the offense to find a rhythm and settle into the game.

Vick needed to quickly return to the field after an interception. He led the Eagles to another touchdown—this time, it was an 11-yard shovel pass to McCoy, a play that had become a Reid staple.

One problem: Vick's vision became obscured. Vick wore a tinted visor on his helmet. It rained that night, and he could not keep his visor dry. He made the decision that it needed to come off. The unmasked helmet was Vick's most vivid memory.

"Everything was crystal clear," Vick said. "It made the night more vibrant and visible. I could remember everything because

I saw it clear. I didn't see it behind the tint of a visor. I saw it in the right perspective. And I'm glad it happened."

It was crystal clear when Jerome Harrison rushed for a 50-yard touchdown to give the Eagles a 28–0 lead by the end of the first quarter.

By the first play of the second quarter, it seemed like Vick had been playing a video game on rookie setting. He threw a 48-yard touchdown to Jeremy Maclin, one of the most memorable moments of the game for Vick. It was not just the precision with which the ball was thrown on a deep pass down the right sideline with the touch and loft to allow Maclin to turn his body and adjust to the ball in the air.

"I put it in a position where only Maclin could get it," Vick said. "He caught it and fell out of bounds.... It was him or nobody."

The television commentators were in awe. Mike Tirico, who did play-by-play for *ESPN Tonight*, told viewers that he had "never seen anything like this, ever."

The play was also memorable because the cornerback in coverage was DeAngelo Hall. Hall was a teammate of Vick's at both Virginia Tech and Atlanta—and one with whom Vick shared a nice embrace after the game—but in the moment, Vick wanted to pick on Hall. Earlier in the season, when Washington beat Philadelphia, Vick was injured when he was sandwiched at the goal line by Hall and another defender.

"The only way to get even with him was to beat him deep," Vick said.

The Eagles had a 35–0 lead. Similarly impressive, a Vick pass had not hit the ground. In fact, Vick completed his first 10 pass attempts that night.

"I don't think I ever went that long without throwing an incomplete pass," Vick said. "I know I had a lot of streaks of passes without an interception, but this one was by far the coolest."

By halftime, the Eagles had a 45–14 lead. And he was not finished. Vick was most proud of his first touchdown of the second half. He led the Eagles on an 11-play, 71-yard drive that included three third-down conversions. He kept the drive alive by running 13 yards on third-and-10. It was a Vick exhibition—not the types of highlight-reel plays that most come to mind when thinking about Vick, but the efficient quarterbacking for which he is not often credited. Third downs in the red zone are considered four-point plays in the NFL, representing the difference between a field goal and a touchdown. On a third-and-goal from the 3-yard line, Washington wanted to limit the damage by holding the Eagles to a field goal.

As was the case throughout the night, they could not stop Vick.

Benefiting from a superb offensive line, Vick had the time in the pocket to pump twice while he let the play develop. A left-handed quarterback, Vick ran to his right. That is away from his dominant hand, which is not often the direction he went. But it bought time to allow Jason Avant to find space in the back of the end zone. Vick did not run, as he is known to do, and as he did as well as any quarterback in NFL history to that point. He used his legs to extend the play only to rifle a pass across the formation, which Avant caught for Vick's sixth touchdown of the night.

"When I hit Jason, especially after the scramble and feel of the pocket presence and feel of the game, it exemplified where I was at," Vick said. "That play set me up for success for the rest of the season because I felt more than capable with the feel of the game, movement, pocket presence, poise. I felt I had it after the play."

The Eagles' sizable lead meant there was no stat-padding for the remainder of that evening. Vick could not technically set records for touchdown passes or touchdown runs. However, his six total touchdowns were the most of any game in his career. His 150.7 passer rating was the best of any start in his career. It was, by his admission, the best he ever played in the NFL.

"You can't play much better than that," Vick said.

That is true. When Vick's career in Philadelphia is remembered, it will be that game that stands out above all others.

"There was so much motivation to show the world, show people," Vick said, "I still had it on the big stage on Monday night."

32

The Snow Bowl

A Week 14 meeting against the Detroit Lions when each team enters the game with seven wins does not often have the makings for something memorable 11 years later. But to this day, if you mention "Snow Bowl" to anyone familiar with that era of Eagles history, they will instantly know what you're referencing. And they've likely seen the famous freeze frame—pun intended—of LeSean McCoy leaping over a Lions defender with snow falling all around on his way to a franchise-record 217 rushing yards. It remains one of the indelible images in recent franchise history.

The Snow Bowl moniker stretches back to the hours after the game, making this literally an instant classic. In fact, the Eagles put an ad on page D6 of *The Philadelphia Inquirer* the next morning that read: The snow made it hard to see you, but we sure heard you! Thank you fans. #Snowbowl2013

Ahead of games, the Eagles always monitor weather forecasts. From game strategy to event management, it is important to know if it will be sweltering or frigid, rainy or snowy, windy or serene. On December 8, 2013, the franchise prepared to host the Detroit Lions in a Week 14 game that called for snow.

The team received updates every six hours that weekend. Forecasts suggested that the snow would not arrive until just before halftime. A written report received at 9:00 AM called for precipitation around 2:00 PM. The Eagles planned accordingly. But the snow came sooner than anticipated—during pregame warm-ups. The field was coated with powder, although it was more akin to what might make for a careful commute—not warranting cancelling school. When players and coaches retreated to the locker room, a blizzard descended onto South Philadelphia. They returned to the field before kickoff to a whiteout. Chip Kelly, then the head coach, turned the corner in the tunnel in the bowels of Lincoln Financial Field and thought, "This is interesting."

Jason Kelce shared a similar sentiment.

"When we came back out," Jason Kelce told reporters after the game, "I remember they had only shoveled the lines and the numbers, and I remember trying to run and cut on a patch where they hadn't shoveled and I just slid like three yards. 'Oh, this is going to be interesting.'"

When the game started, the Eagles (and Lions) quickly realized that whatever plans were made during the week needed to be shoveled away. The Eagles punted on four of their first five drives, with an interception mixed in between. They could not move the ball. The Eagles had zero first downs on their first four drives, one on their fifth before finally moving the ball before halftime. Their 8–0 halftime deficit showed that the weather had frozen a scorching offense.

"Everybody has a plan, and then the first snap, it kind of goes awry," Kelly said after the game. "It's how you react to it. At times during a game, the crap is going to hit the fan."

So the Eagles adjusted. They realized they would not be able to move well laterally because it was hard to gain footing even though players, such as McCoy, changed cleats so they could have longer spikes. They stopped kicking the ball, realizing there was a higher percentage of converting a fourth down or two-point conversion than trust all that it would take to send a kick through the snow—and through the uprights.

The Eagles focused on north-south runs in the second half, and the results showed. After tough sledding early in the third quarter, the Eagles scored on five consecutive drives. McCoy totaled 166 rushing yards after halftime, with touchdown runs of 40 and 57 yards. Even running between the tackles, though, McCoy made moves that amazed teammates and remained a part of his lore in Philadelphia. You cannot discuss McCoy without bringing up that game, and McCoy even referenced it when he retired.

"You just didn't have the normal footing and traction that you get when stopping and cutting," McCoy said after the game. "Sometimes I couldn't really plant. I can usually plant on a dime, but it all worked. The [offensive linemen] were giving me so much room."

The Eagles' passing game even worked in the second half with an adjustment that one would not expect in the snow. Cornerback Cary Williams told Kelly to throw more post routes and corner routes because the defenders could not make up speed based on how hard it was to change direction in the snow. Foles completed a 44-yard deep ball to Riley Cooper and a 17-yard touchdown to DeSean Jackson to help put the Eagles on the board.

"When I was making throws, I couldn't really zip them, because if you zip them in that weather it is hard to see the ball and with the glove on the hands, it would slip right through," Foles said. "As the course of the game went on, I got more and more comfortable with it, and we adjusted and made some big plays."

The Eagles' 34–20 win and second-half offensive onslaught were part of the bookkeeping of the game, but the memories from the day are about the snow-covered field and how much fun the players appeared to have, as if school had been canceled and a bunch of friends had gathered in a park.

"I think our guys embraced [the snow]," Kelly said. "They probably went back to when they were little kids running around out there. It was interesting just to see how those guys were excited about playing in it."

Even those used to snow on the team were taken aback. McCoy, who had played all his football in Pennsylvania to that point, said it was the worst he had seen. Connor Barwin, who grew up in Detroit, remarked the same. The Philadelphia International Airport recorded eight inches of snow, but it was the rate of the precipitation that made it remarkable.

Late in the fourth quarter, when tight end Brent Celek caught a 27-yard pass on fourth down that could have resulted in a touchdown, Celek knew to take a knee before the end zone so the clock could expire. But Celek added a little snow-day panache to the formality. He slid in the snow like a schoolboy at recess. And who could blame him?

As Celek told *The Philadelphia Inquirer* after the game, "They'll talk about this game forever. 'Remember when it snowed?'"

They sure do.

Epilogue

On June 3, 2024, Brian Dawkins hosted a charity golf tournament in suburban Philadelphia. Former teammates from the great Eagles teams in the early 2000s came to support him—from Brian Westbrook to Jeremiah Trotter to Jevon Kearse.

By late afternoon, the NFL released its daily transaction wire. Under the Philadelphia section, the retirements of Jason Kelce and Fletcher Cox officially processed.

Back at the NovaCare Complex, the Eagles prepared for the start of their mandatory minicamp. They adjusted to life without Kelce and Cox. Brandon Graham participated in his final minicamp before his final season.

Among the rookies on the Eagles' roster? Jeremiah Trotter Jr. This day represented the life cycle of an NFL franchise.

Cox long said that he was just renting a spot, and there's truth to that sentiment. Legacies last and memories linger. But there's always somebody else. Shortly after Kelce retired, the locker stall he occupied for much of his career was given to Cam Jurgens, the center drafted to replace Kelce. Perhaps a version of this book in 2049 would include a chapter on Jurgens.

The players, coaches, and executives come and go. The franchise—and the devoted fanaticism—endures.

That was part of the fun of curating this book. As I wrote in the introduction, the challenge wasn't what to include. It was what was left out. Trent Cole deserves his own chapter. So does Asante Samuel. Stars from the start of the 25-year period such as Hugh Douglas and Troy Vincent are worthy. And stars from the end of this period deserve one, too—if this book was written this summer, A.J. Brown would get his own space. Jordan Mailata and Landon Dickerson are ascending. So is DeVonta Smith. And what about the shooting stars, whose stints were brief but their imprint enduring, like Terrell Owens and Haason Reddick?

Andy Reid, who won his third Super Bowl in February 2024, is now more closely associated with the Chiefs than the Eagles. Narratives are always changing. In Philadelphia, he was able to win everything but the Super Bowl. With Bill Belichick out of the NFL, Reid is now the NFL's most accomplished active head coach. I asked him in the days before the 2024 Super Bowl what he would tell the man who accepted his first head-coaching job to much scrutiny 25 years earlier.

"Well, that's a good question," Reid said. "I'm not sure what I would tell him. But I'm glad he's still around."

There are invariably times in this job when those you write about are upset about the coverage. A response I often give is that the coverage is a reflection of the moment. The sentiment about Howie Roseman was different in 2017 than it was 2020 than it was in 2023. As Roseman has explained on a few occasions, if you don't keep trying to get better, "You get your ass kicked." (And as Kelce likes to say, your actions allow you to craft your own narrative.)

Even though this book allowed me to broaden the lens from a player or a game or a season to a 25-year period in the franchise history, it's fair to say the tone is also a reflection of the moment. Most of the book was put together in the summer of 2023, when the Eagles were still in the afterglow of a Super Bowl appearance and were among the favorites entering the 2023 season. The manuscript (save for two chapters) had been submitted before a late-season collapse that sullied the fan base's enthusiasm and led to major changes on the Eagles' coaching staff.

The 2024 offseason continued reinforcing how the Eagles' storied history—including from this 25-year period—informs how decisions are interpreted. As Shakespeare wrote, what's past is prologue. The Eagles signed high-profile running back Saquon Barkley for their biggest investment in the position in a decade. And what was used as precedent? The contracts they had once given LeSean McCoy and Westbrook—two players profiled in this book. The team's first- and second-round picks were both cornerbacks. What draft came to mind? The spring of 2002, of course, and the Eagles would be so lucky if Quinyon Mitchell and Cooper DeJean turned into the Lito Sheppard and Sheldon Brown combination two decades later. The front office was quick to sign top players to contract extensions this offseason—Smith, Brown, Dickerson, and Mailata all fit this category—and it brought to mind Joe Banner's approach of acting quickly to set the market instead of chasing the market. By signing ascending pass rusher Bryce Huff, the Eagles are hoping they channel the success of finding Reddick on a similar trajectory.

Yet with so many headlining moves during the roster churn, the skeptical spin is to beware of the "Dream Team" season from 2011. Or, seeing how the Eagles are trying to meld a new offensive philosophy with a returning head coach, there's curiosity about whether it could combust the way offensive changes were received in 2020.

In all these examples—both the good and the bad—the constant is they were not constant. Westbrook moved on for McCoy to take on a bigger role. McCoy was later traded after a shift in the front office. Sheppard and Brown were replaced, just like they replaced Vincent and Bobby Taylor. Some contracts aged well; others didn't. But all contracts aged. The Eagles rebounded from the Dream Team and from the disastrous 2020 seasons.

Time, as always, wins.

Even ownership of the franchise will evolve. Jeffrey Lurie's son, Julian, has taken on a formal role in the organization that will only grow. This type of book in 25 years will presumably include Julian Lurie's presence.

During an interview with Jeffrey Lurie in the summer of 2023, I posed the question about the next quarter-century in the franchise's history. He mentioned the tenets of what has created the success of the past 25 years. He discussed how the Eagles Autism Foundation, which was founded in 2018, can leave a "profound" influence on taking action against autism.

But he also recognized that he does not want the franchise of the next 25 years to be the franchise of the past 25 years. Principles will remain. Actions will be different.

"I think we will continue—and I would expect this to—as the game evolves, for the franchise to evolve in terms of what will make it correlate with big success," Lurie said. "And don't be stuck in what we did 25 years earlier. It may be that that lasted until 2032, who knows what it is? But be open-minded to what could take place. I think the use of artificial intelligence is going to probably improve the ability to acquire and manage resources and talent.

"But I think overall, the beauty of sports is that it's live, it's human. You do not what the future is going to hold.... And I just think if you're self-analytic, if you're looking at your strengths, your weaknesses at all times, both personally and as a franchise, it'll bode well for the franchise."

In the introduction, I noted that evidence of the last 25 years would suggest the Eagles will find ways to stay relevant "on a consistent basis." Except a Super Bowl in 2017 won't mean success in 2027, just as it would have seemed farfetched in 1994 to think the Eagles would make their fourth consecutive NFC Championship Game in 2004. Lurie said that he wants the organization to adapt, stay innovative, and that the story in 25 years is that "they've been consistently good."

"All that means is this will be a fun sequel to write in 2049," the introduction read.

Let's check back in 25 years ago to see how it went.

Acknowledgments

THE JOY OF SEEING A BOOK IN PRINT AND THE GRATIFICATION of knowing someone devoted time to reading it—or at least placing it on a bookshelf—tends to overshadow the memory of what it took to *write* the book. This is especially true with a full-time job bordering on an obsession, a side gig teaching a college course, and an incredible wife and two children who shouldn't care if a chapter on Nick Foles takes more time than planned.

This is a roundabout way of saying that acknowledgment sections seem self-indulging until you're ready to put a book to bed and realize it cannot be done by the author alone.

I sat in the Veterans Stadium stands for Week 1 of the 1999 season at age 13 and dreamed of covering the Philadelphia Eagles. For more than half of the 25-year period chronicled in this book, I've lived that dream. When you cover an NFL beat for 13 years, the franchise becomes a part of your life. I appreciate so many in the organization, from Jeffrey Lurie to the newest practice squad player, for all their time and perspective. There are too many players, coaches, and executives to single out by name, and all must be included because I value the insight from every one of them. These are their stories I'm sharing. A special thank you to the media relations staff, who needed to endure more than a decade of my pestering requests for more access and information.

As I wrote in the introduction, this was originally supposed to be a Super Bowl book for Triumph Books. I'm grateful to Noah Amstadter and Bill Ames for their interest in signing me up for that project, and their confidence in me to pivot to a different topic when that did not become a reality. Michelle Bruton has been patient and helpful throughout the editing process, and I know too well that all writers need good editors. Thank you to Preston Pisellini, Bianca Maldonado, and Cammie Fein for the help behind the scenes.

I'm honored that Malcolm Jenkins agreed to write the foreword for this book. In this job, you cannot have favorites—everybody has a worthwhile story to tell and deserves a fair shake from reporters—but there's no player I've respected more during my time covering the team than Malcolm. He was honest, intelligent, and accountable and forced me to be on top of my game whenever I came by his locker. (Plus, I read his book and his foreword. He can write far better than I can play football.)

My time on the beat has spanned three different employers, and coverage from each of those periods is reflected in the book. John Quinn, Pat McLoone, Gary Potosky, and Gary Miles were ever helpful and supportive during my time at *The Inquirer.* At The Athletic, I was fortunate to work with Pete Sweigard, Adam Hirshfield, and Josiah Turner in editing my Eagles coverage. And I appreciate Dan Uthman, a trusted editor since I interned for *The Washington Post,* for permitting me to take on this project. Everybody at PHLY has been so good to me since I joined and while I pushed this book past the finish line.

I don't know what it's like to work on a beat alone. I learned how to cover a franchise from Mike Garafolo. For seven years, Jeff McLane was an incredible partner. (And Les Bowen and Paul Domowitch for those last two years.) I've been lucky to spend the last five years working with Bo Wulf, who has been a wonderful colleague, co-host, and friend. (And Sheil Kapadia has been a part of this, too.) The entire Eagles beat corps is like extended family, challenging me to remain on top of my game every day and providing laughs and friendship throughout the seasons.

Matt Gelb has been a journalism confidant and friend for two decades, and his guidance was so helpful with this project. Same with Mike Sielski, whose perspective about book-writing is always valued.

This book is dedicated to my grandfather, who has championed my work, was my first editor, and believed in me for 38 years. These pages are a reflection of that confidence. I'm so lucky to have two loving grandmothers who always think I write well even after a lousy article. The love and support extends to my incredible family.

My five siblings (and now their five significant others!) are my closest confidants and the people who keep me humble. They'll presumably make fun of the acknowledgments, but they could be worthy of an entire chapter.

Nothing I write—and especially this book—would be possible without my mother, who encouraged me to take on the challenge with the same belief used to convince me to join the Germantown Academy newspaper 25 years ago. I'm so thankful to her and Chuck for the role they play in my life (and allowing me to write this down the shore!). Same with David and Jody, who treat and support me like a son.

My father is with me every day; I hope I honored him with the work ethic required to take on this project and appreciating those who allow me to do so.

I wrote in the acknowledgments section six years ago that the only thing I enjoy more than writing and reading is being married to Emily and the father to Reid. Six years later, that's an understatement. (And incomplete—Sloane is now a part of our quartet.) Emily's belief in me propels all my work, and her patience in allowing me to write 87,000 words during my free time is just one of many reasons why I'm a lucky husband.

And Reid and Sloane—one day I hope you enjoy this book half as much as *Dog Man* and *Amelia Bedelia*.

Sources

Books

Berman, Zach. *Underdogs: The Philadelphia Eagles' Emotional Road to Super Bowl Victory*. Running Press, 2018.

Didinger, Ray, and Robert Lyons. *The New Eagles Encyclopedia*. Temple University Press, 2014.

Eckel, Mark. *The Big 50: Philadelphia Eagles: The Men and Moments That Made the Philadelphia Eagles*. Triumph Books, 2016.

Ertz, Zach. *Focus and Finish: How Football Taught Me Grit, Teamwork, and Integrity*. Harvest Kids, 2019.

Foles, Nick, with Joshua Cooley. *Believe It: My Journey of Success, Failure, and Overcoming the Odds*. Tyndale Momentum, 2018.

Frank, Reuben. *Game Changers: The Greatest Plays in Philadelphia Eagles Football History*. Triumph Books, 2009.

Gargano, Anthony L. *A Sunday Pilgrimage: Six Days, Several Prayers, and the Super Bowl*. Middle Atlantic Press, 2005.

Jenkins, Malcolm. *What Winners Won't Tell You: Lessons from a Legendary Defender*. Simon & Schuster, 2023.

Pederson, Doug, with Dan Pompeii. *Fearless: How an Underdog Becomes a Champion*. Hachette Books, 2018.

Vick, Michael. *Finally Free: An Autobiography*. Worthy Books, 2012.

Newspapers, Periodicals, and Wire Services

The Athletic
Bleacher Report
ESPN
NBC Sports Philadelphia
The New York Times
NFL.com
The Philadelphia Daily News
PhiladelphiaEagles.com
The Philadelphia Inquirer
Philadelphia Magazine
Sports Illustrated
The Washington Post

Videos

NFL Films
NFL on NBC
NFL Network
PhiladelphiaEagles.com

Podcasts

Kelce, Jason, and Travis Kelce. *New Heights.*
Dimitroff, Thomas. *The GM Journey.*
Long, Chris. *Green Light.*